Ice Cream

Ice Cream

Over 400 variations, from simple scoops to spectacular desserts, from fresh fruit sorbets to parfaits and bombes, with meringues and sauces plus low calorie and special recipes

Hilary Walden

FIRESIDE

A Fireside Book published by Simon and Schuster
New York

CREATED AND PRODUCED BY PHOEBE PHILLIPS EDITIONS

A Fireside Book
Published by Simon & Schuster, Inc.

Simon & Schuster Building
Rockefeller Center
1230 Avenue of the Americas
New York, New York 10020

FIRESIDE and colophon are registered trademarks of Simon & Schuster, Inc.

Printed and bound in Belgium by Offset-Printing van den Bossche N.Y.

1 2 3 4 5 6 7 8 9 10

Library of Congress Cataloging in Publication Data

Walden, Hilary.
  Ice Cream.
  A Fireside Book.
  Includes index.
  1. Ice Cream, Ices, etc.   1. Title
TX795.W23   1985   641.8'62   85-2234
ISBN 0-671-60094-X

Contents

Flavors

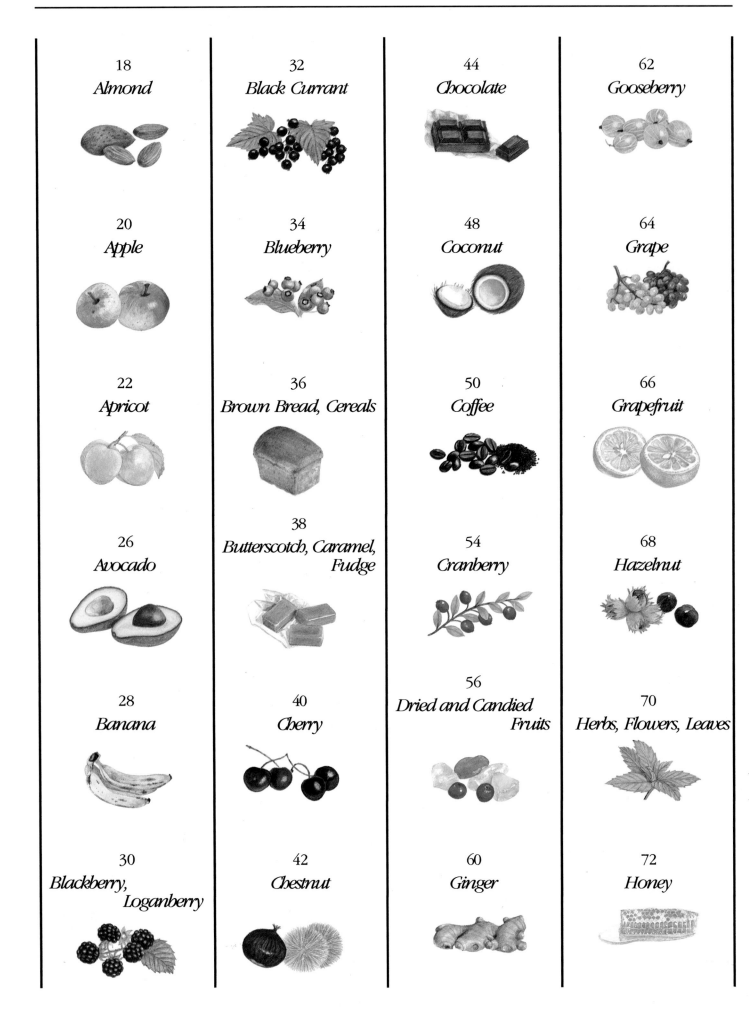

18
Almond

20
Apple

22
Apricot

26
Avocado

28
Banana

30
*Blackberry,
Loganberry*

32
Black Currant

34
Blueberry

36
Brown Bread, Cereals

38
*Butterscotch, Caramel,
Fudge*

40
Cherry

42
Chestnut

44
Chocolate

48
Coconut

50
Coffee

54
Cranberry

56
*Dried and Candied
Fruits*

60
Ginger

62
Gooseberry

64
Grape

66
Grapefruit

68
Hazelnut

70
Herbs, Flowers, Leaves

72
Honey

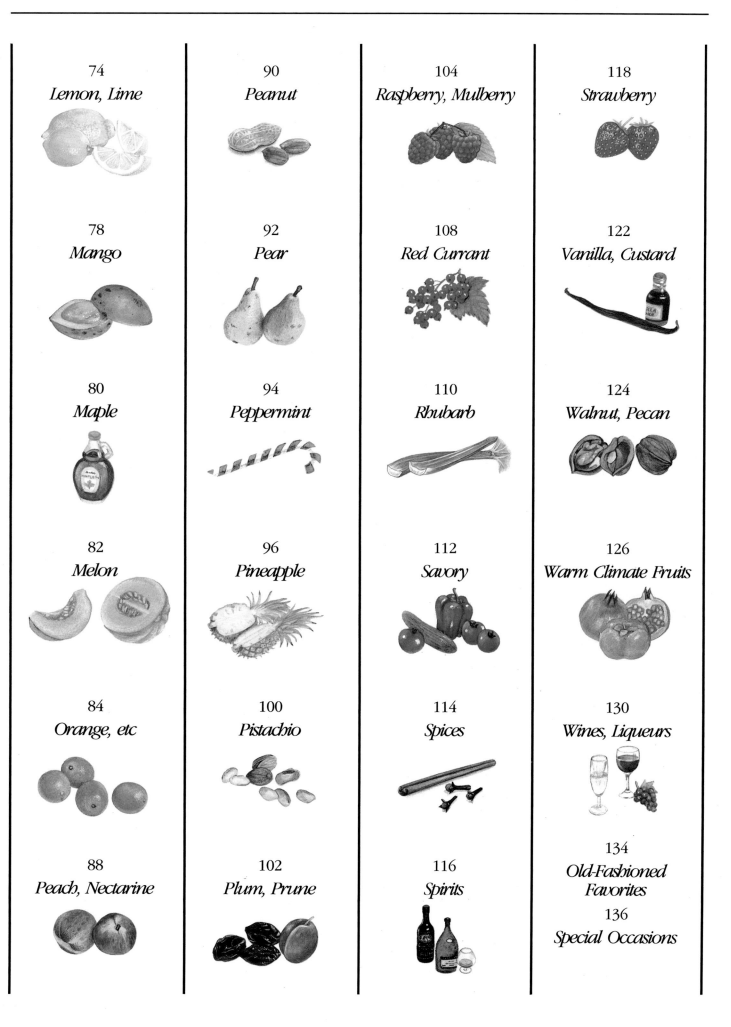

Introduction

Homemade ices and ice creams have a subtlety, purity and intense flavor that just don't exist in commercial products. And, thanks to modern refrigeration techniques, the whole range of iced desserts from refreshing, palette-cleansing sorbets to rich, foaming mousses, from light-as-air soufflés to crystal-clear water ices can be prepared at home by any cook who is capable of whipping cream or making an egg custard.

This had been a virtual impossibility until recently. Although the Romans are known to have cooled their wines with snow and ice, it was the mid-16th century before their freezing technique was improved upon – by a Sicilian who discovered that adding saltpeter to ice would speed up the process and produce a smoother, less crystalline iced mixture. The next development was in the second half of the 18th century when egg yolks and sugar syrups were used as the basis for ices and ice creams. Iced desserts became more elaborate, and bombes and other spectacular creations were served at banquets and fashionable dinner parties.

However, the majority of cooks still did not make their own ices. Although ice cream churns were comparatively early inventions (and have their devotees to this day), they required a supply of ice and were laborious to use – the mixture had to be churned by hand for almost an hour. As a result, most people had to be content with what restaurants and ice cream parlors could supply.

Making ice creams and ices at home only became really practical during this century. Today ice creams can be frozen quickly and easily in a freezer or in the ice-making compartment of a refrigerator – all that is necessary is to beat the mixture occasionally while it freezes. Electric machines, the latest development in ice cream making, even do away with this chore.

Food processors, blenders and electric hand beaters are useful additional aids. However, there are so many kinds of ices that special equipment is not essential. Iced mousses, iced soufflés and very rich mixtures can be left to freeze undisturbed with no risk that ice crystals will form and make the mixture hard. Freezing an ice in individual containers speeds up the process and also ensures a smooth texture.

One of the delights of making your own iced desserts is the opportunity it gives to experiment with your favorite ingredients, alone or combined with contrasting or complementary flavors. Try fresh-tasting yogurt to add a tang and only a few calories, low-fat cottage or farmer's cheese (or tofu, its vegetarian equivalent) for lightness, egg yolks for richness and a golden glow, cream – light, sour, whipping, heavy or crème fraîche – for creaminess, or full-fat cream cheese for smoothness.

Homemade ices can also be made from the most basic of store cupboard ingredients – canned milk, for example – and are perfect for using up gluts of cheap, or even free, fruit. On the other hand, the flavor and texture of the finest, most luxurious and exotic ingredients are emphasized to truly delicious effect.

Author's Notes

The main part of the book consists of recipes for ices and ice creams grouped by flavor, in alphabetical order. These are followed by a selection of popular, old-fashioned recipes and finally a section on iced desserts for special occasions.

Many of the recipes include dessert or serving suggestions, varying from easy combinations of different-flavored ices to more complicated creations and simple ideas in which presentation is all-important. Cakes, cookies, decorations, etc. called for in these suggestions are highlighted with an asterisk, and recipes for these are in the final part of the book (pages 145 to 152). Here you will also find instructions for the various techniques (pages 152 to 155) involved in some of the more complicated desserts. Check with the index for exact page numbers, if necessary. I have not given quantities in these suggestions as they can be varied in order to use up leftover ices.

The book starts with information on making ice creams and ices, using an old-fashioned ice cream churn as well as refrigerators, freezers and electric machines. This is followed by a section on ingredients and where and how you can make substitutions. Then there are definitions of the various kinds of iced mixtures and, finally, recipes for traditional ice cream bases.

Many recipe groupings start with a simple idea for combining the main flavor with these basic recipes or, provided they mix well, with a good-quality commercial vanilla ice cream.

I have included a selection of recipes for low-fat and other dietary needs. These are all highlighted in the index.

As all products labelled 'yogurt' should be natural and 'live', I prefer to call unflavored, unsweetened yogurts 'plain' rather than the quite frequently used 'natural' which I feel is confusing (it refers to the flavor rather than the product).

I would like to thank everyone who has contributed towards making this book possible – too many to mention individually. My very real gratitude goes to the friends and colleagues who made and tasted different versions of the recipes, and to the many people who designed and organized the project from the beginning, who typed and edited, corrected and photographed, who answered endless queries and generously offered advice.

I'd also like to give a special vote of thanks to ICTC and Sheila Fitzjones, their representative in Britain, who lent us the miraculous Gelato-Chef which made our work so much easier. Ice cream making machines are still relatively new. As most people use either the freezing compartment of a refrigerator or a freezer, the recipes in this book have been written with them in mind.

Finally, I would like to dedicate this book to ice cream fanatics everywhere – a largely anonymous group of people whose enthusiasm in searching out (and often creating) the perfect parfait, the fruitiest sorbet, the finest frozen mousse and the simplest, most subtle of flavors has made this book possible.

Making Ice Creams and Ices

Refrigerators, freezers and electric ice cream makers have revolutionized ice cream making at home. Instead of relying on time-consuming techniques using ice cream churns or even ice blocks, it has now become a practical proposition to make the most delicious of all ice creams – homemade ones.

Ice Cream Churns

The introduction of ice cream churns was an important development at the time. They are tedious to operate but necessary if you have no freezer or refrigerator.

Ice cream churns consist of two containers. One fits inside the other and the space between is packed with cracked ice and rock salt in the proportion of three parts ice to one part salt. (The salt lowers the temperature at which the iced mixture freezes and so produces a smoother result.)

The procedure is as follows: first fit the inner metal container into position in the bucket. Pack in the ice and salt tightly in layers. Leave for a few minutes until the metal container is well chilled. Pour the chilled ice cream mixture into the container, filling it not more than three-quarters full. The ice and salt must be well above the level of the ice cream mixture. Fit in the paddle or 'dasher'. Line the lid with waxpaper and put it in place. Start turning the handle, slowly at first and then at a steady pace until turning becomes difficult. This will take about 30 to 45 minutes. At this point remove the paddle and scrape it down. This is when nuts, candied fruits, etc., are added. Wipe the lid, put it back on and plug the hole with a cork.

Pour away the melted ice from the bucket and replace it with more ice and salt. Cover the bucket with newspaper or a blanket and leave for at least an hour for the ice cream to mature.

Refrigerators and Freezers

Making ices in the ice-making compartment of a refrigerator or in a freezer calls for a certain amount of attention but is not time consuming or complicated. It is a good idea to use maximum freezing power because ice cream has a smoother texture if it is frozen quickly. Also, chill all the equipment and ingredients such as yogurt, fruit juices and purées before starting.

Freezers
After the mixture has been made, pour it into a suitable freezing container – a shallow metal tray is best – and cover it with its own lid or with foil. Freeze rich whipped mixtures immediately, but if the mixture is not rich or whipped, chill it for 30 minutes or so in the refrigerator, then place it in the freezer.

When there is a border of hardening mixture about an inch deep round the container, beat the mixture thoroughly, preferably with a hand-held electric beater or in a food processor or blender, to prevent the formation of ice crystals and to incorporate air into the mixture. But try not to let it melt. Return the mixture to the freezing container, and put it back in the freezer compartment. Leave for 20 to 60 minutes, depending on the ingredients in the mixture and the temperature of the freezer, before beating again. If necessary beat a third or even a fourth time during the freezing process to ensure the end result is really smooth. If the mixture freezes too hard between beatings, place it in the refrigerator until it is soft enough to beat.

If the mixture is frozen in a shallow container, transfer it to a chilled bowl each time it is beaten. This is unnecessary if you have used a larger container – but remember to scrape the ice crystals that have formed on the sides and base towards the center.

Freeze until firm. Freezing times will vary according to the recipe and the amount to be frozen. A 5 cup mixture will take from two to three hours to set depending on the recipe. When it is ready, reset the dial to its normal setting.

Refrigerators
Recipes in this book refer to making ice creams in freezers, but they can just as easily be made in the ice-making compartment of a refrigerator.

Set the refrigerator dial at the coldest setting at least an hour before making the iced mixture, and remember to remove items that might be damaged by too low a temperature, such as eggs, from the refrigerator if your compartment does not have a separate control.

Freeze the mixture until firm. Freezing times vary. A general guide is that a 2½ cup mixture for four people will take up to four hours to freeze completely, and a 5 cup mixture for six to eight people will take up to five hours. Once the ice is made, return the refrigerator to its normal setting.

Whether using a freezer or the ice-making compartment of a refrigerator, it is almost always necessary to allow the ice to soften slightly in a refrigerator.

The more airy and rich a mixture, the less attention it will require. The time spent whipping can be reduced by using a food processor or by making a rich mixture, and can even be eliminated entirely by making very rich ice creams, iced mousses or soufflés, or by freezing the mixture in individual dishes (this speeds up the freezing process). As a general rule, add flavorings before folding in the whipped egg whites and whipped cream.

Electric Ice Cream Makers

Electrically powered ice cream makers or sorbetières take the effort out of making ice creams.

There are two kinds of machine: free-standing ones and those that are placed in a freezer or in the ice-making compartment of a refrigerator. Both types have an electrically powered paddle that slowly and rhythmically turns the mixture to prevent the formation of ice crystals. In most models these will lift up automatically when the mixture reaches a consistency that can be safely left undisturbed, on average after about 10 to 15 minutes for a sorbet, and

20 to 30 minutes for an ice cream, depending on the recipe and machine. This is the time to add nuts, dried and candied fruits, etc. and to fold in whipped egg whites and whipped cream. Sorbets should just about be ready for serving at this point, but ice creams will need another one to two hours before they are completely frozen. They can be left in the machine during this time, provided the paddles are removed, or the mixture can be turned into a container, covered and returned to the freezer.

The free-standing ice cream makers produce very good results and allow you to use less rich ingredients and still get smooth, soft ices. Although they are fairly large – and fairly expensive – they are the ultimate labor-saving device for ice cream enthusiasts.

'Freezer' machines are less expensive but the results are not as good, often no better than if the ice had been made by hand. Also, they take up room in a freezer and must be placed on a flat surface to work efficiently, which can be a problem if you are using a chest freezer or the ice-making compartment of a refrigerator. The interiors of some of these machines are in the shape of a decorative mold so that the ice is ready for serving.

A modern, electric (and reasonably priced) version of the old-fashioned ice churn is also available. A free-standing model, it has an outer, plastic container that is packed with a mixture of iced water, ice cubes and salt and an inner, metal container for the ice cream ingredients. The iced mixture will freeze after about 25 to 50 minutes, depending on the richness of the ingredients; it is ready when the ice cream seems to wrap itself around the paddle. It is generally necessary to fill up the level of the iced water/ice/salt mixture after about 15 to 20 minutes and the ice cream must be removed once it has reached the correct consistency.

As the recipes in this book describe ices made in a freezer, follow the manufacturer's directions if you are using an ice cream machine.

Serving

Before serving, most machine or handmade ices should be transferred to the main part of the refrigerator, unless a recipe specifically states otherwise. Allow the ice to 'come to' and soften slightly; if it is too cold it will be hard and will not taste as good as it should. The actual time needed in the refrigerator depends on the richness of the mixture, whether it has been kept in a freezer or the ice-making compartment of a refrigerator, how long it has been kept, the size of the container, the temperature in the refrigerator and how soon the ice cream will be brought to the table.

On average, allow about 30 to 40 minutes for sorbets and simple ice creams, and 20 to 30 minutes for rich ice creams, iced mousses and soufflés; add a little extra time if the ice has been kept for a while in the freezer. Mixtures frozen in small molds should be left in the refrigerator for only 5 to 10 minutes and can be served immediately if they are rich or whipped or if the surroundings in which they will be eaten are warm.

For special occasions, ices can be frozen in all kinds of decorative molds; for suggestions, see page 155.

Storage

Because homemade ices do not contain all the additives found in most commercial products, they cannot be kept for the same length of time. Water ices and sorbets, especially fruit ones, are at their best if eaten within a day of being made. Light mixtures such as yogurt ices should, preferably, be eaten after a couple of days, while rich ices may benefit from two or three days' 'ripening' in a freezer. At the most, they should not be kept for longer than a few weeks if their full glory is to be enjoyed. Granitas, of course, should be eaten at once.

Ingredients

Part of the fun of making ice creams at home is choosing the ingredients and deciding whether or not you want to improve on classical flavors or to try out new combinations to create an exotic or unusual taste.

Cream

Cream is synonymous with ice cream, even though it is not used in all ices. Originally heavy cream was used, but nowadays we use the whole spectrum of creams. In ascending order of richness, these are: sour, light, whipping cream, crème fraîche and, of course, heavy cream. The different fat contents of these creams influence the texture as well as the flavor of the finished dish. The higher the fat content, the smoother and richer the ice cream; sour cream and crème fraîche will vary the flavor.

In recipes where no particular type of cream is specified, you can use whichever you prefer, depending on the kind of ice you want to make and what is available. Even when a particular type of cream is specified, another can usually be substituted, although there will be a change in the texture and flavor. As fat masks other flavors it may be necessary to adjust other ingredients accordingly.

Light cream has a lower fat content than heavy cream and cannot be whipped on its own.

Heavy cream is thick textured, mild tasting and ideal for whipping.

Sour cream is made from light cream with the addition of bacterial culture; its hint of acidity adds sharpness to flavoring.

Whipping cream has a fat content in between light and heavy cream, and can of course be whipped. Make

Evaporated milk and sweetened condensed milk are sometimes recommended as 'everyday' alternatives to cream. However, because they taste of caramel (and the condensed version is very sweet), they are best used in ices with a complementary flavor – butterscotch or caramel – or when making ices for children.

If you are substituting evaporated or condensed milk for ordinary milk or cream, reduce the amount of sugar and taste the prepared mixture to see whether other flavorings need to be increased.

Skim milk and buttermilk contain even less fat than ordinary milk and must be thoroughly beaten during freezing. 'Cultured' buttermilk is more widely available than the uncultured variety. It is slightly thicker and adds a refreshing acidity that blends particularly well with fruit ices.

Soybean milk is a vegetarian, lower calorie, no cholesterol version of milk and can easily be substituted for cow's milk. It produces softer, more 'creamy' ices as it has more body. Commercial soybean milks are often, although not always, sweetened and nearly all are mild flavored. (They remind me of milk that has been very thoroughly blended with ground almonds.)

Soybean milk ices can be made almost as creamy as cream ices by the inclusion of 2 tablespoons oil (such as sunflower oil) to 1¼ cups soybean milk.

Yogurt

Ices made with yogurt have a fresh, light flavor. Most are low in calories, with the exception of those using yogurt made from full-cream milk or with added cream. These full-fat yogurts add smoothness and richness to ices, and retain their characteristic fresh flavor when frozen; use them if calorific value is of no consequence. Add gelatin or whipped egg white to mixtures with low-fat yogurt to soften an ice which would otherwise be hard.

Yogurt can be used on its own or blended with milk, creams or soft cheeses.

Soft Cheeses

Although soft cheeses are not traditionally used, I find them extremely useful for their versatility and for the variety and interest they add.

Cream cheese has a fat content ranging from 45 to 65 per cent, and is made from drained set cream. Other soft cheeses are made from drained milk curds and their fat content ranges from almost nothing to 45 per cent. They can be used on their own, in combination with each other, or with milk, cream or yogurt, to vary flavor and texture. Beat high fat soft cheeses until they are smooth before use.

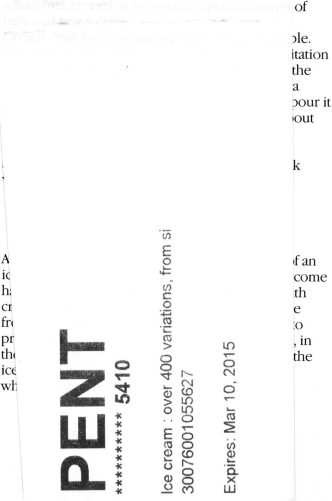

Cottage and farmers' cheeses should be strained to ease blending and for a smooth iced mixture.
Ricotta is a soft, mild Italian cheese traditionally made from sheep's milk and now also made in other countries and from cow's milk. It has a low fat content.
Quark is a fresh cheese with a low fat content.
Tofu is a vegetarian cheese. Made from soybean milk, it does not contain any cholesterol and is low in calories and fat. Its protein content is high. It can be used in any recipe to replace soft cheese. Beat tofu with other ingredients until smooth.
Fromage frais is a French cheese with a lighter texture and sharper flavor than American soft cheeses. It can have a high or low fat content. Fromage frais with a high fat content can be used as a rich alternative to yogurt.
Fromage blanc is also from France and has a very low fat content.

Sugar

As well as its obvious sweetening effect, sugar also affects the hardness of an ice. Too much will make the ice sickly and will also slow down freezing. But bear in mind that freezing takes the edge off sweetness, and if too little sugar is used the ice will not be as soft and will be lacking in flavor.

It is important to dissolve sugar completely by stirring over direct heat, or by beating either over heat or vigorously with an electric beater. Undissolved crystals give a grainy texture to the frozen mixture.
Confectioners' sugar should be used in recipes where the sugar is simply stirred into the ingredients, as with some fresh fruit sorbets.
Brown sugar affects both the color and taste. Although its crystals are slow to dissolve, it adds a new character and dimension to flavors such as rhubarb, apple, butterscotch and brown bread.
Sugar syrup is the foundation of water ices, and of most sorbets, iced mousses and soufflés.

Put the sugar and water in a heavy-based pan and heat gently. Stir until the sugar has dissolved then bring to the boil. Allow to boil for the length of time specified or until the required temperature is reached. The best way to test this is to use a candy thermometer. The proportion of sugar to water will vary according to the sweetness and richness of the other ingredients and the type of ice being made.
Fructose is the sweetest of the natural sugars. It cannot be used to make a sugar syrup, but can otherwise be substituted for sugar. You need about half as much fructose as other sugars, unless the mixture is particularly acidic, and it is therefore useful if you want to reduce your sugar intake. Fructose is suitable for diabetics, who should take medical advice on exact amounts.

Liquid Sweeteners

These give a smooth texture and add individuality and character to ices.
Honey has a distinctive flavor. Use a mild-tasting one that will not dominate the ice, unless it is being used as the main flavor.
Maple syrup is very popular both as a flavor and as a sauce. It has a smooth, rich, sweet taste. The best grades are pale in colour.
Corn syrup may be light or dark, the former being the more refined and less strongly flavored. Twice as much syrup as sugar is needed to obtain the equivalent degree of sweetness.
Molasses is a dark, thick, sticky syrup that combines acidity with sweetness.

Artificial Sweeteners

Many artificial sweeteners and very low-calorie sweeteners lose their sweetness when heated above a certain temperature or beyond a certain time, and can only be used in recipes that do not require sugar syrup. When making a custard-based ice cream, add the sweetener to the custard after it has cooled.

Normally, 3–4 artificial sweeteners are the equivalent of 2 tablespoons sugar, but some sweeteners react differently with different flavors and ingredients; they are enhanced by fruits, for example, and diminished by fats. Tasting and personal experience with a particular sweetener are the best guides to the amounts to use. Remember, though, that the mixture should taste a little over-sweet before it is put into the freezer.

Eggs

The more yolks there are in a recipe, the richer and smoother the frozen mixture will be. When making custard-based mixtures the number of egg yolks used is generally in inverse proportion to the amount and richness of the cream – in other words, the creamier the custard, the fewer the egg yolks. Beaten yolks will add lightness to a mixture. If you are following a recipe that only requires egg yolks, save the whites and use them to make an iced soufflé.

Egg whites also add lightness, and in addition they prevent the formation of ice crystals, and make a mixture go further. They are usually whipped to maximize their effectiveness.

Definitions

The definitions that follow are based on classical sources such as Larousse and Escoffier, combined with accepted modern usage. However, most of them are frequently misused or very loosely applied.

Ice Cream

This is a generic name for a frozen mixture, always containing milk or cream, based on egg custards, cream or mousse. It is often used to describe a variety of desserts, including iced mousses, iced soufflés and parfaits.

Water Ice

A water ice is a simple frozen dessert containing a basic sugar syrup, and flavoring such as fruit juice or puréed fruit. It may also be flavored with wine, liquor, liqueur, coffee or an infusion of tea, spices, black currant leaves, and so on.

Granita

A granita is made from a light sugar syrup and flavoring. Ice crystals are allowed to form during freezing, giving the ice a grainy, granular texture. It should be served when it is still at the slushy, semi-frozen stage.

Sorbet, Sherbet

Smoother than a granita, a sorbet is made from a more concentrated sugar syrup and is beaten several times during the freezing process to break up the ice crystals and create a smooth texture. It should be served when it is one stage harder than being slushy, and just capable of being molded.

A sherbet is a sorbet that has egg white or cream or milk added. (In the latter two cases, the dishes could also be referred to as cream ices or milk ices, respectively.)

There is a great deal of confusion about the terms sorbet and sherbet. The traditionalists, Larousse and Escoffier, always added egg white to the mixture in the form of Italian meringue, which is made by whipping boiling sugar syrup into the egg whites, then cooking the mixture over a pan of hot water. They called this a sorbet. They also called the mixture a sorbet when they added cream to it as it was just beginning to freeze. But nowadays a sorbet need not contain egg white or cream, and many of today's top chefs claim that these ingredients mask the clarity and purity of both the flavor and appearance of a sorbet. In fact modern fruit sorbets are the simplest and freshest tasting of all ices, as they often contain no more than fruit and sugar – not even syrup.

To add to the confusion, the English translation of sorbet from French cookbooks is sherbet. Yet the term sherbet is more frequently used in the United States than in England, which usually uses the term sorbet whether or not egg white, cream or milk is added.

Spoom, Spumone

A spoom is a very light, frothy water ice made from fruit juice or wine. It is based on a more highly concentrated sugar syrup than a sorbet, and includes twice the amount of Italian meringue.

Iced Mousse

An iced mousse is a light-textured but fairly rich dessert based on well-beaten egg yolks, often with the addition of whipped cream and sometimes with egg whites. It is often frozen in the dish in which it will be served with a deep collar of foil or waxpaper supporting the mousse as it stands above the rim. The collar is removed when the mousse is served and the exposed sides can be decorated with, for example, finely chopped nuts or macaroons.

Iced Soufflé, Soufflé Glacé

An iced soufflé is a very light, airy dessert made from whipped egg whites and whipped cream. Like iced mousses, a soufflé is often frozen in the container in which it is to be served.

Parfait

The term parfait originally referred to a coffee-flavored dessert made from beaten egg yolks and sugar syrup, but today it is used much more widely, and encompasses all manner of other flavors.

Bombe

A bombe is a shaped and layered molded iced dessert. It is composed of two or more flavors or textures, with the harder ice forming an outer case – the jacket – and the softer ice the inner layer. The name comes from the mold that is traditionally used. It is dome shaped and made of copper, which, being a good conductor of heat and cold, not only accelerates the freezing but also makes unmolding easier. It has a tight-fitting lid, and should have small feet or a screw-on pedestal so that it stands upright during freezing. This facilitates turning out the dessert because the hole left when the pedestal or feet are removed releases any air lock that may have formed.

There are over 50 classical combinations, many of which are named after people, usually women. They include Coppelia (coffee jacket with a praline center), Marie-Louise (chocolate jacket with a vanilla center), Josephine (pistachio inside a coffee jacket).

Whenever I see these names I wonder who inspired them and whether there was any particular reason for the choice of ingredients. What qualities did Miss Heylett have that brought forth vanilla surrounded by raspberry to create the Miss Heylett bombe? And what of the portentous Gladstone bombe with its outer jacket of ginger and interior mixture flavored with gin, diced ginger and angelica?

Cream ice

A cream ice is a sorbet mixture enriched with whipped cream.

Basic Mixtures

These are the foundations on which iced mixtures are created.

Whipped Cream

The simplest base for an ice cream is whipped cream with sweetening and flavoring folded in. You can use heavy or whipping cream, a combination of the two, or a combination of light and heavy creams.

Folded-in whipped egg white makes a less rich ice cream and increases the number of portions that can be served. A cream base is particularly good with fruits, especially berries such as raspberries, loganberries, blueberries and cranberries.

Basic Whipped Cream Ice Cream

1¼ cups cream (heavy, whipping or crème fraîche;
  heavy and light; heavy and whipping; heavy and
  sour cream)
Approximately ½ cup sugar
Flavoring: about ¾–1 pound/1 cup fruit, puréed and
  strained; ¼ pound whole or segmented fruit;
  approximately ⅔–1 cup chopped nuts; other
  flavorings to taste
1 teaspoon vanilla extract (see method)
1–2 egg whites, optional

In a cold bowl, whip the cream until soft peaks are formed. Fold in the sugar and flavoring; only add the vanilla if it will blend with, or complement, the main flavoring. If egg white is used, whip in a clean bowl until stiff but not dry, then fold into the cream. No beating is necessary during freezing, and 'softening' will take 15–35 minutes depending on the flavoring used. Allow the longer time for ice creams flavored with fruit.

Serves 4 (without egg whites), 5 (1 egg white), 6 (2 egg whites)

Custard

An egg custard base produces very smooth, velvety ice creams and is the foundation most frequently used in professional kitchens. The custard can be made with milk or light, whipping or heavy cream or a mixture of any of these. The richness of the custard will determine the smoothness of the ice cream. For a lighter result, fold whipped cream or whipped egg whites into the custard when it is cold. Yolks or whole eggs can be used to thicken the custard. The richer creams normally require fewer egg yolks, although some very luxurious recipes call for a high proportion of both cream and egg yolks.

A custard base can be made from a number of different ingredients combined in all sorts of different ways, but this is the recipe I find most useful.

Basic Custard Ice Cream

1¼ cups light cream
Vanilla pod
3 egg yolks
Approximately ⅓–½ cup sugar
Flavoring: ¾–1 pound/1 cup fruit, puréed and
  strained; ⅔–1 cup chopped nuts; other flavorings to
  taste. See note below.
⅔ cup cream, whipped

In a heavy-based saucepan gently heat the light cream with the vanilla pod to just on simmering point. Remove from the heat, cover and leave to infuse for 15–30 minutes, depending on the strength of vanilla flavor desired.

In a bowl, beat the egg yolks with the sugar until thick and light, then strain in the warm cream. Return the mixture to the rinsed pan and cook over a very low heat, stirring constantly, until the custard thickens, but do not allow it to boil as it will curdle.

As this stage of making the ice cream is very critical and a little tricky, until you are experienced you may prefer to use a longer but safer method for cooking the custard. Place the bowl containing the egg yolks and milk over a pan of hot, not boiling, water. Put the pan over low heat and beat constantly until the sauce thickens and coats the back of a spoon.

Whether cooking the custard in a saucepan or in a bowl, plunge the base immediately into cold water to prevent further cooking, or pour the custard into a cold bowl.

Straining the custard will give a smoother-textured ice cream. Leave the custard to cool. To prevent a skin forming, cover the surface tightly with plastic wrap or waxpaper, or stir the sauce occasionally.

Pour the mixture into a shallow metal container, cover and chill for 30 minutes before freezing. Beat twice if making the ice cream by hand. Fold in the whipped cream after the last beating, if making by hand, or when the machine has stopped working if using an electric ice cream maker. 'Soften' for 15–35 minutes, depending on the richness of the custard and the flavoring used. Allow the longer time if a fruit flavoring is used.

Serves 4–6

Note: Acidic fruits such as puréed rhubarb and plums and most other flavorings are usually added when the custard is cold (acidic fruits must never be mixed into a hot custard or it will curdle). The exceptions are ingredients such as real vanilla, coffee and spices, which impart extra flavor if they are added to the custard while it thickens.

Iced Mousse

As with the custard base, ingredients and the proportions in which they are used can vary. The following is a good, basic recipe.

Basic Iced Mousse

3 egg yolks
Approximately 1/3 cup sugar
Flavoring: 3/4–1 pound/1 cup fruit, puréed and strained; 2/3–1 cup chopped nuts; other flavorings to taste
1 teaspoon vanilla extract (see method)
1 1/4 cups cream, whipped
2 egg whites

In a large bowl placed over a pan of hot, not boiling, water beat the egg yolks with the sugar until well increased in volume, and thick and light in color.

Remove the bowl from the heat, and continue to beat the mixture until it is cool, then fold in the flavorings and whipped cream with a metal spoon. Only add the vanilla if it will blend with, or complement, the main flavoring. Whip the egg whites until stiff, then lightly fold them into the mixture until the ingredients are evenly blended.

Spoon the mixture into a shallow metal container, mold or cake pan. Cover and freeze until firm. No beating is necessary and 'softening' will take 15–35 minutes depending on the type of flavoring and size of the container.

Serves 4–6

Iced Soufflé, Soufflé Glacé

The following is a good, all-round base.

Basic Iced Soufflé

4 egg whites
1/2 cup sugar
Flavoring: 3/4–1 pound/1 cup fruit, puréed and strained; 1/4 pound whole or segmented fruit;
*   2/3–1 cup chopped nuts; other flavorings to taste*
1 teaspoon vanilla extract (see method)
1 1/4 cups cream, whipped

Place a large bowl over a pan of hot, not boiling, water. Put in the egg whites and whip with the sugar to a stiff meringue. The heat improves the stability of the meringue.

Remove the bowl from the heat, and continue whipping until the meringue is cold. Lightly fold in the flavoring and whipped cream. Only add vanilla if it

will blend with, or complement, the main flavoring. Spoon into a shallow metal container, mold, cake or loaf pan or prepared soufflé dish. Cover.

If the surface of the mixture is above the level of the dish, place the dish in a rigid container with a lid. Alternatively, leave the soufflé to freeze until firm, then protect the top with a dome of foil.

Serves 4–6

Sorbet

I have not included a basic sorbet recipe, as the proportions of sugar to water for the sugar syrup will vary according to the recipe – fruits differ in the amount of sugar and water they contain. Quantities are given in individual recipes.

Adding Italian meringue, as in the classic sorbets of Escoffier and Larousse, is a comparatively lengthy process that few domestic cooks, and certainly not all professional ones, feel inclined to undertake when making a sorbet.

The easier alternative is simply to whip a couple of egg whites as normal then fold or whip them into the mixture when it is halfway through the freezing process. Egg whites will prevent hard ice crystals from forming, a function that dissolved gelatin will also perform.

The more water there is in a recipe, the more vital egg whites are for its success. They are also more necessary if a sorbet is prepared by hand rather than with the assistance of an electric ice cream maker or sorbetière. The more watery mixtures also require more frequent and more vigorous beating during freezing.

Chilling the mixture before freezing it, and using shallow metal trays, will help to make the mixture freeze smoothly.

Almond

Almonds can be used in all their different forms to make a wide range of ices, each with very different characteristics. They can be slivered or finely or coarsely chopped for different degrees of crunchiness, or ground for smoothness. Plain nuts add a delicate flavor, or they can be toasted for a more nutty taste – bake peeled almonds in a moderate oven (350°F) for about 8–10 minutes. Almonds can also be made into praline, which can be crushed to a fine powder or broken into pieces to add crackle.

Simple Almond Ice Cream
Add ¾ cup finely chopped toasted almonds to any of the Basic Recipes*, or to a good-quality bought vanilla ice cream.

Biscuit Tortoni

1¼ cups light cream
1¼ cups heavy cream
½ cup confectioners' sugar, sifted
½ cup almond cookies, crushed
½ cup sweet sherry
Crushed almond cookies, for decoration

Put the creams in a bowl and whip until soft peaks form then whip in the sugar lightly. Fold in the cookies and sherry.

Pour the mixture into a 2 pound loaf pan, cover and freeze until firm.

About 30 minutes before serving, turn the tortoni out onto a cold plate and leave in the refrigerator. Sprinkle the crushed cookies over the top just before serving.

Serves 4–6

Serving suggestions
Serve with Chunky Marmalade Sauce or a Compote* of fresh apricots or oranges.*

Kulfi (Indian almond ice cream)

2½ cups milk
2 eggs
2 egg yolks
½ cup sugar
⅓ cup ground almonds
¼ teaspoon almond extract
1 tablespoon rosewater
¼ cup whipping cream
Finely chopped pistachio nuts, for decoration

In a heavy-based pan, bring the milk slowly to boiling point. Beat the eggs, egg yolks and sugar together in a bowl until evenly blended then gradually stir in the hot milk. Pour the mixture back into the pan and cook gently, stirring constantly, until the custard thickens – do not let it boil. Leave to cool.

Stir in the ground almonds, almond extract and rosewater. Pour the mixture into a container, cover and chill for at least 30 minutes. Freeze until slushy. Beat well in a bowl.

Whip the cream in a bowl until soft peaks form and fold into the custard. Spoon back into the container, cover and freeze until firm. Leave for at least 12 hours.

About 30 minutes before serving, transfer to the refrigerator. Serve decorated with the nuts.

Serves 8

Flavor variations
Add ¼ cup chopped pistachio nuts.

Use half milk and half cream instead of all milk for the custard.

Praline Ice Cream

1 cup milk
3 egg yolks
1 cup sugar
1¼ cups cream, whipped
⅔ cup shelled, unpeeled almonds

In a heavy-based pan, gently bring the milk to simmering point. Beat the egg yolks and half the sugar together in a bowl until thick and light then gradually stir in the milk. Pour the mixture back into the rinsed pan and cook gently, stirring constantly, until the custard thickens but do not allow it to boil. Leave to cool. Fold in the cream, spoon into a container, cover and freeze until just firm.

To make the praline, dissolve the remaining sugar in ⅓ cup water in another heavy-based pan. Add the almonds and boil for about 10 minutes until golden brown. Pour onto a cold, oiled surface and leave to set. Place the praline in a thick plastic bag or clean cloth and hit with a rolling pin to break it into small pieces.

Beat the ice cream in a bowl, and fold in all but 1 tablespoon of the praline. Spoon the mixture back into the container, cover and freeze until firm.

About 20 minutes before serving, transfer the ice cream to the refrigerator. Serve decorated with the reserved praline.

Serves 4–5

Serving suggestion
Serve with Cigars Russe.*

Dessert suggestion
Make into a bombe with Traditional Coffee Parfait (page 50) or Fresh Coffee Ice Cream (page 53) in the center. Decorate the outside of the turned-out bombe with whipped cream flavored with coffee liqueur, sugar-coated coffee beans and crushed praline.

Toasted Almond Ice Cream

1/4 pound full fat cream cheese, softened
1/2 pound cottage cheese, strained
2 tablespoons ground almonds
2 tablespoons orange or lemon juice
1 cup confectioners' sugar
1/3 cup toasted almonds, finely chopped
1 egg white

For decoration
Toasted slivered almonds
Coffee sugar crystals

Put the cream cheese and the cottage cheese into a bowl and beat until smooth. Beat in the ground almonds and orange or lemon juice and sugar. Stir in the toasted almonds. Whip the egg white until stiff and fold into the mixture.

Spoon the mixture into individual dishes. Cover and freeze until firm.

About 30 minutes before serving, transfer the ice cream to the refrigerator and decorate with the slivered almonds and sugar crystals.

Serves 4

Serving suggestion
Scoop into individual glass dishes and decorate with whipped cream and toasted, slivered almonds. Top with a wafer biscuit.

Additional recipes using almonds: Iced Orange and Almond Mousse (page 85), Coffee Almond Ice Cream (page 52).

Apple

Both eating and cooking apples are suitable for ices, but it is important to use only well-flavored varieties like Delicious, Jonathan and Winesap. To add color and texture to the ice cream, leave the skin on the apples when you purée them in a blender or food processor. Alternatively, if the fruit is peeled, or the skin is not in good condition, add a few drops of green food coloring to the mixture. You can use bought or homemade applesauce – canned, frozen or bottled – if fresh fruit is not available.

Simple Apple Ice Cream
Add 1¼ cups applesauce, bought or homemade, to any of the Basic Recipes*.

Apple and Walnut Ice Cream

4 cups dessert apples, peeled, cored and sliced
4 tablespoons sweet butter
2 tablespoons orange juice
¼ cup sugar
2 eggs, separated
⅔ cup heavy cream
⅔ cup light cream
¼ cup chopped walnuts
1 red-skinned apple, thickly sliced and dipped in
  lemon juice, for decoration

Cook the apples gently in a covered saucepan with the butter and orange juice until soft. Add the sugar and reduce to a purée. Beat the egg yolks until light and frothy and stir into the purée. Return the mixture to the pan and cook over a low heat, stirring, until the mixture thickens slightly. Pour into a bowl and leave to cool.

Whip the creams together in a bowl until thick and fold into the purée with the nuts. Turn into a 2 pound loaf pan, cover and freeze for about 1–1½ hours until half frozen.

Turn the ice cream into a bowl. Whip the egg whites until stiff but not dry and carefully fold into the ice cream. Return the ice cream to the loaf pan, cover and freeze until firm.

About 30–40 minutes before serving, turn out onto a cold plate, decorate with the apple slices and leave in the refrigerator.

Serves 5–6

Serving suggestion
Spoon into the center of small, hollowed-out brioche, sprinkle with chopped candied ginger and serve with a sauce of cream whipped with ginger wine.

Apple and Elderflower Ice Cream

3 cups tart apples, peeled, cored and chopped
2 tablespoons butter
¼ cup sugar
2 sprigs of elderflowers
Finely grated zest of 1 orange
⅔ cup plain yogurt
2 egg whites
6 small elderflower sprigs for decoration

Gently cook the apples, butter, sugar, elderflowers and orange zest in a covered saucepan until the apples are very soft. Leave until cold. Remove the elderflowers and purée the apple mixture. Chill the mixture then fold in the yogurt. Spoon into a container, cover and freeze to the slushy stage.

Whip the egg whites in a bowl until stiff but not dry. Beat the apple mixture in a bowl and fold in the egg whites.

Spoon into a 1 pound loaf pan, cover and freeze until firm.

About 30 minutes before serving, unmold the ice cream onto a cold plate and leave in the refrigerator. Decorate with elderflowers just before serving.

Serves 6

Apple and Apricot Ice Cream

1½ cups good-quality dried apricots, soaked overnight
  in the minimum of water
4 cups tart apples, peeled, cored and coarsely chopped
Finely grated zest and juice of 1 lemon or orange
½ cup brown sugar
2 large eggs, separated
⅔ cup cream, whipped

Drain the apricots and measure out 1¼ cups of the soaking liquid. Put this with the apricots and apples and the zest and juice into a saucepan and simmer gently, covered, until the apricots are tender. Purée the fruit with the liquid and return to the rinsed pan. Add the sugar and egg yolks and cook over a low heat, stirring constantly, until the **mixture thickens**. Leave to cool, stirring occasionally. Pour into a container, cover and freeze until just becoming firm. Put into a bowl and beat well.

Fold in the cream. Whip the egg whites until stiff but not dry and fold into the fruit cream.

Spoon the mixture back into the container, cover and freeze until firm.

About 30 minutes before serving, transfer the ice cream to the refrigerator.

Serves 4–6

Apple and Raisin Ice Cream

1/3 cup raisins
1/3 cup apple brandy or hard cider, warmed
6 cups tart apples, peeled, cored and roughly chopped
Juice and grated zest of 1 orange
1/2 cup caster sugar
4 egg yolks
1 1/4 cups light cream

For decoration
Slices of apple, preferably of a red-skinned variety,
*   dipped in lemon juice*
Small mint leaves

Soak the raisins in the apple brandy or cider. In a covered saucepan cook the apples with the orange juice and zest and half the sugar over a low heat until a dryish purée is formed. Leave until cold.

Put the egg yolks and remaining sugar in a bowl and beat together until thick and light. In a heavy-based pan, heat the cream to simmering point then gradually beat into the egg yolks. Pour the mixture back into the pan and cook over low heat, stirring constantly until the custard thickens – do not allow it to boil. Leave to cool then mix with the apples. Pour into a container, cover and freeze until just becoming firm. Transfer to a bowl, beat well and fold in the raisins and apple brandy or cider. Spoon the mixture into a 2½ pound loaf pan, cover and freeze until firm.

About 20 minutes before serving, turn the ice cream out onto a cold plate and leave in the refrigerator. Decorate with the apple slices and mint leaves just before serving.

Serves 6–8

Serving suggestions
Serve as a sundae with Toasted Oat and Nut Ice Cream (page 36), poached apricots and Chunky Marmalade Sauce*.

Spoon into the center of a doughnut soaked in apple brandy or whiskey and studded with hazelnuts. Just before serving spoon over a little cider sauce: use the Wine Sauce* substituting hard cider for the wine. Decorate with fine strips of orange peel.

To reduce your sugar intake
Replace the sugar with half the quantity of **fructose** or with an **artificial sweetener**, provided the recipe does not call for a sugar syrup. Normally, 3–4 artificial sweeteners are the equivalent of 2 tablespoons sugar but always check that you have the right degree of sweetness. Artificial sweeteners must be added to custard-based ice creams after the custard has cooled.

Apple Cream Ice

6 cups tart apples peeled, cored and sliced
3/4 cup sugar
Thinly grated zest of 1 lemon
Juice of 2 lemons
1 1/2 inch cinnamon stick
Green food coloring, optional
1/4 cup brandy, optional
2/3 cup cream, whipped

Poach the apples with the sugar, lemon zest and juice, cinnamon and 2½ cups water until tender. Remove the cinnamon stick and reduce the mixture to a purée. Leave to cool.

Add the coloring and brandy, if you are using them, and freeze until just becoming firm around the edges. Beat the mixture in a bowl, fold in the cream and pour back into the container. Cover and freeze until firm.

About 30 minutes before serving, transfer the cream ice to the refrigerator.

Serves 4

Serving suggestion
Serve with Burnt Honey Sauce*.

Dessert suggestion
Line a loaf tin with the cream ice. Fill the center with Blackberry Sorbet (page 30) or Cider Sorbet (page 134).

Applesauce Yogurt Ice

1 1/4 cups very thick applesauce, chilled
Large pinch of grated nutmeg
Large pinch of ground cinnamon
1/2 cup confectioners' sugar
Finely grated zest and juice of 1 orange
1 1/4 cups thick plain yogurt, whipped

Put the applesauce in a bowl with the nutmeg, cinnamon and confectioners' sugar and beat until light. Fold in the orange zest and juice and then the yogurt. Pour into individual containers, cover and freeze until firm.

About 25 minutes before serving, transfer the ice cream to the refrigerator.

Serves 4

Additional recipe using apples: Chestnut and Apple Meringue Mousse (page 42).

Apricot

All the forms in which apricots are available – fresh, dried, canned and even good-quality apricot jam – are suitable for making ices. Each imparts its own character – dried apricots give a deep richness, fresh fruit the taste of sun and summer and canned apricots a sweeter, less pronounced (but very smooth) fruit flavor. About 1¼ pounds fresh apricots will yield 1¼ cups purée.

Simple Apricot Ice Cream
Add 1 cup canned apricots, drained and chopped, to any of the Basic Recipes*.

Dried Apricot Ice Cream

¾ cup dried apricots, soaked overnight in cold, strained tea
Long strip of lemon peel
3 egg yolks
⅓ cup sugar
1¼ cups cream, whipped
2 egg whites

Cook the apricots and lemon peel in just enough soaking liquid to cover until the fruit is soft. Remove the peel and purée the apricots with the soaking liquid. Boil to reduce, if necessary, until you have ⅔ cup purée. Set aside to cool.

Beat the egg yolks with the sugar in a bowl placed over hot water until they are thick and light. Remove the bowl from the heat and continue beating until the mixture is cool. Fold in the apricot purée and the cream.

Whip the egg whites until stiff, then lightly fold them into the apricot mixture. Spoon into a container, cover and freeze until firm.

About 30 minutes before serving, transfer the ice cream to the refrigerator.

Serves 4–6

Apricot Sorbet

¾ pound very ripe apricots, peeled and pitted
Juice of 1 large lemon
½ cup sugar

Purée the apricots into a bowl. Add the lemon juice and whip in the sugar with a wire whisk. Pour into a container, cover and freeze until firm, beating 3 times at 45-minute intervals. About 30 minutes before serving, transfer the sorbet to the refrigerator.

Serves 4

Serving suggestion
Place small spoonfuls in the centers of cold ripe apricots from which the pits have been removed. For an extra special touch sprinkle the apricots with a little cognac.

Apricot and Wine Ice Cream

12 large, plump dried apricots
Approximately 1 cup dry white wine
2 tablespoons honey
Approximately ¼ cup sugar
Long strip of lemon peel
¼ pound full fat cream cheese
1 cup cottage cheese, strained
2 egg whites
Crushed Gingersnaps, for decoration*

Put the apricots in a bowl and pour in the wine, there should be sufficient to cover the fruit, and soak for 8 hours or overnight.

Put the apricots and the soaking wine in a saucepan. Add the honey, sugar and lemon peel and simmer gently for about 20 minutes until tender. Remove the lemon peel and purée the fruit and liquid – if there is a lot of excess liquid reduce it by boiling rapidly.

Beat the cheeses together in a bowl until very smooth then beat in the apricot purée. Taste and adjust the sweetness if necessary. Spoon into a container, cover and freeze to the slushy stage. Beat well in a bowl. In another bowl, whip the egg whites until stiff but not dry and fold into the apricot mixture. Return to the container, cover and leave until firm.

About 35–40 minutes before serving, transfer the ice cream to the refrigerator. Serve each portion with some crushed gingersnaps sprinkled over.

Serves 4

Apricot Ice Cream (with pie filling)

1¼ cups cream
1 pound can apricot pie filling
1 egg white

Whip the cream until soft peaks are formed, then fold in the pie filling. In a clean bowl whip the egg white until stiff but not dry and fold into the cream and apricot mixture. Pour into a container, cover and freeze until firm.

About 20 minutes before serving, transfer the ice cream to the refrigerator.

Serves 4–5

To reduce your calorie intake
Tofu can be substituted for any soft cheese (see page 13); beat with the other ingredients until smooth. It has no cholesterol and is low in fat.

Iced Apricot Mousse

1/3 cup sugar
3 egg yolks
1 1/2 pounds fresh apricots, pitted, puréed and strained
3/4–1 cup confectioners' sugar
Juice of 1 lemon
1 1/4 cups crème fraîche
3 tablespoons brandy, optional

Put the sugar and 1/2 cup water in a heavy-based saucepan and stir to dissolve. Bring to the boil and boil until the temperature reaches 234°F.

Meanwhile, beat the egg yolks until thick in a bowl. Slowly pour in the syrup, beating constantly. Continue beating until the mixture is very thick and light.

Flavor the apricot purée with confectioners' sugar and lemon juice and fold into the egg yolks.

In another bowl, whip the crème fraîche with the brandy, if you are using it, until thick, and fold into the apricot mixture. Pour the mixture into a container, cover and freeze until firm.

About 30 minutes before serving transfer the mousse to the refrigerator.

Serves 5–6

Dessert suggestion
Make into a bombe or freeze in a can or loaf pan, with a jacket of Champagne Ice Cream (page 132). Decorate with Benedictine-flavored whipped cream and Chocolate Shapes.*

Iced Apricot Soufflé

2 egg whites
1 cup confectioners' sugar
1 1/4 cups cream, whipped
1 cup apricot purée

Put the egg whites in a bowl and whip until stiff. Gradually add the sugar, whipping well after each addition, and continue whipping until a thick meringue is formed. Fold in the cream and apricot purée until just evenly blended. Pour into a container, cover and freeze until firm.

About 20 minutes before serving transfer the soufflé to the main part of the refrigerator.

Serves 4

Serving suggestion
Serve in Coupelles to which 3 tablespoons finely chopped slivered almonds have been added.*

Apricot Ice Cream

1 1/4 cups fresh apricot purée
Squeeze of lemon juice
Approximately 3/4 cup confectioners' sugar
1 1/4 cups cream, whipped

Flavor and sweeten the purée with lemon juice and sugar, adjusting the amounts of each to give a good balance. Fold the cream into the purée and pour into a container. Cover and freeze until firm, beating twice at hourly intervals.

About 30 minutes before serving transfer the ice cream to the refrigerator.

Serves 4–5

Serving suggestion
After the second beating, pour the mixture into a pie or cake pan with a removable rim, lined with crushed hazelnut Macaroons. Just before serving, remove the rim and surround with poached, halved apricots, their centers filled with a swirl of brandy-flavored whipped cream and topped by half a hazelnut.*

Apricot Yogurt Ice

3/4 cup dried apricots
1/4 cup clear honey
1 1/4 cups plain yogurt
2 egg whites, whipped until stiff
Fine strips of twisted lemon peel, for decoration

Soak the apricots in 1 1/4 cups hot water for at least 4 hours or overnight.

In a saucepan cook the apricots gently in the soaking liquid with the honey for about 20 minutes until soft. Purée the apricots with the liquid and the yogurt. Leave to cool completely. Fold in the egg whites and pour into individual containers. Cover and freeze until firm.

About 20 minutes before serving transfer the ice to the refrigerator. Decorate each portion with a twist of lemon peel as it is served.

Serves 4

Low calorie version
Substitute fructose, or a low calorie or artificial sweetener for the honey, adding it to the cold purée.

Dessert suggestion
Swirl with an equal quantity of Banana Custard Ice Cream (page 28), Butterscotch Ice Cream (page 39) or Maple Mousse (page 81). Freeze in a can or in an ice-cube tray with the ice-cube divider in place.

Apricot Jam Water Ice

1 pound jar good-quality apricot jam
¼ cup brandy or whiskey
2–3 tablespoons lemon juice

Mix the jam with the brandy or whiskey and 1¼ cups water in a blender or food processor. Pass through a strainer and add lemon juice to taste. Spoon the mixture into a container, cover and freeze until firm, beating twice at hourly intervals.

About 30 minutes before serving, transfer the water ice to the refrigerator.

Serves 4

Dessert suggestion
Remove the pits of fresh apricots, enlarge the hollows, and fill with the water ice. Sandwich the apricot halves together, brush with beaten egg white then roll in shredded coconut. Place in the freezer for about 45 minutes. Transfer to the refrigerator about 5 minutes before serving.

Quick Apricot Ice Cream

Approximately 1 pound can apricots
Approximately 1 pound can condensed milk
Juice and finely grated zest of 1 large, juicy lemon
⅔ cup cream, whipped

Drain the apricots, purée the flesh and make up to 1½ cups with some of the juice. Whip the purée with the condensed milk and lemon juice and zest in a bowl or mix in a food processor or a blender. Fold in the cream. Pour the mixture into a container, cover and freeze until firm, beating well after about 1½ hours.

About 30 minutes before serving transfer the ice cream to the refrigerator.

Serves 4–6

Serving suggestion
Serve with a Compote* of lemons and Gingersnaps*.

Apricot and Ratafia Ice Cream Dessert

1 pound can apricots
¼ cup sugar
2 eggs, separated
2 teaspoons gelatin
1¼ cups heavy cream
2 tablespoons crushed ratafias
2–3 tablespoons Amaretto liqueur

For decoration
Whipped cream
Ratafias

Purée the apricots with their syrup. Put the purée in a small saucepan with half the sugar and bring to the boil. Beat the egg yolks and gradually stir in the purée. Return the mixture to the pan and heat gently, stirring and taking care not to let it boil, until it thickens slightly. Pour into a bowl, sprinkle the gelatin over the surface and stir it in so that it dissolves. Leave in a cool place until beginning to set.

Put the egg white in a bowl and whip to a stiff foam. Gradually whip in the remaining sugar to make a soft meringue. In another bowl, whip the cream to a similar consistency and fold it into the purée followed by the meringue.

Lightly stir the ratafias and Amaretto together and leave until the liqueur is just absorbed. Fold into the apricot cream mixture and spoon into a plastic bowl. Cover and freeze until firm.

To serve, turn out the ice cream by gently pulling the sides of the bowl away from it so that it loosens, then invert it onto a cold plate and shake. Decorate with whipped cream and ratafias. Leave in the refrigerator for about 15–20 minutes.

Serves 8–10

Additional recipes using apricots: Apple and Apricot Ice Cream (page 20), Apricot and Hazelnut Meringue Cake (page 140)

To reduce your sugar intake
Replace the sugar with half the quantity of **fructose** or with an **artificial sweetener**, provided the recipe does not call for a sugar syrup. Normally, 3–4 artificial sweeteners are the equivalent of 2 tablespoons sugar but always check that you have the right degree of sweetness. Artificial sweeteners must be added to custard-based ice creams after the custard has cooled.

Avocado

With their smooth, rich flavor and texture, and delicate green colour, avocados are ideal ingredients for both sweet and savory ice creams. They soon lose their color once they have been peeled and cut, so wait until the last moment before preparing them. It is also important to freeze the mixture as soon as it is ready, in order to preserve its attractive appearance. Citrus juices will delay discoloration but will not stop it altogether.

Iced Avocado Mousse

1 large ripe avocado
Juice of 1/2 lemon
1/4 pound full fat cream cheese, softened
2/3 cup sour cream
Finely grated zest of 1 orange
1/2 cup confectioners' sugar
1 tablespoon gelatin dissolved in 2 tablespoons water
1 egg white

Purée the avocado flesh with the lemon juice. Put the cheese in a bowl and beat until smooth. Gradually beat in the sour cream and the avocado purée. Add the orange zest and sugar. Taste and add more sugar, if necessary. Blend in the dissolved gelatin. In another bowl, whip the egg white until stiff but not dry and fold into the mixture.

Pour the mixture into a container. Cover and freeze until firm.

About 10 minutes before serving, transfer the mousse to the refrigerator.

Serves 4

Dessert suggestion
Layer with Coconut Cake* sprinkled with lime juice. Spread advocaat-flavored whipped cream over the turned-out dessert and decorate with shapes cut from lime peel, and Chocolate Shapes* or Curls*.

Savory Avocado Ice Cream

2 ripe avocados
2 tablespoons lemon juice
2/3 cup sour cream
1/2 teaspoon French mustard
1 tablespoon chopped chives
Salt and freshly ground black pepper

For garnish
Lemon twists
Parsley sprigs

Cut the avocados in half, remove the stones and scoop out the flesh into a bowl. Rub the inside of the shells with some of the lemon juice and set aside. Mash the avocado flesh with the sour cream, remaining lemon juice, mustard, chives and seasoning.

Spoon the mixture into a container. Cover and freeze until firm, beating the mixture twice at 45-minute intervals. Freeze the avocado shells separately.

About 30 minutes before serving, transfer the avocado ice cream and shells to the refrigerator. Just before serving scoop the ice cream into the shells. Garnish with the lemon twists and parsley sprigs.

Serves 4

Serving suggestion
Serve as a first course for a light summer lunch, with finely sliced raw zucchini sprinkled with a light lemon vinaigrette or with poached fresh salmon steaks.

Avocado Ice Cream

2 eggs, separated
1/3 cup sugar
1 1/4 cups light cream
2 avocados
Finely grated zest and juice of 1 large orange
1 1/4 cups heavy cream, whipped

Put the egg yolks with the sugar in a bowl and beat until thick. Put the light cream in a heavy-based saucepan, and heat to just below simmering point then beat into the egg yolks. Return to the rinsed pan and cook over low heat, stirring constantly, until thickened. Set aside to cool, stirring occasionally.

Remove the flesh from the avocados and purée with the orange zest and juice and put in a bowl. Beat in the cooled custard and fold in the whipped cream. Spoon into a container, cover and freeze until just becoming firm. Beat well in a bowl. Whip the egg whites until stiff but not dry and fold into the avocado mixture.

Spoon the mixture back into the container. Cover and freeze until firm.

About 30 minutes before serving, transfer the ice cream to the refrigerator.

Serves 6–8

Serving suggestion
Fill chilled avocado shells with scoops of Avocado Ice Cream intermingled with scoops of Lemon Sorbet (page 74). Serve with Cigars Russe*.

Avocado Sorbet

2 large ripe avocados
Juice of 2–3 limes or lemons
3–4 tablespoons sugar

For decoration
Thick plain yogurt
Shapes cut from lime or lemon peel

Peel the avocados, put the flesh in a blender and immediately add the lime or lemon juice. Add the sugar and blend until smooth. Taste and add more lime or lemon juice or sugar if required. Pour the mixture into a container. Cover and freeze until firm, beating 3 times at 30-minute intervals.

About 30 minutes before serving, transfer the ice cream to the refrigerator.

Top each portion with 1–2 teaspoons yogurt and decorate with lime or lemon peel shapes.

Serves 4

Serving suggestion
Spoon the sorbet into chilled avocado shells and decorate with lemon slices.

Additional recipe using avocados: Lime and Avocado Ice Cream (page 75).

Banana

Bananas make delicious ice creams – and have the additional advantage that they are available all the year round. They start turning brown as soon as they have been peeled, so don't prepare bananas until you are ready to add them to the mixture – and blend them immediately with lemon, lime or orange juice. This will protect them against discoloration and also help to 'lift' the flavor.

Simple Banana Ice Cream
Mash enough bananas to make about 1¼ cups purée, blend with citrus juice and add to any of the Basic Recipes* or to a good-quality bought vanilla ice cream.

'Irish Coffee' Banana Ice Cream

1¼ cups cream, whipped
3 bananas, sliced
⅓ cup walnuts, chopped
¼ cup sugar
5 tablespoons Irish Velvet liqueur
3 egg whites

Put the cream in a bowl and fold in the bananas, walnuts, sugar and 2 tablespoons of the liqueur. Whip the egg whites until stiff but not dry and fold into the cream mixture. Spoon the mixture into a container. Cover and freeze until firm.

About 15 minutes before serving transfer the ice cream to the refrigerator. Spoon a little of the remaining liqueur over each portion of ice cream as it is served.

Serves 6

Serving suggestion
Serve in Ice Cream Cones* coated in shredded coconut, with a little Jamesons Irish Velvet Irish Coffee liqueur spooned over each portion.

Banana Ice Cream

1 vanilla pod
1¼ cups milk
3 egg yolks
¼ cup sugar
¼ cup plain flour
3 ripe bananas
Finely grated zest and juice of 1 orange
1¼ cups cream, whipped

In a heavy-based saucepan, heat the vanilla pod in the milk just to simmering point. Remove from the heat, cover and leave to infuse for 45 minutes.

Put the egg yolks, sugar and flour in a bowl and blend together until smooth.

Remove the vanilla pod and bring the milk to simmering point. Stir the milk into the egg yolk mixture. Return the mixture to the rinsed pan and bring to the boil, stirring constantly. Then simmer gently until the mixture thickens. Remove from the heat and leave to cool, stirring frequently to prevent a skin forming.

In another bowl, mash the bananas with the orange zest and juice. Beat in the custard. Spoon the mixture into a container. Cover and freeze, beating twice at hourly intervals in a bowl. Fold in the whipped cream and spoon the mixture back into the container. Cover and freeze until firm.

About 30 minutes before serving transfer the ice cream to the refrigerator.

Serves 4

Serving suggestion
Serve with Bitter Chocolate Sauce*, Burnt Honey Sauce*, Hot Fudge Sauce*, Marshmallow Sauce*, Caramel Sauce* or Milky Way Sauce*.

Banana Custard Ice Cream

Approximately 1¾ cups sweetened condensed milk
2 tablespoons cornstarch
3 eggs, separated
Sugar, to taste
4 bananas
Juice of 1 lime or lemon
Few drops of vanilla extract

Make up the condensed milk to 1 quart with water. Put the cornstarch in a cup and stir in a little milk until smooth. In a heavy-based saucepan, bring the remaining milk to the boil. Pour into the blended cornstarch, stirring. Return the mixture to the boil again, stirring constantly. Continue to cook until the mixture thickens. Check for sweetness.

Beat the egg yolks, with sugar if needed, in a bowl and stir in the hot milk. Mash the bananas with the lime or lemon juice and beat into the custard with the vanilla extract. Leave to cool, stirring occasionally. Pour the mixture into a container, cover and freeze until just becoming firm. Beat well in a bowl. Whip the egg whites until stiff but not dry and fold into the custard. Spoon the mixture back into the container. Cover and freeze until firm.

About 30 minutes before serving transfer the ice cream to the refrigerator.

Serves 6–8

Dessert suggestions
Ripple with Apricot Yogurt Ice (page 24), or freeze in a ring mold and fill the center with Orange Water Ice (page 84).

Banana Yogurt Ice

2 cups mashed bananas
1 tablespoon lime or lemon juice
¼ cup brown sugar
1¼ cups thick plain yogurt
Praline* broken into small pieces, for decoration

Put the bananas in a bowl and blend in the lime or lemon juice and the sugar. Beat in the yogurt. Spoon the mixture into a container. Cover and freeze until firm, beating 3 times at 45-minute intervals.

About 30 minutes before serving transfer the ice cream to the refrigerator. Serve decorated with the praline.

Serves 4

Serving suggestion
Serve with crème fraîche decorated with strips of lemon or lime peel.

Low calorie version
Replace the brown sugar with fructose, or a low calorie or artificial sweetener. Serve with Low Calorie Topping*.

Banana and Honey Ice Cream

2 cups mashed ripe bananas
⅔ cup heavy cream
⅔ cup plain yogurt
2 tablespoons lemon juice
5 tablespoons honey
2 egg whites
Toasted slivered almonds, for decoration

Put the bananas in a bowl. Blend in the cream, yogurt, lemon juice and honey until smooth. Pour the mixture into a container, cover and freeze, beating twice at 45-minute intervals. Whip the egg whites until stiff but not dry then carefully fold into the banana cream after the second beating. Pour the mixture into a container. Cover and freeze until firm.

About 30 minutes before serving, transfer the ice cream to the refrigerator. Serve each portion decorated with toasted slivered almonds.

Serves 6

Serving suggestion
Put into sundae dishes with black grapes and Ginger Wine Sorbet (page 60). Top with warm Orange Flower Sauce* just before serving and sprinkle with chopped hazelnuts.

Banana and Chocolate Fudge Ripple Ice Cream

2½ cups milk
4 egg yolks
½ cup sugar
⅔ cup heavy cream
4 bananas

For the chocolate fudge
2 squares bitter chocolate, chopped
2 tablespoons light corn syrup
½ cup sugar
1 tablespoon cocoa
2 tablespoons sweet butter

In a heavy-based saucepan, gently heat the milk to simmering point. Put the egg yolks and sugar into a bowl and beat together then stir in the hot milk. Return the mixture to the rinsed pan and cook over a low heat, stirring constantly, until the mixture thickens. Leave to cool, stirring occasionally.

Strain the custard into a shallow metal container, cover and chill for 30 minutes before freezing until just becoming firm.

Meanwhile, make the chocolate fudge. Put the chocolate, corn syrup, sugar, cocoa and ⅓ cup water in a heavy-based saucepan over a low heat. Stir until the chocolate has melted then bring to the boil and simmer for 5 minutes, stirring. Remove from the heat and beat in the butter. Leave to cool, stirring occasionally.

Remove the semi-frozen custard from the freezer, pour into a bowl and beat well. Whip the cream in another bowl until soft peaks form. Purée the bananas and fold into the custard with the cream. Lightly fold in the chocolate fudge to give a rippled effect, spoon back into the container, cover and freeze until firm.

About 35 minutes before serving, transfer the ice cream to the refrigerator.

Serves 6

Recipes for cakes, sauces, etc., asterisked in the dessert and serving suggestions, are given on pages 145 to 152. For directions on layering, lining and other techniques involved in creating desserts, see pages 152 to 155. Basic recipes are on pages 16 and 17.

Blackberry, Loganberry

There are two kinds of blackberries – plump, juicy ones with a delicate, slightly perfumed flavor, and hard, less juicy berries that are almost bitter. The first make beautiful ices, the second may need some help from rosewater, blackberry liqueur or eau-de-vie (and give out less juice). One recipe specifically calls for loganberries but they can be used instead of blackberries in any of the recipes.

Simple Blackberry Ice Cream
Lightly crush 1 cup blackberries, sweetening them with confectioners' sugar if necessary, and add to any of the Basic Recipes*.

Blackberry Snow Cream

3 cups blackberries
Blackberry eau-de-vie, optional
1/2 cup sugar
6 ounces full fat cream cheese
2 egg whites

In a saucepan, gently cook the blackberries in 1/2 cup water until they begin to fall apart. Purée the fruit then pass through a strainer. Measure the purée and make up to 1 1/4 cups, if necessary, with water or, preferably, with blackberry eau-de-vie. Pour the mixture into a container and leave to cool. Cover and freeze to the slushy stage.

Put half the sugar and the cheese in a bowl and beat until smooth. Then beat the mixture into the semi-frozen purée. Return to the freezer until just firm.

Just before serving, whip the egg whites until stiff but not dry then whip in the remaining sugar. Fold the egg whites lightly into the blackberry cream to give a swirled effect. Serve immediately in frosted glasses.

Serves 4

Serving suggestion
Put the cream into a bowl, surround with whipped cream and decorate with fresh blackberries.

Blackberry Custard Ice

5 cups blackberries
1/3 cup sugar
1 1/4 cups canned dairy custard
2/3 cup cream, whipped
Whole fresh blackberries, for decoration

Poach the blackberries with 2 tablespoons water until they begin to fall apart. Purée then strain the fruit into a bowl. Stir in the sugar and leave to cool.

Beat the custard into the purée then fold in the cream. Pour the mixture into a container. Cover and freeze until firm, beating twice at hourly intervals.

About 30 minutes before serving, transfer to the refrigerator. Decorate with fresh blackberries.

Serves 4–5

Blackberry Rose Ice Cream

1 cup sugar
6 cups blackberries, puréed and strained
2 tablespoons crème de cassis
2 tablespoons rosewater
Squeeze of lemon juice, to taste
2 cups cream, whipped
Whole blackberries, for decoration

In a heavy-based saucepan, dissolve the sugar in 2 cups water. Bring to the boil and boil rapidly for 2 minutes. Set aside to cool.

Stir the blackberry purée, crème de cassis, rosewater and lemon juice into the syrup. Gradually pour the syrup into the cream and fold together lightly until evenly blended.

Pour the mixture into a container. Cover and freeze until firm, beating twice at hourly intervals.

About 30 minutes before serving, transfer the ice cream to the refrigerator. Decorate each portion with whole blackberries.

Serves 6–8

Serving suggestion
Scoop balls into Meringue Baskets, intermingled with fresh blackberries. Serve with a sauce made from strained blackberry purée and cream flavored with a touch of rosewater.*

Blackberry Sorbet

4 cups ripe blackberries
1/2 cup sugar
2 tablespoons rosewater, optional

For decoration
Blackberry leaves
Whole blackberries

Cook the blackberries with 1 tablespoon water in a covered pan over a very low heat until the juices just begin to run and the fruit softens. Purée the fruit then pass through a fine strainer. Stir in the sugar and rosewater.

Pour the mixture into a container. Cover and freeze until firm, beating 3 times at 45-minute intervals.

About 35 minutes before serving, transfer the sorbet to the refrigerator. Serve decorated with blackberry leaves and whole berries.

Serves 4

Serving suggestion
Surround with fresh blackberries and serve with Cigars Russe.*

Dessert suggestion
Make into a bombe (or freeze in a cake or loaf pan) with a jacket of Apple Cream Ice (page 21).

Loganberry Cream Ice

½ pound cream cheese
1 cup confectioners' sugar
⅔ cup cream, lightly whipped
Juice of 1 small lemon
5 cups loganberries, puréed and strained
Frosted* whole loganberries, for decoration

Beat the cheese in a bowl until it is smooth and soft
then beat in the sugar. Fold in the cream, lemon juice
and loganberry purée until evenly blended. Pour the
mixture into a container.

Cover and freeze until firm, beating the mixture
once after 1½ hours.

About 20 minutes before serving, transfer the cream
ice to the refrigerator. Decorate each portion with
frosted berries.

Serves 4

Dessert suggestion
*Just before serving, layer with circles or rectangles of
Meringue* starting and finishing with meringue.
Decorate with whipped cream, slivered almonds and
frosted berries.*

Additional recipe using blackberries: Blackberry
and Orange Layer Cake (page 139).

Black Currant

Black currants, with their wonderfully concentrated flavor, make some of the most delicious of all ices. Puréed fruit must be strained; one pound black currants will make about 1¼ cups purée.

Simple Black Currant Ice Cream
Add 1¼ cups black currant purée, sweetened if necessary, to any of the Basic Recipes*.

Black Currant Yogurt Ice

3 cups black currants, cooked
1¼ cups plain yogurt
Juice of ½ lemon
Approximately ½ cup confectioners' sugar
1 tablespoon gelatin
2 egg whites

For decoration
Frosted black currant leaves
Whole black currants

Purée the black currants then pass through a strainer into a bowl. Beat in the yogurt, lemon juice and sugar.

Dissolve the gelatin in 4 tablespoons water in a small bowl placed over a pan of hot water. Blend this with the black currant mixture and leave in a cool place until just beginning to set. Pour into a container, cover and freeze, beating twice at 45-minute intervals.

Whip the egg whites until stiff but not dry and carefully fold into the black currant mixture after the second beating. Spoon the mixture into a container. Cover and freeze until firm.

About 15 minutes before serving, transfer the ice to the refrigerator. Serve decorated with frosted black currant leaves and whole black currants.

Serves 4

Low calorie version
Substitute fructose, or a low calorie or artificial sweetener for the sugar. Use yogurt or Low Calorie Topping instead of cream for serving.*

Black Currant Sorbet

4 cups black currants
¾ cup sugar
2 teaspoons lemon juice
Crème de cassis, for serving

In a covered saucepan, gently cook the black currants with 6 tablespoons water until the juices run and the fruit is soft. Reduce to a purée, with the liquid, then pass through a strainer. In a heavy-based saucepan dissolve the sugar in 1¼ cups water and bring to the boil for 10 minutes. Cool slightly, stir in the lemon juice and strain.

Mix the syrup with the black currant purée and make up to 3 cups with water, if necessary. Pour the mixture into a container. Cover and freeze until firm, beating 3 times at 45-minute intervals.

About 45 minutes before serving, transfer the sorbet to the refrigerator. Pour a spoonful of crème de cassis over each portion as it is served.

Serves 6

Serving suggestion
For a refreshing summer first course serve intermingled with balls of honeydew or cantaloupe melon. Decorate with mint leaves.

Black Currant Ice Cream (with soft cheese)

6 ounces soft cheese/ricotta
⅓ cup sugar
1¼ cups milk
1 cup strained thick black currant purée
Squeeze of lemon juice

Put the cheese with the sugar in a bowl and blend until smooth. Gradually beat in the milk making sure the mixture remains smooth. Lastly, beat in the black currant purée and lemon juice.

Pour the mixture into a container. Cover and freeze until firm, beating twice at hourly intervals.

About 20 minutes before serving, transfer the ice cream to the refrigerator. Serve in frosted glasses.

Serves 4

Serving suggestion
Serve in a Meringue Basket with lid. Decorate with crème de cassis-flavored whipped cream and black currants. Serve with a sauce of strained black currant purée.*

Black Currant Ice Cream

4 cups black currants
⅔ cup sugar, to taste
1½ cups cream, whipped

For decoration
'Pairs' of Frosted black currants*
Frosted black currant leaves*

In a saucepan, gently cook the black currants with the sugar and ⅔ cup water until they are soft. Reduce to a purée then pass through a fine strainer and set aside to cool. When cold fold in the cream.

Pour the mixture into a container. Cover and freeze until firm, beating twice at hourly intervals.

About 30 minutes before serving, transfer the ice cream to the refrigerator. Decorate each portion with frosted black currants and black currant leaves.

Serves 4

Serving suggestion
Put into thin-stemmed wine glasses, layered with swirls of whipped cream. Decorate with fresh black currants and angelica.

Dessert suggestion

Layer with Peppermint Ice Cream (page 95), with crushed Meringues* between each layer. Decorate the turned-out dessert with whipped cream flavored with crème de menthe or crème de cassis, black currants and mint leaves. Serve with Sponge Fingers*.

Iced Black Currant Mousse

5 cups black currants
5 eggs, separated
³/₄ cup sugar
²/₃ cup cream, whipped

For decoration
Whipped cream
Crème de cassis
Long thin strips of orange peel

In a saucepan, cook the black currants in ½ cup water until soft. Purée the black currants and cooking liquid and strain into a bowl. Set aside to cool. Beat the egg yolks with the sugar until thick and light, fold into the black currant purée with the cream. Whip the egg whites until stiff but not dry and fold into the black currant mixture.

Pour the mixture into a container. Cover and freeze until firm.

About 30 minutes before serving, transfer the mousse to the refrigerator. Serve each portion topped by a swirl of whipped cream, with a little crème de cassis poured over and finished by thin shreds of orange peel.

Serves 6

Serving suggestion

Create a sundae with scoops of Pistachio and Green Chartreuse Ice Cream (page 101), Black Currant Sorbet (page 32) and tiny Meringues*. Top with cream and slivered almonds.

Dessert suggestion

Enclose the mousse in a lining of Litchi Ice Cream (page 127). Serve with fresh (or canned) litchis and strained black currant purée.

Additional recipes using black currants: Black Currant Leaf Water Ice (page 71), Black Currant, Rose Petal and Champagne Roll (page 136).

Blueberry

Plump, juicy and richly flavored, the blueberry has been described as an aristocrat among fruits. Originally gathered in the wild, blueberries are now cultivated in many parts of the world. Canned, bottled or frozen berries can be used when the fresh fruit is not available.

Simple Blueberry Ice Cream
Add 1 cup stemmed whole blueberries to any of the Basic Recipes*.

Blueberry Yogurt Ice

3 cups blueberries, puréed and strained
1¼ cups plain yogurt
Juice of ½ lemon
Approximately ½ cup confectioners' sugar
1 tablespoon gelatin, dissolved in 4 tablespoons water
2 egg whites

Put the blueberry purée, yogurt, lemon juice and sugar in a bowl and beat together until smooth. Blend in the dissolved gelatin.

In another bowl, whip the egg whites until stiff but not dry then fold into the yogurt mixture. Freeze in individual dishes until firm.

About 20 minutes before serving, transfer the ices to the refrigerator.

Serves 4

Low calorie version
Use fructose or a low calorie or artificial sweetener instead of sugar. Serve with Low Calorie Topping.*

Blueberry Ice Cream (with whole berries)

2 eggs, separated
3 tablespoons syrupy blueberry jam
⅓ cup sugar
1¼ cups cream, whipped
2 cups fresh blueberries, stemmed

Beat the egg yolks until thick in a bowl. Beat in the blueberry jam and the sugar and continue beating until thick and light.

In another bowl, whip the egg whites until stiff. Fold the cream into the egg yolks followed by the egg whites and lastly the blueberries.

Pour into a container. Cover and freeze until firm.

About 30 minutes before serving, transfer the ice cream to the refrigerator.

Serves 4

Dessert suggestion
Freeze in a lining of Coconut and Lime Ice Cream (page 49). Warm some blueberries in brandy or bourbon, place them on the dessert and flambé. Serve with extra blueberries and Sponge Fingers.*

Iced Blueberry Snow

5 ounces full fat cream cheese, beaten
⅓ cup caster sugar
⅔ cup sour cream
4 cups blueberries, puréed and strained
2 egg whites

For decoration
Sweet geranium leaves
Geranium flowers or crystallized roses

Put the cheese in a bowl and gradually beat in the sugar and then the soured cream. Fold in the blueberry purée. Taste and add more sugar, if necessary.

Pour the mixture into a container. Cover and freeze to the slushy stage. Beat well in a bowl.

Whip the egg whites until stiff but not dry and fold into the blueberry cream. Spoon into a container, cover and freeze until firm.

About 30 minutes before serving, transfer the snow to the refrigerator. Decorate each portion with sweet geranium leaves and small geranium flowers or crystallized roses.

Serves 4

Dessert suggestion
Freeze in individual ring molds, then pipe slightly softened Strawberry Soufflé (page 120) into the center and return to the freezer. To serve, arrange blueberries around the base of the turned-out dessert and pipe small rosettes of whipped cream around the top. Place one or two strawberry slices in the center of each soufflé.

Blueberry Sorbet

1 pound jar or can of blueberries
Finely grated zest and juice of 1 lemon

Purée the contents of the jar or can of blueberries with the lemon zest and juice. Pour the mixture into a container. Cover and freeze until firm, beating 3 times at 45-minute intervals.

About 15 minutes before serving, transfer the sorbet to the refrigerator.

Serves 4

Serving suggestion
Serve in Coupelles or in long-stemmed frosted wine glasses with strips of lemon and lime peel hanging from the edges. Decorate each serving with triangular segments of the lemon and lime.*

Blueberry Ice Cream

2 cups fresh blueberries, stemmed
¹/₂ cup sugar
2¹/₂ cups light cream
Fresh blueberries, for decoration

Mix the blueberries and sugar in a saucepan and cook, stirring occasionally, until the sugar dissolves and the mixture simmers. Remove from the heat and leave to cool.

Stir in the cream, mixing well. Pour the mixture into a container and cool completely. Cover and chill for at least an hour before freezing until firm, beating twice at hourly intervals.

About 20 minutes before serving, transfer the ice cream to the refrigerator. Serve decorated with the blueberries.

Serves 6

Serving suggestion
Serve as a sundae with Muesli Ice Cream (page 37).
Top with white Wine Sauce*.

Blueberry Tofu Ice Cream

3 cups fresh or unsweetened frozen blueberries
1¹/₄ cups tofu
1 tablespoon fructose, or to taste
Few drops of vanilla extract

In a covered heavy-based saucepan, cook the blueberries over a low heat until the juice starts to run and bubble around the edges. Purée the blueberries and pass through a fine strainer. Blend the blueberry purée with the tofu, fructose and vanilla extract until smooth.

Pour the mixture into a shallow, metal container, cover and freeze until just becoming firm.

Tip the semi-frozen mixture into a bowl and beat well then return to the container, cover and freeze until firm.

About 30 minutes before serving, transfer the ice cream to the refrigerator.

Serves 3–4

Blueberry Ripple Ice Cream

1¹/₄ cups milk
1 vanilla pod
3 egg yolks
¹/₂ cup sugar
2¹/₂ cups fresh or unsweetened frozen blueberries
1¹/₄ cups cream, whipped

In a heavy-based saucepan, bring the milk and vanilla pod to simmering point. Remove from the heat, cover and leave for 15 minutes. Remove the vanilla pod. Put the egg yolks and half the sugar in a bowl and beat until light, then beat in the milk. Pour the mixture into the rinsed pan and cook over a low heat, stirring constantly, until the mixture thickens. Do not allow it to boil.

Strain the custard into a bowl and leave to cool, stirring occasionally. Pour into a shallow container and chill for 30 minutes. Cover and freeze until just becoming firm.

In a covered heavy-based saucepan cook the blueberries with the remaining sugar over a low heat until the juices run and just begin to simmer. Purée the fruit then pass through a fine strainer and leave to cool.

Tip the semi-frozen custard into a bowl and beat well. Fold in the cream. Lightly fold the blueberry purée into the mixture to give a rippled effect then spoon into a washed can. Cover the ends with plastic wrap and freeze until firm. About 30 minutes before serving, remove the ice cream from the can and leave in the refrigerator. Serve in slices.

Serves 6–8

Serving suggestion
Serve with Cigars Russe*.

To reduce your sugar intake
Replace the sugar with half the quantity of **fructose** or with an **artificial sweetener**, provided the recipe does not call for a sugar syrup. Normally, 3–4 artificial sweeteners are the equivalent of 2 tablespoons sugar but always check that you have the right degree of sweetness. Artificial sweeteners must be added to custard-based ice creams after the custard has cooled.

Brown Bread, Cereals

Brown bread and cereals like oatmeal and muesli add an interesting texture to ices. Toasting both breadcrumbs and oatmeal, with sugar, gives an intriguing flavor – but watch closely and stir them with a fork while they are heating, so that they brown evenly and don't burn.

Quick Brown Bread Ice Cream

3/4 cup dried brown breadcrumbs
3 cups heavy cream
2/3 cup sugar
Pinch of salt
Few drops of vanilla extract

Put the breadcrumbs in a bowl with 2 cups of the cream and leave to soak for 15 minutes. Stir in the sugar, salt, vanilla extract and the remaining cream.

Pour the mixture into a container. Cover and freeze until firm, beating twice at hourly intervals.

About 30 minutes before serving, transfer the ice cream to the refrigerator.

Serves 6–7

Serving suggestions
For each serving, place a tablespoonful of Butterscotch Sauce* in the bottom of a glass, top with a scoop or two of ice cream and trickle over some Benedictine.

Serve with fresh orange segments, pith and membrane removed.

Rich Brown Bread Ice Cream

2 cups fresh brown breadcrumbs
1/2 cup light brown sugar
2 1/2 cups heavy cream
7–8 tablespoons brandy
1 orange, for decoration

Mix the breadcrumbs and sugar together, spread out on a cookie sheet. Place in a 375°F oven for 30 minutes or until an even golden brown, stirring frequently with a fork. Leave until cold.

Pour the cream into a bowl and whip until soft peaks form then gently fold in the brandy and cold crumbs. Spoon the mixture into a container, cover and freeze to the slushy stage. Then, if necessary, whip vigorously to break down any ice crystals. Turn into a loaf pan lined with plastic wrap and press down firmly. Cover and freeze until firm.

To prepare the decoration, carefully remove the peel from the orange and cut it into 1 inch lengths and then into fine strips. Place the strips in a small saucepan of boiling water and simmer for 5 minutes. Drain, rinse in cold water and drain again. Leave to cool.

About 30 minutes before serving, transfer the ice cream to the refrigerator. Just before serving, turn the loaf out onto a cold plate, peel away the plastic wrap and decorate with the orange strips.

Serves 4–5

Serving suggestion
Spoon a little hot chopped candied ginger in syrup beside each portion of ice cream as it is served.

Variation
For a lighter ice cream, fold 2 whipped egg whites into the mixture after whisking. This quantity would then serve 6.

Flavor variation
Use sherry, a coffee liqueur or crème de noyau (almond-flavored liqueur) instead of brandy.

Toasted Oat and Nut Ice Cream

1/2 cup oatmeal
1/4 cup firmly packed light brown sugar
1/4 cup hazelnuts, chopped
2/3 cup milk
2 eggs, separated
1/3 cup brown sugar
Approximately 3/4 cup evaporated milk, well chilled
Brandy or orange liqueur, for serving

Mix the oatmeal, light brown sugar and hazelnuts together and place under the broiler until crisp and lightly toasted. Set aside to cool.

Pour the milk into a heavy-based saucepan and bring gently to simmering point. In a bowl, beat the egg yolks and brown sugar together until thick and light then beat in the milk. Return the mixture to the rinsed pan and cook over a low heat, stirring constantly, until thickened. Remove from the heat and set aside to cool, stirring occasionally.

In a bowl, whip the evaporated milk until thick and light. In another bowl, whip the egg whites until stiff but not dry. Fold the evaporated milk and oatmeal mixture into the custard followed by the egg whites.

Spoon the mixture into a container. Cover and freeze until firm.

About 30 minutes before serving, transfer the ice cream to the refrigerator. Serve with a spoonful of brandy or orange liqueur poured over.

Serves 4–6

Serving suggestions
Serve with Coffee Sauce*, Sweet and Sour Molasses Sauce* or a sauce made from strained, puréed blackberries.

Dessert suggestions
Ripple with Pineapple Sorbet (page 98) or Caribbean Sorbet (page 99).

Muesli Ice Cream

1/2 cup brown sugar
1/2 cup muesli
Grated zest of 1 orange
1 1/4 cups thick plain yogurt
2/3 cup cream, whipped

In a heavy-based saucepan, dissolve the sugar in
1 1/4 cups water. Bring to the boil and boil until the
temperature reaches 230–234°F then leave to cool.

Mix the muesli and orange zest together then whip
the yogurt into the cream followed by the syrup. Fold
in the muesli and orange zest and pour into a
container. Cover and freeze until firm, beating 3 times
at 45-minute intervals.

About 45 minutes before serving, transfer the ice
cream to the refrigerator.

Serves 4–6

Serving suggestion
*For each serving, place two or three scoops on a
banana sliced lengthwise. Pour over Chunky
Marmalade Sauce*.*

Dessert suggestion
Freeze as the outer layer of a bombe with Orange

*Sorbet De Luxe (page 84) or Valencia Orange Sorbet
(page 86) in the center. Arrange thin slices (not
segments) of orange, pith and membrane removed,
over the surface of the turned-out dessert and pipe
whipped cream around the base. Serve with
Gingersnaps* shaped like Cigars Russe*.*

Atholl Brose

2/3 cup oatmeal, toasted
1/2 cup light brown sugar
1 1/4 cups cream, whipped
6–8 tablespoons whiskey

Mix the oatmeal and sugar together and fold into the
cream with the whiskey. Pour the mixture into a
container. Cover and freeze until firm, beating after
1 1/2 hours.

About 20 minutes before serving, transfer the Atholl
Brose to the refrigerator.

Serves 4

Serving suggestion
*Create a coupe with Egg Nog Ice Cream (page 117)
and Bitter Chocolate Sauce*.*

Additional recipe using cereals: Maple Granola Ice
Cream (page 81).

Butterscotch, Caramel, Fudge

All-time favorites, these flavors appeal to children and adults alike. Butterscotch and caramel blend perfectly with a variety of bases to make simple treats or sophisticated desserts, while the crunchy texture of fudge complements the peanuts in one of my favorite ice creams.

Simple Caramel Ice Cream
Add ¼ pound caramels (finely chopped in a blender or food processor) to any of the Basic Recipes* or to a good-quality bought vanilla ice cream.

Simple Chocolate Caramel Ice Cream
Add 3 ounces finely chopped caramels to Chocolate Ice Cream (page 44).

Peanut Chocolate Fudge Ice Cream

½ cup milk
3 eggs, separated
½ cup sugar
3 ounces semi-sweet chocolate, chopped
2 tablespoons sweet butter
4 tablespoons smooth peanut butter
Few drops of vanilla extract
1 cup dark corn syrup
½ cup roasted unsalted peanuts, coarsely chopped

In a heavy-based saucepan, gently bring the milk to boiling point. Beat the egg yolks with the sugar in a bowl until thick. Beat in the milk. Return the mixture to the rinsed pan and cook gently over a low heat, stirring constantly, until the custard thickens. Remove from the heat.

Melt the chocolate with the sweet butter in a bowl set over a pan of hot water. Remove from the heat and beat in the peanut butter, vanilla extract and corn syrup. Slowly beat in the custard and leave the mixture to cool. Pour into a container, cover and freeze until just becoming firm. Beat well in a bowl.

Whip the egg whites until stiff but not dry. Fold the egg whites into the custard with the peanuts.

Spoon the mixture back into the container. Cover and freeze until firm.

About 20 minutes before serving, transfer the ice cream to the refrigerator.

Serves 5–6

Dessert suggestion
Freeze in a cake or loaf pan surrounded by Genoise Cake. Decorate the outside of the cake with peanut-butter-flavored whipped cream and peanut brittle. Serve with Sweet and Sour Molasses Sauce*.*

Caramel Ice Cream (with evaporated milk)

½ cup sugar
¾ cup evaporated milk

In a heavy-based saucepan, dissolve the sugar in ⅔ cup water and cook over a low heat until it turns a rich golden brown. Remove from the heat and gradually stir in another ⅔ cup water. Cover your hand while doing this as the caramel splatters. Return the pan to the heat and stir until the caramel has dissolved.

Put the milk in a bowl and whip until thick and light. Pour the caramel in, still whipping. Pour the mixture into a container. Cover and freeze until firm, beating well after 1½ hours.

About 30 minutes before serving, transfer the ice cream to the refrigerator.

Serves 4

Dessert suggestion
Layer with Walnut Ice Cream (page 124) and Coffee Ice Cream (page 50). Decorate the base and top of the turned-out dessert with coffee-liqueur-flavored whipped cream and crushed caramel.

Butterscotch Parfait

4 egg yolks
2 tablespoons butter
⅓ cup brown sugar
1¼ cups cream, whipped

Put the egg yolks in a bowl and beat until light and thick. Melt the butter and sugar in a small heavy-based saucepan. Bring to the boil and boil for 1 minute. Stir in ⅔ cup hot water – take care as the mixture will splatter – and heat until the butterscotch has dissolved. Pour onto the egg yolks, beat, and return the mixture to the pan. Stir well to ensure all the butterscotch is incorporated and continue to stir over a low heat until the mixture thickens but do not allow it to boil. Set aside to cool.

Fold in the cream and pour the mixture into a container. Cover and freeze until firm.

About 30 minutes before serving, transfer the parfait to the refrigerator.

Serves 4

Serving suggestion
Sprinkle the top of the parfait with crushed almonds or Praline

Dessert suggestion
Make a bombe or freeze in a loaf or cake pan, with the parfait encased in a layer of Rich Hazelnut Ice Cream (page 69) followed by a layer of Orange Ice Cream (page 85).

Iced Caramel Mousse

2 eggs, separated
2 egg yolks
1¼ cups sugar
2½ cups milk, warmed
4 teaspoons gelatin
3 tablespoons lemon juice
1¼ cups whipping cream
Roughly broken walnuts, for decoration

Put all the egg yolks and 4 tablespoons sugar in a bowl and beat together until thick. Gradually stir in the warmed milk. Pour into a heavy-based saucepan and heat gently, stirring and taking care not to let the mixture boil, until the custard thickens slightly. Leave to cool.

Dissolve the remaining sugar in ⅓ cup water in a heavy-based saucepan. Bring to the boil and boil to a rich, dark caramel then immediately pour in another ⅓ cup water to prevent the caramel darkening further – cover your hand while doing this as the caramel splatters. Stir over a low heat to blend in the water. Stir the caramel into the custard.

Dissolve the gelatin in the lemon juice in a small bowl placed over a pan of hot water. Remove from the heat and stir in a little of the custard then pour this mixture into the custard, stirring constantly. Leave in a cool place until just beginning to set.

Whip the egg whites and lightly whip half the cream then fold into the custard. Pour into a 2 quart ring mold, cover and freeze until firm.

About 15 minutes before serving turn the mousse out onto a cold plate and decorate with the remaining cream and the broken walnuts. Leave in the refrigerator.

Serves 6

Serving suggestion
Arrange scoops in a coffee-flavored Meringue Basket*. Top with sliced peaches and, perhaps, some crushed Praline*.

Butterscotch Ice Cream

½ cup brown sugar
¼ cup light corn syrup
4 tablespoons butter
1¼ cups heavy cream or 50/50 light and heavy
2 ounces butterscotch candies, crushed

To make the butterscotch sauce, heat the sugar, syrup and butter in a small heavy-based saucepan until the butter has melted and the sugar dissolved. Raise the heat, bring to the boil and boil for 2 minutes. Remove from the heat and stir in 2 tablespoons hot water – take care as the mixture will splatter. Leave for about an hour to cool.

Pour the cream into a bowl and whip until it stands in soft peaks. Stir in the butterscotch sauce.

Pour the mixture into a container. Cover and freeze until firm, beating well and folding in half the butterscotch candies after 1½ hours.

Serve straight from the freezer decorated with the remaining crushed butterscotch candies.

Serves 4–6

Serving suggestion
Serve in Gingersnap Baskets*, intermingled with scoops of Apple and Raisin Ice Cream (page 21).

Dessert suggestion
Ripple with Apricot Yogurt Ice (page 24).

Caramel Ice Cream

⅔ cup sugar
1 cup heavy cream
1½ cups milk
4 egg yolks

Heat the sugar in a heavy-based saucepan, stirring constantly, until it melts and turns a rich golden brown. Remove from the heat immediately and plunge the base of the pan into cold water; take care as the caramel may splatter. In another saucepan, bring cream and milk to the boil. Slowly pour the mixture into the caramel, stirring constantly, making sure the caramel is dissolved and the mixture is smooth.

Put the egg yolks in a bowl and beat until thick then slowly beat in some of the hot cream and caramel mixture. When the yolks have become warm beat them into the cream mixture. Cook over a very low heat until the mixture thickens slightly. Leave to become cold. Pour the mixture into a container. Cover and freeze until firm, beating twice at hourly intervals.

About 30 minutes before serving, transfer the ice cream to the refrigerator.

Serves 4

Dessert suggestion
Freeze in a crust of ground amaretti and very finely chopped hazelnuts bound with melted butter. Decorate the turned-out bombe with Chocolate Curls*.

Additional recipe using fudge: Banana and Chocolate Fudge Ripple Ice Cream (page 29).

CANDIED FRUITS: see DRIED and
*   CANDIED FRUITS*
CEREALS: see BROWN BREAD,
*   CEREALS*
CHAMPAGNE: see WINES, LIQUEURS

Cherry

The dark varieties of cherries make the prettiest-colored ices, but do make sure the flavor matches up to the color.

Simple Cherry Ice Cream

Add 2 cups pitted black cherries, puréed and strained, to any of the Basic Recipes* or to a good-quality bought vanilla ice cream.

Victorian Cherry Ice

2 cups dark sweet cherries
1¼ cups sugar
6 blanched almonds
Juice of 1 lemon
4 tablespoons kirsch, optional
2 egg whites

Remove the pits from the cherries, crack them and remove and bruise the kernels. In a saucepan, dissolve the sugar in 2½ cups water. Add the kernels and the almonds and bring to the boil. Remove from the heat, cover and leave to infuse for 30 minutes.

Remove and discard the kernels and almonds. Purée the cherries with the syrup. Stir in the lemon juice and kirsch, if you are using it. When cold pour the mixture into a container. Cover and freeze until just becoming firm. Lightly whip the egg whites and fold into the purée. Cover and freeze until firm. About 35 minutes before serving, transfer the ice to the refrigerator.

Serves 4–5

Dessert suggestion
Encase in Iced Kirsch Soufflé (page 131). Decorate the turned-out dessert with piped, very slightly softened Cherry Ice Cream (page 41).

Black Cherry Ice Cream (with pie filling)

1 pound can black cherry pie filling
2 tablespoons kirsch
2 tablespoons plain yogurt
1¼ cups cream, whipped
Large Macaroons*, for serving

Put the pie filling and kirsch in a bowl and beat together. Fold the yogurt into the cream then fold into the pie filling. Pour the mixture into a container. Cover and freeze until firm, beating after 1½ hours.

About 20 minutes before serving, transfer the ice cream to the refrigerator. Serve with macaroons.

Serves 4

Dessert suggestion
Freeze in a jacket of Genoise Cake*, sprinkled with kirsch. Decorate the turned-out dessert with mint-flavored whipped cream and sieved cocoa powder.

Cherry Frost

1½ cups ripe cherries, preferably a dark variety, pitted
⅓ cup sugar
1¼ cups plain yogurt
5 ounces soft cheese/ricotta or ⅔ cup crème fraîche, whipped
2 egg whites
2 tablespoons confectioners' sugar
6 pairs of cherries joined together by their stems, for decoration

Put the cherries with the sugar in a saucepan. Add about ¼ cup water and simmer for about 4 minutes. Reduce to a purée and leave until cold.

Put the yogurt and cheese in a bowl and beat until smooth or whip it lightly with the crème fraîche. Fold into the fruit purée. Pour the mixture into a container. Cover and freeze to the slushy stage. Beat well in a bowl. Whip the egg whites until stiff. Gradually whip in the confectioners' sugar and continue whipping until stiff peaks are formed. Carefully fold into the fruit mixture. Spoon back into the container, cover and freeze until firm.

About an hour before serving, transfer the cherry frost to the refrigerator. Serve decorated with pairs of cherries.

Serves 6

Serving suggestion
Freeze in individual containers. Serve on white plates, accompanied by Sponge Fingers*.

Low calorie version
Use fructose or a low calorie or artificial sweetener instead of sugar.

Black Cherry Ice Cream

2 cups ripe black cherries, pitted
Approximately ⅔ cup caster sugar
1¼ cups heavy cream, whipped
Lemon juice, optional

For decoration
Frosted* black cherries
Frosted* mint leaves

Purée the cherries with the sugar into a bowl. Fold in the cream then taste the mixture and add more sugar or some lemon juice, if necessary. Pour the mixture into a container. Cover and freeze until firm, beating well after 1½ hours.

About 30 minutes before serving, transfer the ice cream to the refrigerator. Serve decorated with frosted cherries and mint leaves.

Serves 4

Serving suggestions
Serve in chocolate-coated Meringue Baskets* or chocolate-covered Ice Cream Cones*.

Dessert suggestion
Freeze in a Chocolate Case* then decorate the top with whipped cream flavored with Cherry Heering and Chocolate Shapes* or Curls*. Arrange black cherries around the base.

Cherry Ice Cream

1¼ cups milk
3 egg yolks
⅔ cup sugar
⅔ cup light cream
⅔ cup crème fraîche
2 cups ripe cherries, pitted
Pairs of cherries joined together by their stems, for decoration

In a heavy-based saucepan, heat the milk to just below boiling point. Put the egg yolks and sugar in a bowl and beat together until thick and light then beat in the hot milk. Return to the rinsed pan and cook over a low heat, stirring constantly, until the mixture thickens. Cool, stirring occasionally.

Stir in the light cream and crème fraîche. Pour the mixture into a container. Cover and freeze until firm, beating twice at hourly intervals, and adding the cherries after the second beating.

About 30 minutes before serving, transfer the ice cream to the refrigerator. Serve decorated with pairs of cherries.

Serves 4–6

Serving suggestion
Ripple with Vanilla Ice Cream (page 123) and serve with Sponge Fingers*.

Chestnut

Chestnuts can be used fresh, dried, puréed or – for a touch of luxury – in the form of marrons glacés (candied chestnuts). The purée is available in cans and can be either sweetened or unsweetened. Check which kind a recipe calls for and make sure you buy the right one.

Simple Chestnut Ice Cream
Add either ¼ pound chopped marrons glacés or about ⅔ cup unsweetened chestnut purée to any of the Basic Recipes*.

Chestnut and Chocolate Ice Cream

1 cup dried chestnuts
Vanilla pod
2 tablespoons honey
2 eggs
2 egg yolks
⅓ cup brown sugar
2½ cups milk
1¼ cups cream, whipped
6 squares semi-sweet chocolate

For decoration
Grated chocolate
Crystallized violets

Put the chestnuts in a saucepan with the vanilla pod and honey. Cover with water and simmer for about 2 hours until tender, adding a little more water if necessary. Remove the vanilla pod and purée the chestnuts, adding a little more water if the mixture is too dry.

Put the eggs, egg yolks and sugar in a bowl and beat together. Put the milk in a heavy-based saucepan and heat to just below boiling point then stir into the eggs. Return the mixture to the rinsed pan and cook over a low heat, stirring constantly, until the mixture thickens. Leave to cool.

Fold in the cream. Melt the chocolate in a bowl over a pan of hot water then blend into the chestnut purée. Fold into the custard. Pour the mixture into a container. Cover and freeze until firm, beating twice at hourly intervals.

About 30 minutes before serving, transfer the ice cream to the refrigerator. Decorate each portion with grated chocolate and crystallized violets.

Serves 6–8

Dessert suggestion
Freeze in a loaf or cake pan around a center of Ginger Wine Sorbet (page 60). Decorate the turned-out dessert with lavish swirls of whipped cream, chopped candied ginger and Chocolate Shapes.*

Chestnut and Apple Meringue Mousse

1 cup unsweetened chestnut purée
½ cup confectioners' sugar
⅔ cup apple juice
⅔ cup heavy or whipping cream, whipped
2 egg whites
*¼ cup roughly broken Meringues**

For decoration
Whipped cream
Marrons glacés

Put the chestnut purée in a bowl with the sugar and beat until smooth. Gradually beat in the apple juice to give a soft, smooth consistency. Pour the mixture into a container, cover and freeze until just becoming firm. Fold in the whipped cream.

Whip the egg whites until stiff but not dry and carefully fold into the chestnut cream. Lastly fold in the meringues. Spoon the mixture back into the container. Cover and freeze until firm.

About 30 minutes before serving, transfer the ice cream to the refrigerator. Decorate each portion with whipped cream and marrons glacés.

Serves 4

Serving suggestion
Serve with poached apple chunks sprinkled with chopped Praline.*

Dessert suggestion
Put into apple shells and freeze. Decorate with slices of marrons glacés.

Flavor variations
Use Macaroons or hazelnut macaroons instead of meringues.*

To reduce your sugar intake
Replace the sugar with half the quantity of **fructose** or with an **artificial sweetener**, provided the recipe does not call for a sugar syrup. Normally, 3–4 artificial sweeteners are the equivalent of 2 tablespoons sugar but always check that you have the right degree of sweetness. Artificial sweeteners must be added to custard-based ice creams after the custard has cooled.

Recipes for cakes, sauces, etc., asterisked in the dessert and serving suggestions, are given on pages 145 to 152. For directions on layering, lining and other techniques involved in creating desserts, see pages 152 to 155. Basic recipes are on pages 16 and 17.

Chestnut and Cinnamon Circle

1 cup unsweetened chestnut purée
2 eggs
1¼ cups light cream
⅓ cup sugar
½ teaspoon ground cinnamon
1 pound whole fresh chestnuts
2 tablespoons Grand Marnier or other orange liqueur

Put the chestnut purée, eggs, cream, ¼ cup of the sugar and cinnamon in a bowl and beat together until thoroughly blended. Pour into a container, cover and freeze until just becoming firm. Beat well. Pour into a cold 1 quart ring mold, cover and freeze until firm.

With a small, sharp knife cut a cross through the skins of the chestnuts. Put the chestnuts in a saucepan, cover with water and boil for 10 minutes. Drain and remove the skins. Return the chestnuts to the pan, cover with water and simmer for 20–25 minutes until tender. Drain well.

In a heavy-based saucepan, heat the remaining sugar until it caramelizes and turns golden brown. Remove from the heat and stir in the Grand Marnier and 2 tablespoons water – take care as it will splatter. Reheat, stirring, until the caramel dissolves. Stir in the chestnuts and leave to cool.

Thirty to forty minutes before serving, turn the chestnut ring out onto a cold serving plate and leave in the refrigerator. Immediately before serving spoon the chestnuts into the center of the ring and trickle the syrup over the ice cream.

Serves 6–8

Chestnut and Molasses Ice Cream

¼ cup sugar
½ cup cooked, peeled chestnuts, chopped and toasted
3 large eggs, separated
⅓ cup molasses
¼ cup confectioners' sugar
Few drops of vanilla extract
1 cup heavy cream, whipped

Dissolve the sugar in ¼ cup water in a small heavy-based pan. Then boil until it becomes a light caramel. Stir in the chestnuts until evenly coated. Pour the mixture onto a cold oiled surface. Leave until cold. Break into small pieces that resemble coarse breadcrumbs.

Put the egg yolks into a bowl and beat until very thick and pale. Beat in the molasses. In another bowl, whip the egg whites until they stand in soft peaks. Whip in the confectioners' sugar and vanilla extract a little at a time and continue whipping until the mixture is very thick. Carefully fold the cream into the egg yolks with the crumbled chestnuts, followed by the egg whites. Pour the mixture into a container. Cover and freeze until firm.

About 30 minutes before serving, transfer the ice cream to the refrigerator.

Serves 4

Dessert suggestion
Encase in a jacket of Sponge Cake*. Decorate the turned-out dessert with whipped cream and raisins, soaked in rum if liked.

Nesselrode Pudding

¼ cup sugar
2 egg yolks
1¼ cups light cream
⅔ cup whipping cream
⅔ cup unsweetened chestnut purée
⅓ cup seedless raisins
2 tablespoons chopped candied orange and lemon peel
2 tablespoons roughly chopped candied cherries
Vanilla syrup made by dissolving a little sugar in a small amount of water and adding a few drops of vanilla extract

For decoration
Whipped cream
Marrons glacés

Beat the sugar and egg yolks together in a bowl until thick. In a heavy-based saucepan, bring the light cream to just below boiling point. Gradually pour the hot cream onto the egg yolks, stirring constantly. Return the mixture to the rinsed pan and heat gently, stirring constantly and taking care that the mixture does not boil, until it thickens slightly. Leave to cool, stirring occasionally to prevent a skin forming.

Whip the whipping cream in a bowl until thick. Gradually beat the custard into the chestnut purée then fold in the whipped cream.

Pour the mixture into a container. Cover and freeze until just becoming firm but not hard.

Lightly poach the dried fruit, peel and candied cherries in enough vanilla syrup to cover them for 15 minutes. Remove with a slotted spoon and leave to drain and cool. Gently fold into the chestnut ice cream making sure they are evenly distributed. Spoon the ice cream into a fluted mold, cover and freeze until firm.

About 15 minutes before serving turn out onto a cold plate and decorate with whipped cream and marrons glacés, either whole or cut in half. Leave in the refrigerator.

Serves 4

Additional recipes using chestnuts: Chestnut and Chocolate Bombe (page 142).

Plain or lavish, chocolate ices are among the most luscious of all ice creams. They can be made from semi-sweet, bitter and white chocolate, but milk chocolate is not really suitable. Cooking chocolate must be heated in cream or milk to avoid giving a raw, grainy flavor to the finished ice.

Powdered cocoa mixes and malted chocolate drink powders are also useful – and are very simple to use. They are invariably sweetened, so you may have to reduce the amount of sugar called for in a recipe. Cocoa, like cooking chocolate, must be cooked in milk or cream for several minutes.

To melt chocolate, heat it in milk or cream, or in a bowl placed over a pan of hot water – never over direct heat.

Simple Chocolate Ice Cream

Add ½ cup very finely chopped semi-sweet chocolate to any of the Basic Recipes* or to a good-quality bought vanilla ice cream.

Chocolate Ice Cream

½ cup sweet butter, chopped
1 cup milk
⅓ cup sugar
Few drops of vanilla extract
¼ cup semi-sweet chocolate, chopped

Put the butter, milk and sugar in a saucepan and stir to dissolve over low heat. Then bring to just boiling point. Pour into a blender and mix in 4 bursts of 10 seconds each. Add the vanilla extract and chocolate and blend until smooth. Pour the mixture into a container. Cover and freeze until firm, beating twice at hourly intervals.

About 30 minutes before serving, transfer the ice cream to the refrigerator.

Serves 3–4

Serving suggestion
For each serving, place a pear half, rounded side up, on a circle of Genoise Cake* sprinkled with kirsch. Coat in the ice cream followed by Meringue*. Place under a hot broiler just long enough to brown the surface.

Chocolate Ice Cream (with condensed milk)

½ cup semi-sweet chocolate, broken into small pieces
¾ cup condensed milk
½ teaspoon vanilla extract
1¼ cups whipping or heavy cream

Dissolve the chocolate in the condensed milk in a bowl over a pan of hot water, stirring occasionally. This takes about 10 minutes. Remove from the heat

and gradually stir in the vanilla extract and 4 tablespoons water. Leave until completely cold.

Pour the cream into a bowl and whip until soft peaks form then fold into the chocolate mixture. Pour the mixture into a container. Cover and freeze until firm.

About 20 minutes before serving, transfer the ice cream to the refrigerator.

Serves 6

Dessert suggestion
Layer with Iced Orange and Almond Mousse (page 85). Decorate the turned-out dessert with orange-liqueur-flavored whipped cream, slivered almonds and slices of candied orange peel.

Carob, Soybean Milk and Tofu Ice Cream

3 tablespoons unsweetened carob powder
1 pound tofu
1 cup soybean milk
½ cup vegetable oil
⅓ cup brown sugar
Few drops of vanilla extract

Blend all the ingredients together in 2 or 3 batches until smooth. Pour into a container, cover and freeze until firm, beating 3 times at 45-minute intervals.

About 30 minutes before serving, transfer the ice cream to the refrigerator.

Serves 6

Chocolate-Mint Ice Cream

2 tablespoons sugar
6 ounces chocolate-covered mint creams
3 egg yolks
⅔ cup heavy cream
¼ cup cognac, optional

Put the sugar and ½ cup water into a small saucepan and stir to dissolve over low heat. Bring to the boil and boil for 3 minutes. Pour the syrup into a blender, add the mints and blend until smooth.

Put the egg yolks in a bowl and beat until very light. Fold in the chocolate mixture. Lightly whip the cream with the cognac, if used, and lightly fold into the chocolate mixture.

Pour the mixture into a container. Cover and freeze until firm.

About 20 minutes before serving, transfer the ice cream to the refrigerator.

Serves 4–6

Rich Chocolate Ice Cream

1/2 pound good-quality semi-sweet chocolate, chopped
2 eggs
1/4 cup sugar
2/3 cup heavy cream
1/3 cup light cream
1 tablespoon Grand Marnier, optional
Twisted fine strips of orange peel, to decorate

Melt the chocolate in a bowl over a pan of hot water. Put the eggs and sugar into a bowl and beat together until very light and fluffy then quickly but lightly fold in the chocolate.

In another bowl, lightly whip the creams and Grand Marnier, if used, together and fold into the chocolate mixture. Pour the mixture into a loaf pan, cover and freeze until firm, beating well after 1½ hours.

About 15 minutes before serving, turn the ice cream out onto a cold plate and leave in the refrigerator. Serve decorated with twists of orange peel.

Serves 4

Dessert suggestion
Freeze in a crust of ground almonds worked to a stiff paste with sugar and egg white, around a center of Iced Nectarine Mousse (page 89). Decorate the turned-out dessert with Chocolate Shapes* and nectarine slices.

Cocoa Ice Cream

3 tablespoons cocoa
3 cups milk
3/4 cup sugar
6 egg yolks
1/4 cup finely chopped toasted hazelnuts

Put the cocoa in a heavy-based saucepan. Blend in a little milk until smooth. Then stir in the remaining milk. Bring to the boil over a medium heat.

Put the sugar and egg yolks in a bowl and beat until thick and light. Stir in the hot milk. Return the custard to the pan and gently heat, stirring constantly, until thickened, but do not allow it to boil. Remove from the heat and leave to cool, stirring occasionally, to prevent a skin forming. Stir in the nuts and chill for about an hour. Pour the mixture into a container. Cover and freeze until firm, beating twice at hourly intervals.

About 20 minutes before serving, transfer the ice cream to the refrigerator.

Serves 6

Serving suggestion
Serve as a sundae with Pina Colada Ice Cream (page 98), chopped marshmallows, lightly toasted chopped hazelnuts and Sweet and Sour Molasses Sauce*.

Iced Chocolate Soufflé

6 squares bitter chocolate, chopped
4 egg whites
1½ cups confectioners' sugar
2 tablespoons orange liqueur
2 cups cream, whipped

Melt the chocolate in a bowl over a pan of hot water. Leave to cool.

Put the egg whites in a bowl and whip until stiff. Gradually add the sugar, whipping well after each addition. Continue to whip until a thick, light meringue is formed. Carefully fold in the liqueur, chocolate and then the cream. Pour into a container. Cover and freeze until firm. About 15 minutes before serving, transfer to the refrigerator.

Serves 8

Dessert suggestion
Freeze in individual containers, then turn out and coat in Rich Hazelnut Ice Cream (page 69). Decorate with Chocolate Shapes* and small scrolls of whipped cream flavored with hazelnut liqueur.

Chocolate-Peppermint Ripple

2/3 cup semi-sweet chocolate, chopped
2 tablespoons milk
4 eggs
1/2 cup sugar
2 cups whipping cream
1¼ cups plain yogurt
1 teaspoon peppermint oil
Green food coloring, optional

Melt the chocolate in the milk in a bowl placed over a pan of hot water. Stir until smooth and remove from the heat. Put the eggs and sugar in a bowl and beat together until thick and light.

In another bowl, whip the cream and yogurt together until soft peaks are formed then fold into the egg mixture. Fold two-thirds of the egg and cream mixture into the melted chocolate. Stir the peppermint oil and a few drops of green coloring, if you are using it, into the remaining mixture.

Place the chocolate mixture into a container, cover and place in the freezer for about an hour. Put the peppermint mixture in the refrigerator. Swirl the peppermint mixture through the chocolate to give a rippled effect then freeze until firm.

About 30 minutes before serving, transfer the ice cream to the refrigerator.

Serves 8

Serving suggestion
Freeze in a can. Serve with Marshmallow Sauce* and Cigars Russe*.

Chocolate Ice Cream (with evaporated milk)

1³⁄₄ cups evaporated milk, well chilled
³⁄₄ cup milk or light cream
¹⁄₂ cup sugar
4 tablespoons powdered chocolate drink mix

Pour the evaporated milk and milk or cream into a bowl. Add the sugar and whip until very light and thick. Beat in the chocolate drink mix until just evenly combined. Pour the mixture into a container. Cover and freeze until firm, beating well after 1½ hours.

About 30 minutes before serving, transfer the ice cream to the refrigerator.

Serves 4

Dessert suggestion
Serve in a checkerboard with Vanilla Ice Cream (page 123).

Flavor variation
Use a malted chocolate drink powder instead of the chocolate drink mix.

Chocolate Cream Ice

2¹⁄₂ cups light cream
1 vanilla pod
¹⁄₂ cup sugar
¹⁄₂ cup semi-sweet chocolate, melted

Put the cream with the vanilla pod in a heavy-based saucepan and heat gently to just below simmering point. Remove from the heat, stir in the sugar, cover and leave for 30 minutes.

Remove the vanilla pod then gradually stir the cream into the melted chocolate. Pour the mixture into a container. Cover and freeze until firm, beating twice at hourly intervals.

About 30 minutes before serving, transfer the cream ice to the refrigerator.

Serves 4

Serving suggestion
Serve in Ice Cream Cones* coated in shredded coconut. Accompany with Chunky Marmalade Sauce*.

To reduce your sugar intake
Replace the sugar with half the quantity of **fructose** or with an **artificial sweetener**, provided the recipe does not call for a sugar syrup. Normally, 3–4 artificial sweeteners are the equivalent of 2 tablespoons sugar but always check that you have the right degree of sweetness. Artificial sweeteners must be added to custard-based ice creams after the custard has cooled.

White Chocolate Ice Cream

4 egg yolks
¹⁄₄ cup sugar
1 cup milk
¹⁄₂ pound white chocolate, chopped
1¹⁄₄ cups cream, whipped
2 tablespoons Cointreau, optional
Grated bitter chocolate, for decoration

Put the egg yolks and sugar in a bowl and beat until thick and light. Pour the milk into a heavy-based saucepan and heat to just below simmering point. Beat the milk into the egg yolks and return the mixture to the rinsed pan. Cook over a low heat, stirring constantly, until the mixture thickens. Remove from the heat.

Put the chocolate into a bowl over a pan of hot water and stir in the custard. When the chocolate has melted remove the bowl from the heat and leave to cool, stirring occasionally. Fold in the cream and Cointreau, if you are using it. Pour the mixture into a container. Cover and freeze until firm, beating twice at hourly intervals.

About 30 minutes before serving, transfer the ice cream to the refrigerator. Serve each portion decorated with grated bitter chocolate.

Serves 6

Dessert suggestion
Form into 6 balls around a small amount of Raspberry Sorbet (page 104) and coat in cocoa. Serve with Langues de Chat*.

Flavor variation
At Inigo Jones restaurant, Garrick Street, in London's Covent Garden, where this recipe was created, they flavor the ice cream with 2 tablespoons truffle juice and 1 finely chopped fresh, small truffle instead of Cointreau. Needless to say, it's quite heavenly.

Additional recipes using chocolate: Simple Chocolate Caramel Ice Cream (page 38), Chestnut and Chocolate Ice Cream (page 42), Ginger and Chocolate Chip Ice Cream (page 61), Mint and Chocolate Ice Cream (page 95), Chestnut and Chocolate Bombe (page 142), Chocolate Truffle and Hazelnut Ring (page 142).

CIDER: see WINES, LIQUEURS
CINNAMON: see SPICES
CLOVE: see SPICES

Coconut

Coconut ices can be made from fresh coconut milk and flesh, creamed coconut (which comes in a solid, compressed block) and coconut cream (a liquid, available in cans). To toast coconut, spread fresh strands or shredded coconut on a tray in a 350°F oven for about 20 minutes. Watch carefully, and stir, to make sure it doesn't get too brown.

Simple Coconut Ice Cream
Add 2 cups shredded coconut to any of the Basic Recipes*.

Coconut Ice Cream

2 cups milk
3 egg yolks
¼ cup light corn syrup, warmed
3 tablespoons butter, melted
Few drops of vanilla extract
1 cup shredded coconut
Toasted coconut, for decoration

Pour the milk into a heavy-based saucepan and bring to just below boiling point. Put the egg yolks with the syrup into a bowl and beat until thick. Beat in the hot milk and the butter.

Return the mixture to the rinsed pan and cook over a low heat until the custard thickens, stirring constantly – do not allow it to boil. Remove from the heat and add the vanilla extract and coconut and leave to cool, stirring occasionally.

Pour the mixture into a container. Cover and freeze until firm, beating twice at hourly intervals.

About 40 minutes before serving, transfer the ice cream to the refrigerator. Serve each portion decorated with a sprinkling of toasted coconut.

Serves 4

Serving suggestions
Serve with Black Cherry Sauce, Hot Chocolate Sauce*, Coffee Sauce*, Milky Way Sauce* or Orange Flower Sauce*.*

Coconut and Lime Ice Cream

5 eggs, separated
1/3 cup sugar
Juice and finely grated zest of 2 limes
1 1/2 cups canned coconut cream or 1/4 pound block creamed coconut dissolved in 1 cup hot water

For decoration
Toasted coconut
Twisted lime or lemon slices

Put the egg yolks, sugar and lime juice in a bowl and beat until very thick and light. Stir in the coconut cream and fold in the lime zest. Pour into a container, cover and freeze until just becoming firm. Beat well in a bowl. Whip the egg whites until stiff but not dry and fold into the coconut mixture.

Spoon the mixture back into its container. Cover and freeze until firm.

About 30 minutes before serving, transfer the ice cream to the refrigerator. Serve each portion decorated with toasted coconut and a twisted slice of lime.

Serves 6–8

Dessert suggestion
Make with lemon juice instead of lime and use as the jacket of a bombe. Follow with a layer of Coconut Cake* soaked in orange liqueur and a center of Iced Apricot Mousse (page 24). Decorate the turned-out dessert with coffee-flavored whipped cream, shreds of toasted coconut and quarters of poached apricots.

Smooth Coconut Ice Cream

1 1/2 cups shredded coconut
1 cup light cream
Approximately 1/2 cup sugar
1 1/4 cups plain yogurt

To serve
Fresh* raspberry sauce
Fresh raspberries
Strands of toasted coconut

Put the coconut and cream in a saucepan and bring slowly to the boil. Turn off the heat, cover the pan and leave to infuse for 30 minutes. Reduce the mixture to as fine a purée as possible in a food processor or blender then pass through a strainer. Pour about 2/3 cup very hot water through the strainer at the end to wash as much of the liquor through as possible. Stir in the sugar. Pour the mixture into a container. Cover and freeze until just becoming firm. Whip in the yogurt and freeze until firm.

About 35 minutes before serving, transfer the ice cream to the refrigerator. Serve with fresh raspberry sauce poured over and surrounded by fresh raspberries. Scatter a few toasted coconut strands over the surface.

Serves 4–5

Serving suggestion
Spoon into Almond Tuiles* and surround with poached cranberries.

Form the ice cream into 4 balls and surround each with swirls of whipped cream. Decorate with butterfly-like Chocolate Shapes* and mint leaves.

Smooth Coconut Ice Cream (with fresh coconut)

1 coconut
2/3 cup milk
1/4 cup coconut cream
1/3 cup sugar
1 1/4 cups cream, whipped
Marshmallows dipped in toasted coconut shreds, for decoration

Crack open the coconut, scrape out the flesh and reserve the milk. Cut the flesh into small pieces and put in a saucepan with the coconut milk, milk, coconut cream and sugar and cook until soft. Reduce to a purée in a blender or food processor then pass through a fine strainer. Fold in the cream. Pour the mixture into a container. Cover and freeze until firm, beating twice at hourly intervals.

About 30 minutes before serving transfer the ice cream to the refrigerator. Serve decorated with the marshmallows dipped in coconut.

Serves 4

Serving suggestion
Form the ice cream into 4 balls, roll in cocoa, and make a small indentation in the top of each. Pour some coffee or chocolate liqueur into the indentation and cap with a coconut-coated marshmallow.

Additional recipes using coconut: Coffee and Coconut Ice Cream (page 53), Mango and Coconut Ice Cream (page 79), Pina Colada Ice Cream (page 98), Pineapple and Coconut Macaroon Cake (page 137).

Recipes for cakes, sauces, etc., asterisked in the dessert and serving suggestions, are given on pages 145 to 152. For directions on layering, lining and other techniques involved in creating desserts, see pages 152 to 155. Basic recipes are on pages 16 and 17.

Coffee

Freshly roasted, freshly ground coffee steeped in milk or cream which is then strained through a fine strainer gives the ultimate in coffee flavor. An infusion of coffee beans is also delicious, but good instant coffees – and even coffee extract – are by no means to be despised or dismissed. For a softer, more rounded flavor, sweeten the ice with vanilla sugar or add a few drops of vanilla extract.

Simple Coffee Ice Cream
Add 2 tablespoons instant coffee to any of the Basic Recipes*.

Coffee Granita

About ¹/₃ cup sugar
1¼ cups fresh, hot, very strong black coffee
4–6 ice cubes
²/₃ cup heavy cream, whipped

Dissolve enough sugar to sweeten in the coffee – the granita should not be very sweet. Add 1¼ cups cold water and the ice cubes and stir until the cubes have melted.

Pour the mixture into a container. Cover and freeze until the mixture has the appearance of a mass of small, light crystals. Stir the granita and spoon into 6 tall glasses. Top each with whipped cream and serve at once with long spoons.

Serves 6

Coffee granita de luxe
Add 1¹/₂ tablespoons Benedictine and adjust the sugar to taste.

Coffee Ice Cream

³/₄ cup sweet butter, chopped
1¹/₂ cups milk
¹/₂ cup sugar
Few drops of vanilla extract
2 tablespoons instant coffee granules

Put the butter, milk and sugar in a saucepan and heat gently until the butter has melted and the sugar dissolved. Then bring to just boiling point. Pour into a blender, add the vanilla extract and coffee and blend in 4 bursts of 10 seconds each. Leave to cool. Pour the mixture into a container. Cover and freeze until firm, beating twice at hourly intervals.

About 30 minutes before serving, transfer the ice cream to the refrigerator.

Serves 4–5

Serving suggestion
Scoop into individual dishes and decorate with grated chocolate and chocolate-covered coffee beans.

Coffee Ice Cream (with condensed milk)

³/₄ cup full cream condensed milk
1¹/₂ tablespoons instant coffee granules, dissolved in 1 tablespoon boiling water
¹/₂ teaspoon vanilla extract
1¹/₄ cups whipping or heavy cream

Put the condensed milk and dissolved coffee in a bowl over a pan of gently simmering water. Cook for 15 minutes, stirring occasionally, until slightly thickened. Remove from the heat, stir in the vanilla extract and leave to cool before chilling in the refrigerator.

Whip the cream until soft peaks are formed then fold into the coffee mixture. Pour the mixture into a container. Cover and freeze until firm, beating well after 1½ hours.

About 15 minutes before serving, transfer the ice cream to the refrigerator.

Serves 4

Serving suggestions
Serve with Black Cherry Sauce, Hot Fudge Sauce* or Burnt Honey Sauce*.*

Traditional Coffee Parfait

¹/₃ cup sugar
4 egg yolks
2 cups heavy cream
Few drops of vanilla extract
2 tablespoons instant coffee granules
Grated semi-sweet chocolate, for decoration

Put the sugar and ¼ cup water in a small heavy-based saucepan. Stir to dissolve over low heat then bring to the boil and boil until the temperature reaches 230°F.

Beat the egg yolks in a bowl until thick and light. Gradually beat in the syrup. Leave to cool then chill for 30 minutes.

Put the cream in a bowl with the vanilla extract and coffee and whip until soft peaks are formed. Carefully fold into the egg yolk mixture. Spoon into tall, freezer-proof glasses, if available, or into individual dishes, and freeze until firm.

About 15 minutes before serving, transfer the parfaits to the refrigerator. Decorate the tops of the parfaits with grated chocolate.

Serves 4–6

Dessert suggestion
Form into 4–6 balls, each with a tablespoonful of Nougat Glace à l'Orange (page 57) in the center. Roll in shredded coconut, crushed hazelnut Macaroons or cocoa.*

Iced Mocha Soufflé

3 tablespoons freshly ground coffee
1¼ cups milk
½ pound bitter chocolate, chopped
4 egg whites
2 cups confectioners' sugar
2 cups cream, whipped
8 Meringue Baskets*

Put the coffee and milk in a saucepan and heat to boiling point. Remove from the heat, cover and leave to infuse for 15 minutes. Strain over the chocolate and stir until the chocolate has melted and the liquid is smooth. Leave to cool.

Whip the egg whites in a bowl over a pan of hot water until thick then gradually whip in the sugar. Continue whipping off the heat until the meringue is thick, very light and cold.

Lightly fold the cream and chocolate together then fold into the meringue. Freeze until firm in individual meringue baskets. Serve straight from the freezer.

Serves 8

Dessert suggestion
Fold ¼ cup chopped walnuts into the soufflé mixture just before freezing. Make a bombe with a jacket of Genoise Cake* sprinkled with rum, followed by a layer of Vanilla Ice Cream (page 123). Fill the center with the soufflé. Decorate the turned-out dessert with coffee- or chocolate-flavored whipped cream and Chocolate Shapes*.

Iced Capuccino

1 tablespoon gelatin
2½ cups strong black coffee
1 square semi-sweet chocolate, chopped
½ cup sugar
1 cup heavy cream
2–3 tablespoons coffee liqueur
Finely grated chocolate, for decoration

Dissolve the gelatin in a little of the coffee in a bowl. Put the chocolate and half the coffee in a saucepan and stir to melt over very low heat. Stir in the sugar and gradually stir the mixture into the gelatin. Stir in the remaining coffee and chill. Stir in the cream and liqueur and pour into a container. Cover and freeze until firm.

About 45 minutes before serving, transfer the ice cream to the refrigerator. Serve decorated with grated chocolate.

Serves 6–8

Serving suggestion
Serve in tall glasses with long-handled spoons, accompanied by Sponge Fingers*.

Coffee and Hazelnut Ice Cream

3 egg yolks
¾ cup confectioners' sugar
2 cups cream, whipped
1 tablespoon hazelnut liqueur or
    2 tablespoons hazelnuts, toasted and chopped
1 teaspoon instant coffee granules
2½ tablespoons raisins
3 tablespoons slivered almonds, toasted
Cocoa, for decoration

Beat the egg yolks and confectioners' sugar together in a bowl until very light. Fold in 1¼ cups of the cream and the liqueur or hazelnuts. Spoon half the mixture into a ring mold or loaf pan, cover and freeze for 2 hours.

Fold the coffee into the remaining cream until evenly blended. Sprinkle the raisins then the almonds evenly over the frozen cream mixture and cover with the coffee cream. Finally, spoon in the remaining hazelnut cream. Return to the freezer until firm.

About 20 minutes before serving, turn the ice cream out onto a cold plate and leave in the refrigerator. Sprinkle a little cocoa over the top just before serving.

Serves 4–5

Dessert suggestion
Freeze in a ring mold. Fill the center of the turned-out mold with small orange segments and chopped marshmallows. Pipe brandy-flavored whipped cream around the base of the dessert and finish with chopped hazelnuts.

Coffee Almond Ice Cream

2 tablespoons coffee extract
2 tablespoons brown sugar
1¼ cups plain yogurt
3 tablespoons ground almonds
2 egg whites

Put the coffee extract, brown sugar and yogurt in a bowl and beat until well mixed. Fold in the ground almonds.

In another bowl, whip the egg whites until stiff but not dry and fold into the coffee mixture. Pour into individual dishes, cover and freeze.

About 20 minutes before serving, transfer the ice cream to the refrigerator.

Serves 4

Low calorie version
Use fructose, or a low calorie or artificial sweetener instead of sugar.

Italian Coffee Ice Cream

4 egg yolks
1/2 cup sugar
1 1/3 cups strong espresso coffee made with milk instead
    of water
1 cup heavy cream, lightly whipped

For serving
Sambuca
Coffee candies

Put the egg yolks and sugar in a bowl and beat until
thick and light. Beat in the coffee then fold in the
cream.

Pour the mixture into a saucepan and warm over
low heat, stirring constantly, until it swells to nearly
twice its original volume. Leave to cool completely.

Pour the mixture into a container. Cover and freeze
until firm, beating twice at hourly intervals.

About 40 minutes before serving, transfer the ice
cream to the refrigerator. Pour a little Sambuca over
each portion and finish with coffee candies.

Serves 6

Coffee and Coconut Ice Cream

1/4 cup coffee beans
2 cups heavy or whipping cream
1 teaspoon vanilla extract
3 large eggs, separated
1/4 cup sugar
3/4 cup lightly toasted shredded coconut
Bitter Chocolate Sauce*, for serving

Put the coffee beans and half the cream in a saucepan
and bring to just below boiling. Remove from the heat,
cover and leave for 30 minutes. Strain the cream,
discard the coffee beans and whip in the remaining
cream with the vanilla extract.

Put the egg yolks in a bowl and beat until thick and
light. In a small heavy-based saucepan, dissolve the
sugar in 1/3 cup water. Then boil until the temperature
reaches 220°F. Pour the syrup onto the egg yolks in a
steady stream, whipping constantly, and continue to
whip until thick and cold.

Fold in the cream and coconut. Whip the egg whites
until stiff but not dry and fold into the mixture. Pour
the mixture into a container. Cover and freeze until
firm.

About 20 minutes before serving, transfer to the
refrigerator. Serve with chocolate sauce.

Serves 4–5

Serving suggestion
*Serve as a sundae with pineapple cubes soaked in
kirsch, Melon-Lime Ice (page 83) and coarsely chopped
semi-sweet chocolate. Top with Coffee Sauce*.*

Fresh Coffee Ice Cream

1/4 cup milk
4 teaspoons finely ground coffee
1/3 cup sugar
2 small eggs, lightly beaten
Pinch of salt
Few drops of vanilla extract
1 1/2 cups light or whipping cream

Put the milk in a heavy-based saucepan and bring just
to boiling point. Stir in the coffee and the sugar. Slowly
pour the coffee-milk mixture onto the eggs, beating
constantly. Pour back into the pan, add the salt and
vanilla extract and cook over a very gentle heat,
stirring constantly, until it thickens, taking care not to
let the mixture boil. Remove from the heat, stir in half
the cream and leave until cool, stirring occasionally.

Strain the custard through cheesecloth. Blend in the
remaining cream and pour into a container. Cover and
freeze until firm, beating twice at hourly intervals.

About 30 minutes before serving, transfer the ice
cream to the refrigerator.

Serves 5

Serving suggestion
*Make ice cream sodas by putting 2 tablespoons
chocolate sauce in the base of a tall glass for each
serving. Mix with soda water, add a scoop of ice cream
and finish with more chocolate topping.*

Dessert suggestion
Carefully fold small Meringues into the ice cream
when it has been beaten for the second time and freeze
in a round cake pan. Decorate the turned-out dessert
with large swirls of slightly softened Chocolate Ice
Cream (page 44). Finish with small Meringues* and
hazelnuts.*

Additional recipes using coffee: Walnut Mocha Ice
Cream (page 125), Coffee Ice Cream Slice (page 137),
Chocolate-coated Coffee Ice Cream Balls (page 138).

Recipes for cakes, sauces, etc., asterisked in the
dessert and serving suggestions, are given on
pages 145 to 152. For directions on layering,
lining and other techniques involved in creating
desserts, see pages 152 to 155. Basic recipes are
on pages 16 and 17.

*CRABAPPLE: see OLD-FASHIONED
                          FAVORITES*

Cranberry

Either fresh or frozen cranberries can be used for the purées in these recipes (which make some of the most beautifully colored of all ices). One pound fresh or frozen cranberries and ½–¾ cup sugar will yield about 1½ cups purée. If the fruit itself is not available cranberry sauce, preferably homemade, is a good store-cupboard stand-by for quick ice creams.

Simple Cranberry Ice Cream
Add 1½ cups cranberry sauce, sweetened if necessary, to any of the Basic Recipes*.

Cranberry Ice Cream (with cranberry purée)

3 eggs, separated
2 tablespoons sugar
1½ cups sweetened cranberry purée
1¼ cups cream, whipped
Whole cooked fresh cranberries, for decoration

Put the egg yolks and sugar in a bowl and beat until very thick and light. Fold in the cranberry purée, then the cream.

In another bowl, whip the egg whites until stiff but not dry and fold into the cranberry cream. Pour the mixture into a container. Cover and freeze until firm.

About 30 minutes before serving, transfer to the refrigerator. Decorate with whole cranberries.

Serves 4–6

Serving suggestion
Freeze in an ice-cube tray with the ice-cube divider in place. Pile in frosted glasses with cream or plain yogurt trickled over, with a scattering of cranberries.

Quick Cranberry Ice Cream

1¼ cups cream, whipped
1¼ cups bought cranberry sauce or 1¼ cups
* sweetened thick homemade cranberry sauce*
1–2 tablespoons chunky orange marmalade

Put the cream in a bowl and fold in the cranberry sauce. Mix until evenly blended. Add marmalade to taste. Pour the mixture into a container. Cover and freeze until firm. About 20 minutes before serving, transfer to the refrigerator.

Serves 4

Texture variation
Use a sauce made with whole cranberries.

Cranberry Ice Cream

1 pound fresh or frozen cranberries
1/2–3/4 cup sugar
1 1/4 cups crème fraîche or whipping cream
2 tablespoons milk if crème fraîche is used or plain
    yogurt if whipping cream is used

Put the cranberries in a saucepan and pour 1 cup
boiling water over. Cover and leave for 5 minutes.
Bring to simmering point, cook for 5 minutes, turn off
the heat and leave for 5 minutes. Bring to simmering
point again and cook for 5 minutes. Remove from the
heat, stir in the sugar and reduce to a purée. This
method produces a purée with an exceptionally good
color. Leave to cool.

   In a bowl, lightly whip the crème fraîche with the
milk or the cream with the yogurt then fold into the
purée. Pour the mixture into a container. Cover and
freeze until firm, beating twice at hourly intervals.

   About 20 minutes before serving, transfer the ice
cream to the refrigerator.

Serves 4

Dessert suggestion
*Freeze Smooth Coconut Ice Cream (page 49) in small
foil dishes or custard cups. Turn out and cover in the
ice cream. Just before serving, decorate with gin-
flavored whipped cream.*

Cranberry Ice Cream
(with cheese and yogurt)

1 pound fresh or frozen cranberries
1/2–3/4 cup sugar
1/2 pound soft cheese/ricotta, beaten
1/2 cup plain yogurt
1 egg white

Cook the cranberries as for Cranberry Ice Cream, then
stir in the sugar, adjusting to taste and leave to cool.

   Put the cheese into a bowl and gradually beat in the
yogurt to make a smooth mixture then stir in the
cranberries. Pour the mixture into a container, cover
and freeze until firm. Tip into a bowl and beat well.
Whip the egg white until stiff but not dry and fold into
the cranberry mixture. Spoon the mixture back into
the container. Cover and freeze until firm.

   About 40 minutes before serving, transfer the ice
cream to the refrigerator.

Serves 4

Dessert suggestion
*Ripple with Orange Frost (see Grapefruit Frost, page
66). Serve with Cigars Russe*.*

Low calorie version
*Use fructose or a low calorie or artificial sweetener
instead of sugar.*

Cranberry and
Pistachio Ripple

1 pound fresh or frozen cranberries
Finely grated zest and juice of 2 oranges
1/2 cup sugar
1 1/4 cups cream, whipped
2 × approximately 1 1/2 ounce packets dessert topping
    mix
1 1/4 cups milk
2 tablespoons pistachio nuts
3 tablespoons Cointreau, optional

Cook the cranberries with the orange zest and juice as
for Cranberry Ice Cream. Purée, strain, stir in the sugar
and leave to cool. Fold in the cream then freeze in a
covered container until just becoming firm.

   Make up the topping mix with the milk in a bowl.
Stir in the nuts and liqueur. Carefully fold through the
cranberry cream to give a rippled effect. Return to the
freezer until firm.

   About 30 minutes before serving, transfer the ice
cream to the refrigerator.

Serves 8–12

Dessert suggestion
*Freeze in individual ring molds. Fill the centers with
cubes of white marshmallow lightly mixed with
cranberry sauce. Pipe small rosettes of whipped cream,
brandy-flavored if wished, around the base of each
serving.*

Additional recipe using cranberries: Cranberry
Snowballs (page 138).

To reduce your calorie intake
Tofu can be substituted for any soft cheese (see
page 13); beat with the other ingredients until
smooth. It has no cholesterol and is low in fat.

CUCUMBER: see SAVORY
CUSTARD: see VANILLA, CUSTARD
DAMSON: see PLUM, PRUNE
DATE: see DRIED and CANDIED
   FRUITS

Dried and Candied Fruits

All kinds of dried fruits – apples, pears, peaches and even bananas – are suitable for ices. They can be the main ingredient, as in the recipes on these pages, or added to other recipes for extra interest (preferably soaked for a while beforehand in a liquor or liqueur, to plump them up).

Candied fruits (steeped in a rich sugar syrup for up to 14 days) and crystallized fruits (steeped in syrup and then given an outer coating of crunchy sugar) make equally delicious ices, either on their own as in a number of the recipes that follow, or combined with dried fruits.

Simple Dried Fruit Ice Cream
Soak ⅔ cup chopped dried fruit overnight in brandy or liqueur. Add to any of the Basic Recipes* or to a good-quality bought vanilla ice cream.

Tutti-Frutti Ice Cream

⅔ cup raisins
2 tablespoons chopped candied cherries
2 tablespoons chopped candied pineapple
2 tablespoons chopped candied orange or citron peel
1 tablespoon chopped candied angelica
Long strip of lemon peel
4 tablespoons brandy or orange liqueur
4 eggs, separated
1 cup confectioners' sugar, sifted
1¼ cups heavy cream, whipped
2½ tablespoons slivered almonds

For decoration
'Leaves' cut from candied angelica
Candied cherries, quartered

Soak the fruits and lemon peel in the brandy or liqueur for at least 4 hours.

Put the egg yolks and sugar in a bowl and beat until thick and light. In another bowl, whip the egg whites until stiff but not dry. Fold the egg whites into the egg yolks with the cream.

Pour the mixture into a container. Cover and freeze until beginning to become firm around the edges.

Remove and discard the lemon peel from the fruits. Mix the fruits, the soaking liquid, and the almonds into the ice cream.

Spoon into a 5 cup bowl. Cover and freeze until firm.

About 20 minutes before serving, turn out onto a cold plate and leave in the refrigerator. Decorate with the angelica 'leaves' and quartered cherries arranged in the shapes of flowers.

Serves 6–8

Dessert suggestion
Fill a Jelly Roll* with the ice cream, then coat the outside in Smooth Pistachio Ice Cream (page 101). Decorate with whole pistachio nuts.

Frozen Fruit Cake

3 eggs, beaten
½ cup sugar
2 cups milk
1 cup golden raisins
½ cup chopped pecans or walnuts
1 cup crushed Macaroons*
¼ cup chopped candied cherries
1 teaspoon vanilla extract
1 cup cream, whipped

Put the eggs and sugar in a bowl and beat until thick and light. Pour the milk into a heavy-based saucepan and bring to just simmering point. Gradually pour onto the eggs, stirring. Return to the rinsed pan and cook over low heat, stirring constantly, until thickened. Remove from the heat and set aside to cool. Pour into a container, cover and freeze to the slushy stage. Turn into a bowl, beat well, then stir in the raisins, nuts, macaroons, cherries and vanilla and fold in the cream. Spoon the mixture back into the container. Cover and freeze until firm.

About 30 minutes before serving, transfer the ice cream to the refrigerator.

Serves 6

Dessert suggestion
Fill a Jelly Roll* with the frozen cake, then coat the outside with Maple Ice Cream (page 81), Rich Hazelnut Ice Cream (page 69) or Chocolate Ice Cream (page 44).

Fruit Cake Ice Cream

2 eggs
¼ cup brown sugar
1 cup milk
1 cup cream
2½ tablespoons marzipan, finely chopped or
    1½ tablespoons ground almonds
½ cup finely chopped fruit cake
1½ tablespoons brandy, sherry or rum

Beat the eggs and sugar together in a large bowl.

Bring the milk and cream to simmering point in a saucepan. Pour onto the eggs in a slow steady stream, beat constantly, and continue to beat until the mixture is very thick and light.

Stir in the marzipan or ground almonds then fold in the fruit cake and brandy, sherry or rum.

Spoon the mixture into a container. Cover and freeze until firm.

About 20 minutes before serving, transfer the ice cream to the refrigerator.

Serves 6

Simple Candied Fruit Ice Cream

3/4 cup mixed candied fruits, chopped if necessary
Grated zest of 1 large lemon
1 × approximately 1 1/2 ounce packet instant dessert
  topping
2/3 cup milk
1 1/4 cups cream, whipped

Mix the candied fruits together with the lemon zest. Make up the dessert topping with the milk in a bowl. Fold in the cream and the fruits.

Spoon the mixture into a container. Cover and freeze until firm, beating twice at hourly intervals.

About 30 minutes before serving, transfer the ice cream to the refrigerator.

Serves 4

Serving suggestion
Sandwich each portion between two Meringues* and freeze. Just before serving, pour a little Milky Way Sauce* over each one, and sprinkle with finely chopped hazelnuts.

Nougat Glace à l'Orange

1/2 cup sugar
2 egg whites
1 quart whipping cream
2 1/2 tablespoons Cointreau
2 1/2 tablespoons chopped candied orange peel
2 tablespoons Praline*
Fresh* raspberry sauce, for serving

In a heavy-based saucepan, dissolve all but 1 tablespoon of the sugar in 2 tablespoons water then boil until a temperature of 250°F is reached.

Whip the egg white in a bowl with the sugar until stiff but not dry. Slowly pour in the syrup, whipping constantly and continue to whip until the mixture is very thick and cold.

In another bowl whip the cream together with the Cointreau until soft peaks form then fold into the meringue with the orange peel and the praline.

Pour into an oblong mold, cover and freeze until firm.

About 20 minutes before serving, turn the ice cream out onto a chilled plate and leave in the refrigerator. Serve cut into slices surrounded with raspberry sauce.

Serves 6

Serving suggestion
Sprinkle with grated chocolate.

Candied Fruit Ice Cream

1 1/4 cups candied fruits
6 tablespoons kirsch, brandy or sherry
8 lady fingers cut into 1/2 inch pieces
3 cups cream, lightly whipped
1 cup confectioners' sugar
Few drops of vanilla extract
Fresh* orange sauce for serving

Soak the fruit in the kirsch, brandy or sherry for 30 minutes.

Put the lady fingers in a bowl and drain the liquor over them. Pour the liquid off again. Whip the liquid into the cream with the sugar and vanilla extract then fold in the fruit and lady fingers. Spoon into a chilled 1 quart domed mold or bowl, cover and freeze until firm.

About 15 minutes before serving, turn the dessert out onto a chilled plate and leave in the refrigerator. Serve each portion with some fresh orange sauce.

Serves 6–8

Winter Fruit Ice Cream

1 cup chopped dried fruits – figs, peaches, dates, pears, apples, etc.
4 tablespoons brandy or rum
2 cups milk
1 cinnamon stick
3 eggs
1/2 cup light brown sugar
2 cups whipping cream

Soak the fruits in the brandy or rum overnight.

Pour the milk into a heavy-based saucepan, add the cinnamon and bring to just below boiling point. Remove from the heat, cover and leave for 30 minutes. Remove the cinnamon stick.

Put the eggs and sugar in a bowl and beat together. Bring the milk to just below boiling point again and slowly pour onto the eggs, stirring constantly. Cook the mixture gently, stirring constantly, until it thickens but do not allow it to boil. Remove from the heat and leave to cool, stirring frequently.

Whip the cream in a bowl until soft peaks form then fold into the custard with the fruits and soaking liquor. Pour into a container. Cover and freeze until firm.

About 30 minutes before serving, transfer the ice cream to the refrigerator.

Serves 6–8

Serving suggestion
Layer with crushed ginger cookies in tall glasses. Pour over Burnt Honey Sauce* or Chunky Marmalade Sauce*.

Candied Peel Ice Cream

1 1/4 cups whipping or heavy cream
4–5 tablespoons advocaat
2–4 tablespoons confectioners' sugar
1–2 tablespoons orange juice
3 heaped tablespoons chopped candied peel
Orange segments or Caramelized* orange strips, for
    serving

Whip the cream in a bowl with the advocaat, confectioners' sugar and orange juice, adjusting the amounts of these to taste, until soft peaks are formed. Spoon into a container, cover and freeze until just becoming firm. Turn into a bowl and beat well. Fold in the candied peel.

Spoon the mixture back into the container. Cover and freeze until firm.

About 20 minutes before serving, transfer the ice cream to the refrigerator. Serve with fresh orange segments or caramelized orange strips.

Serves 4

Date and Fig Ice Cream

1/3 cup chopped dates
1/3 cup chopped figs
2/3 cup sherry
Finely grated zest and juice of 1 orange
1/2 cup brown sugar
1 cup heavy or whipping cream
3/4 cup sour cream
2 egg whites

Put the dates, figs and sherry in a small saucepan and heat gently to just below simmering point. Stir in the orange zest and juice and the sugar, cover and leave for at least 4 hours.

Put the creams in a bowl with the liquid drained from the fruit and whip until soft peaks form. In another bowl, whip the egg whites until stiff. Fold the fruit into the cream and then the egg whites. Spoon the mixture into a container. Cover and freeze until firm.

About 30 minutes before serving, transfer the ice cream to the refrigerator.

Serves 4–6

Serving suggestions
Spoon into small Crêpes* with orange segments soaked in a liqueur or liquor. Deep-fry briefly, sprinkle with a thick coating of confectioners' sugar, and serve with a white Wine Sauce*.

Dessert suggestion
Freeze in a fluted container. Decorate the turned-out dessert with swirls of whipped cream, chocolate bits and walnuts.

Date Ice Cream

1/3 cup chopped pitted dates
4 tablespoons rum
2 eggs, separated
1/2 cup sugar
2/3 cup milk
1 1/2 cups cottage or farmers' cheese
Finely grated zest and juice of 1 lemon
2/3 cup cream, whipped
2 tablespoons finely chopped stem ginger

Soak the dates in the rum for about 4 hours. Put the egg yolks and sugar in a bowl and beat until light. Heat the milk to simmering point in a saucepan then stir into the egg yolks. Return the mixture to the rinsed pan and cook over a low heat, stirring constantly, until thickened. Cool, stirring occasionally.

Process the cottage or farmers' cheese, lemon zest and juice and the rum strained from the dates together in a blender or food processor until smooth then mix with the custard. Pour the mixture into a container, cover and freeze until just becoming firm. Turn into a bowl, beat well, then fold in the cream, dates and ginger. Whip the egg whites in a bowl until stiff but not dry and fold into the fruit mixture.

Spoon the mixture back into the container. Cover and freeze until firm.

About 30 minutes before serving, transfer the ice cream to the refrigerator.

Serves 6

Dessert suggestion
Freeze between layers of chocolate-flavored Meringue*. Cover the turned-out dessert with whipped cream. Decorate with pieces of candied orange peel or shapes cut from fresh orange peel.

Additional recipes using dried and candied fruits: Old English Raisin Ice Cream (page 64), Raisin Ice Cream (page 64), Golden Raisin Ice Cream (page 65), Honey and Fig Sorbet (page 73), Prune Sorbet (page 103), Prune Custard Ice (page 103), Prune Ice Cream with Brandy (page 116), Prune Ice Cream with Wine and Brandy (page 130), Mincemeat Ice Cream (page 141), Cassata (page 135), Iced Christmas Pudding (page 139).

ELDERBERRY: see OLD-FASHIONED
                  FAVORITES
FLOWERS: see HERBS, FLOWERS,
                  LEAVES
FUDGE: see BUTTERSCOTCH,
              CARAMEL, FUDGE
GERANIUM LEAF: see HERBS,
                  FLOWERS, LEAVES

Ginger

Traditionally used in sweet dishes as well as savory ones, ginger makes some of the freshest-tasting of all ices. Ginger wine gives a particularly rich, smooth flavor, while the syrup from a jar of preserved ginger is sweeter but equally refreshing. Chopped candied or preserved ginger provides 'bite' and texture, while freshly chopped fresh ginger root is well worth trying. Powdered or ground ginger can also be used and is probably a more practical ingredient.

Simple Ginger Ice Cream
Add ¼ cup chopped candied or preserved ginger to any of the Basic Recipes* or to a good-quality bought vanilla ice cream.

Ginger Wine Sorbet

1½ cups ginger wine
2 tablespoons lime juice
1 cup sugar
¼ teaspoon cream of tartar
2 egg whites

For decoration
Candied ginger
Long, thin, twisted strips of lemon peel

Mix the ginger wine and lime juice with ¾ cup water and pour into either an 8 inch cake pan or into an ice cream maker and freeze until slushy.

In a heavy-based saucepan, dissolve the sugar with the cream of tartar in ⅓ cup water over low heat. Bring to the boil and boil rapidly for 4 minutes. Remove from the heat.

Whip the egg whites in a bowl until firm then slowly pour in the hot syrup whipping all the time. Beat the ginger wine mixture then fold in the meringue.

Return the mixture to the container, cover and freeze until firm.

About 15–20 minutes before serving, transfer the sorbet to the refrigerator. Decorate each portion with candied ginger and prettily twisted strips of lemon peel.

Serves 6

Serving suggestion
Flake the sorbet and serve on top of a fresh fruit salad.

> Recipes for cakes, sauces, etc., asterisked in the dessert and serving suggestions, are given on pages 145 to 152. For directions on layering, lining and other techniques involved in creating desserts, see pages 152 to 155. Basic recipes are on pages 16 and 17.

Ground Ginger Ice Cream

3 eggs, separated
⅓ cup sugar
1 teaspoon ground ginger
¼ cup full fat cream cheese
⅔ cup milk
2 tablespoons finely chopped candied or preserved ginger

Beat the egg yolks, sugar and ground ginger together in a bowl until very light.

In another bowl, beat the cheese with the milk until fluffy. In a third bowl, whip the egg whites until stiff but not dry.

Fold the cheese and milk into the egg yolk mixture with the chopped ginger. Then fold in the egg whites.

Spoon the mixture into a container. Cover and freeze until firm.

About 30 minutes before serving, transfer the ice cream to the refrigerator.

Serves 4

Dessert suggestion
Layer with Sponge Cake or Sponge Fingers* and Gooseberry Mallow Ice Cream (page 62). Decorate the turned-out dessert with whipped cream and walnuts.*

Ginger Ice Cream (with whiskey and marmalade)

2 tablespoons whiskey
4 tablespoons ginger marmalade
2 tablespoons brown sugar
Finely grated zest of 1 lemon
1¼ cups whipping or heavy cream
2 egg whites

Put the whiskey, marmalade, sugar and lemon zest in a bowl and leave for at least 15 minutes. Whip in the cream until soft peaks are formed.

In another bowl, whip the egg whites until stiff but not dry. Fold into the ginger cream.

Pour into a container. Cover and freeze until firm.

About 20 minutes before serving, transfer the ice cream to the refrigerator.

Serves 4

Serving suggestion
Serve in Almond Tuiles. Decorate with whipped cream, fresh lime segments, pith and membrane removed, and a sprinkling of coffee sugar crystals.*

Note: If you have difficulty finding ginger marmalade, add 1 teaspoon chopped, candied ginger to a good-quality marmalade.

Ginger Crush

3 egg yolks
¼ cup sugar
1¼ cups milk
⅔ cup cream, whipped
¼ cup drained and chopped candied or stem ginger
¼ cup roughly broken Meringues*
Slices of stem ginger, for decoration

Put the egg yolks and sugar in a bowl and beat together until thick and light.

In a heavy-based saucepan, heat the milk to just below boiling point. Slowly pour the milk onto the eggs, beating constantly. Return to the rinsed pan and heat gently, stirring constantly, until the custard thickens – but do not allow it to boil. Allow to cool completely.

Pour the custard into a container, cover and freeze to the slushy stage. Beat well in a bowl.

Whip the cream in a bowl until soft peaks form. Fold the cream into the ice cream with the ginger and meringues. Return the mixture to the container, cover and freeze until firm.

About 30 minutes before serving, transfer the ice cream to the refrigerator. Serve decorated with the slices of stem ginger.

Serves 6

Dessert suggestion
Make into a bombe or freeze in a loaf or cake pan with a center of Pear Sorbet (page 93). Serve with Sponge Fingers*.

Ginger and Lime Granita

1½ cups sugar
½ ounce fresh ginger root, grated
Finely grated zest of 2 limes
Juice of 6 limes

Put the sugar in a saucepan with 2¼ cups water. Stir to dissolve over low heat. Add the ginger and lime zest and bring to the boil. Remove from the heat, cover and leave to infuse for 15 minutes. Add the lime juice and leave to cool completely. Pour into a large, shallow container, cover and chill before freezing. Stir occasionally from the outside edges to the middle until it forms into a mass of ice crystals. Serve immediately – a good palate cleanser between the courses of a long and/or rich meal.

Serves 5–6

Ginger Ice Cream

½ cup sugar
3 large egg yolks
5 tablespoons syrup from jar of preserved ginger
2½ cups cream, whipped
½ cup chopped preserved ginger

In a heavy-based saucepan, dissolve the sugar in ½ cup water. Bring to the boil and boil until the temperature reaches 215°F.

Meanwhile beat the egg yolks in a bowl until very thick. Stir in the sugar syrup in a slow, continuous stream. Stir in the ginger syrup. Fold in the cream and ginger.

Pour the mixture into a container. Cover and freeze until firm, beating the mixture twice at hourly intervals.

About 30 minutes before serving, transfer the ice cream to the refrigerator.

Serves 6

Ginger and Chocolate Chip Ice Cream

1¼ cups milk
3 egg yolks
½ cup sugar
⅔ cup ginger wine
Juice of 1 lemon
1¼ cups heavy cream, whipped
3 squares bitter chocolate, finely chopped

In a heavy-based saucepan, gently heat the milk to just below simmering point.

Put the egg yolks and sugar in a bowl and beat together until thick, then beat in the hot milk. Return the mixture to the rinsed pan and cook over a low heat, stirring constantly, until the mixture thickens. Remove from the heat and leave to cool slightly. Stir in the ginger wine and lemon juice and leave to cool completely, stirring occasionally.

Pour the custard into a shallow metal container, cover and freeze until just becoming firm. Tip the semi-frozen mixture into a bowl and beat well. Fold in the cream and chocolate then spoon back into the container, cover and freeze until firm.

About 20 minutes before serving, transfer the ice cream to the refrigerator.

Serves 6

Gooseberry

Gooseberries are always strained when they are used in ices, so there is no need to go through the time-consuming process of trimming them. If possible, use mid- or late season berries which will give a sweet, full flavor to the ice. For an additional, subtle taste add a sprig of elderflowers to the poaching liquid.

Simple Gooseberry Ice Cream
Add 1¼ cups strained gooseberry purée to any of the Basic Recipes*, or to a good-quality bought vanilla ice cream.

Gooseberry Sorbet

1 pound gooseberries
¾ cup sugar
Juice of ½ lemon
Green food coloring, optional
¼ cup gin, optional

In a saucepan gently cook the gooseberries with the sugar, lemon juice and ⅔ cup water until soft. Reduce to a purée then pass through a strainer. Add a few drops of green coloring, if you are using it. Set aside to cool completely.

Stir in the gin, if you are using it. Pour the mixture into a container, cover and chill. Freeze until firm, beating 3 times at 45-minute intervals.

About 30 minutes before serving, transfer the sorbet to the refrigerator.

Serves 4

Serving suggestion
Serve in Almond Tuiles surrounded by fresh gooseberries marinated in sweet wine. Decorate with sweet geranium flowers or elderflowers.*

Easy Gooseberry Ice Cream

1¼ pounds gooseberries
½ cup sugar
Long strip of orange peel
1¼ cups cream, whipped

In a saucepan, poach the gooseberries with the sugar (adding more or less to taste), orange peel and about 2 tablespoons water until soft. Remove and discard the orange peel. Purée the gooseberries and pass through a fine strainer. Leave to cool.

Fold in the cream and pour into a container. Cover and freeze until firm, beating twice at hourly intervals.

About 30 minutes before serving, transfer the ice cream to the refrigerator.

Serves 4

Dessert suggestion
Sandwich each portion between two graham crackers and freeze. Serve with Orange Flower Sauce.*

Gooseberry Mallow Ice Cream

12 large white marshmallows
¾ cup evaporated milk
1 pound fresh or frozen gooseberries
⅓ cup sugar
⅔ cup cream, whipped
¼ cup light corn syrup
12–16 large Macaroons, to serve*

Melt the marshmallows with the evaporated milk in a bowl placed over a pan of warm water, stirring until smooth.

In a saucepan, cook half the gooseberries in 2 tablespoons water over gentle heat for about 5 minutes or until the skins burst and the fruit softens. Stir in the sugar then strain. Leave to cool.

Fold in the cream and pour into a container. Cover and freeze until firm.

Make a sauce by cooking the remaining gooseberries with the corn syrup and 2 tablespoons water in a covered pan over gentle heat until the fruit softens. Pass through a strainer and set aside.

About 45 minutes before serving, transfer the ice cream to the refrigerator. Just before serving, warm the sauce gently if necessary. Spoon the ice cream between the macaroons and pour the sauce over.

Serves 6–8

Gooseberry and Geranium Leaf Yogurt Ice

1 pound sweet gooseberries
¼ cup sugar
6 sweet geranium leaves
⅔ cup thick plain yogurt
Geranium flowers, for decoration

Poach the gooseberries with the sugar, geranium leaves and 4 tablespoons water in a covered pan until very soft. Remove the geranium leaves. Purée the gooseberry mixture, pass through a strainer into a bowl and leave to cool.

Beat the yogurt into the gooseberry purée. Pour into a container, cover and freeze until firm, beating 3 times at 45-minute intervals.

About 40 minutes before serving, transfer the ice to the refrigerator. Serve each portion decorated with a single geranium flower.

Serves 4

Serving suggestion
Scoop into individual dishes and surround with slices of kiwi fruit.

Low calorie version
Use fructose or a low calorie or artificial sweetener instead of sugar.

Gooseberry Ice Cream

1¾ pounds gooseberries
¾ cup brown sugar
1¼ cups milk
3 large egg yolks
Juice of 1 lemon
⅔ cup cream, whipped
Green food coloring, optional

Poach the gooseberries with half the sugar and about 4 tablespoons water in a covered pan until soft but not mushy. Drain off the excess liquid into a small saucepan and boil until reduced and syrupy. Purée the fruit then pass through a strainer.

In a heavy-based saucepan, bring the milk to just below boiling point. Beat the egg yolks in a bowl with the remaining sugar until thick and light then beat in the hot milk. Return the mixture to the rinsed pan and cook over a low heat, stirring constantly, until thickened – but do not allow to boil. Leave to cool, stirring occasionally.

Beat the gooseberry purée and syrup and the lemon juice into the custard. Fold in the cream and coloring, if you are using it.

Pour the mixture into a container. Cover and freeze until firm beating twice at hourly intervals.

About 30 minutes before serving, transfer the ice cream to the refrigerator.

Serves 6–8

Dessert suggestion
Layer with Moist Ginger Cake*. Decorate with advocaat-flavored cream and fresh orange segments.

Recipes for cakes, sauces, etc., asterisked in the dessert and serving suggestions, are given on pages 145 to 152. For directions on layering, lining and other techniques involved in creating desserts, see pages 152 to 155. Basic recipes are on pages 16 and 17.

Grape

For a truly distinctive taste, choose muscat grapes with their rich, almost exotically perfumed flavor. Black grapes are also suitable – their flesh has a pink tinge which is retained in the finished ice. However, for a really good 'grape' color, use unsweetened grape juice, available in cartons and bottles. Remember to remove the seeds first if you purée the grapes in a blender or food processor; 1 pound fruit will give about 2 cups purée, depending on the type of grape. Or you can use seedless grapes, provided they have a good, strong flavor. Several recipes for dried grapes – raisins – are included in this section.

Simple Grape Ice Cream

Peel, de-seed and halve 1 pound sweet grapes and add to any of the Basic Recipes* or to a good-quality bought vanilla ice cream.

Black Grape Granita

3/4 cup sugar
1 1/2 pounds black grapes, puréed and strained
Juice of 1 lime or lemon
1 1/4 cups dry white wine
Black grapes, for decoration

In a saucepan, dissolve the sugar in 2/3 cup water. Bring to the boil and boil for 1 minute. Leave to cool.

Stir the syrup into the grape purée with the lime or lemon juice and wine. Freeze in a shallow tray, stirring from the sides to the center with a fork to form a mass of small crystals. Serve immediately straight from the freezer.

Serves 6

Flavor variation
Use white instead of black grapes.

Raisin Ice Cream

2/3 cup raisins
5 tablespoons lemon juice
1 3/4 cups evaporated milk, well chilled
Few drops of vanilla extract
1/4 cup sugar

Soak the raisins in the lemon juice for at least 4 hours. Pour the evaporated milk into a bowl and whip until very thick. Beat in the vanilla extract and sugar. Fold in the raisins with their liquor and pour into a container. Cover and freeze until firm.

About 30 minutes before serving, transfer the ice cream to the refrigerator.

Serves 6

Serving suggestion
Serve with fresh orange segments, pith and membrane removed, and Orange Flower Sauce.*

Grape Ice Cream

1/2 cup sugar
1 pound grapes, preferably muscat, peeled and seeds removed
4 tablespoons heavy cream, whipped
Frosted* grapes, for decoration

Dissolve the sugar in 8 tablespoons water in a small saucepan over medium heat. Then pour the syrup into a bowl and leave to cool.

Chop the grape flesh finely (do not worry if you have missed a few shreds of the skin) and mix with the syrup, adding any juice that comes out of the fruit. Pour into a container, cover and freeze until just becoming firm. Turn into a bowl, beat well then fold in the cream. Spoon back into the container, cover and freeze until firm, beating after 45 minutes. If possible, serve the ice cream as soon as it is ready. If prepared in advance, transfer the ice cream to the refrigerator about 30 minutes before serving. Decorate each portion with frosted grapes.

Serves 4

Dessert suggestion
Line a mold or pan with Langues de Chat. Add a layer of the ice cream and fill the center with White Wine Sorbet (page 130). Decorate with black grapes.*

Old English Raisin Ice Cream

1 1/4 cups milk
4 tablespoons clear honey
2 eggs, beaten
1 1/2 teaspoons ground nutmeg
2/3 cup raisins
1/4 cup toasted slivered almonds
1 1/4 cups cream, whipped

In a heavy-based saucepan, heat the milk and honey to just below simmering point. Put the eggs in a bowl and beat until light. Then beat in the milk. Return the mixture to the rinsed pan and cook over low heat until the mixture thickens, stirring constantly. Remove from the heat, stir in the nutmeg and leave to cool, stirring occasionally. Pour into a container, cover and freeze until firm. Turn into a bowl and beat well. Stir in the raisins and almonds and fold in the cream.

Spoon the mixture back into the container. Cover and freeze until firm.

About 30 minutes before serving, transfer the ice cream to the refrigerator.

Serves 4–5

Flavor variation
Soak the raisins in dark rum and add the soaking liquid to the mixture, with the raisins.

Golden Raisin Ice Cream

2 large juicy lemons
1¼ cups heavy cream
1¼ cups light cream
½ cup brown sugar
4 tablespoons advocaat, optional
½ cup golden raisins, soaked in a liquor or liqueur if
    liked
2 tablespoons chopped marrons glacés (or mixed peel)
Sliced marrons glacés or toasted slivered almonds, for
    decoration

Remove the rind from the lemons with a potato peeler
and put in a saucepan with the creams and sugar and
simmer for 5 minutes. Remove from the heat, cover
and leave until cold.

Strain the cream into a bowl. Add the advocaat if
using and beat until soft peaks are formed. Pour into a
container, cover and freeze until just becoming firm.
Turn into a bowl, beat, then fold in the raisins and
marrons or peel. Spoon the mixture back into the
container, cover and freeze until firm.

About 30 minutes before serving, transfer the ice
cream to the refrigerator. Serve each portion
decorated with sliced marrons or toasted slivered
almonds.

Serves 4

Serving suggestion
For each serving, spoon into the center of a liquor-
soaked rum baba or a doughnut studded with slivered
almonds. For a flamboyant flourish, flambé with a
liquor or an orange liqueur.

Grape Yogurt Ice

2 cups puréed and strained grapes
Approximately ½–¾ cup confectioners' sugar
1¼ cups plain yogurt
Squeeze of orange juice
2 egg whites

Blend the grape purée and sugar together in a bowl.
Blend in the yogurt and orange juice. Taste and adjust
the level of sweetness and orange juice.

Pour the mixture into a container. Cover and freeze
to the slushy stage. Beat well in a bowl.

In another bowl, whip the egg whites until stiff. Fold
the egg whites into the grape yogurt ice, return the
mixture to the container, cover and freeze.

About 40 minutes before serving, transfer the yogurt
ice to the refrigerator.

Serves 5–6

Low calorie version
Use fructose or a low calorie or artificial sweetener
instead of sugar.

Smooth Grape Ice Cream

¼ cup sugar
1¼ cups unsweetened grape juice, preferably red
1 teaspoon lime or lemon juice
2½ cups cream, whipped

For decoration
Halved black grapes
Leaf shapes cut from lemon peel

Dissolve the sugar in the grape juice and lime or
lemon juice. Fold into the whipped cream and pour
into a container. Cover and freeze until firm, beating
twice at hourly intervals.

About 20 minutes before serving, transfer to the
refrigerator. Serve decorated with the grapes and
lemon peel 'leaves'.

Serves 6

Dessert suggestion
Layer with Provençal Honey Ice Cream (page 72)
between a base and top of Hazelnut Meringue*.
Decorate the outside of the dessert with orange-
liqueur-flavored whipped cream and seedless green
grapes.

Muscat Sorbet

1 cup sugar
1¼ pounds white muscat grapes, puréed and strained
Juice of 2 lemons
1 tablespoon orange flower water (or use orange
    instead of lemon juice)
3 tablespoons sweet muscat wine
Finely chopped pistachio nuts, for decoration

In a heavy-based saucepan, dissolve the sugar in 2½
cups water. Bring to the boil and boil for 10 minutes.
Remove from the heat, add the lemon (or orange)
juice and leave to cool.

Strain the syrup into the grape purée with the
orange flower water if used and the wine.

Pour the mixture into a container. Cover and freeze
until firm, beating 3 times at 45-minute intervals.

About 30 minutes before serving, transfer the sorbet
to the refrigerator. Serve decorated with pistachio
nuts.

Serves 6–8

Dessert suggestion
Encase in Tea Ice Cream (page 71).

Additional recipe using grapes: Apple and Raisin
Ice Cream (page 21).

Grapefruit

Use large, firm fruit that feels heavy for its size – a light grapefruit has more pith and less juice. The many pink varieties that are now available are comparatively sweet, with a soft, delicate flavor. However, all grapefruit make marvellously refreshing ices, giving sorbets in particular a fresh, tangy taste. Canned grapefruit segments, in syrup or unsweetened, are ideal for serving with the ices, and the unsweetened variety can, if necessary, be used instead of fresh fruit.

Simple Grapefruit Ice Cream
Chop ½ cup drained, canned grapefruit segments (in syrup) and add to any of the Basic Recipes*, or to a good-quality bought vanilla ice cream.

Grapefruit Yogurt Ice

2 large grapefruit
½ cup sugar
1 cup plain yogurt
½ pound low fat soft cheese, beaten
1 tablespoon finely chopped fresh mint
1 egg white

For decoration
Grapefruit segments
Mint leaves

Peel the grapefruit, divide into segments and cut the flesh away from the membranes. Chop the flesh, reserving any juice.

In a heavy-based saucepan, dissolve the sugar in ¾ cup water. Bring to the boil and boil until the temperature reaches 234°F. Set aside to cool.

Stir the grapefruit flesh and reserved juice into the syrup. Blend the yogurt and cheese together until smooth, then mix in the grapefruit mixture and mint.

Pour the mixture into a container, cover and freeze to the slushy stage. Beat well in a bowl.

Whip the egg white in a small bowl until stiff but not dry. Fold into the grapefruit-yogurt mixture.

Spoon the mixture into individual dishes, cover and return to the freezer.

About 40 minutes before serving, transfer the ices to the refrigerator. Decorate each dish with grapefruit segments and mint leaves.

Serves 4

Serving suggestion
Serve in chilled grapefruit or avocado shells, intermingled with small scoops of Avocado Ice Cream (page 27), quartered grapefruit segments, pith and membrane removed, chopped hazelnuts and sprigs of mint.

Low calorie version
Use fructose or a low calorie or artificial sweetener instead of sugar.

Grapefruit Sorbet

½ cup sugar cubes
2 large juicy grapefruit
1 egg white

Rub the sugar cubes over the skins of the grapefruit until they are soaked in the flavoring oil. Dissolve the cubes in ⅔ cup water.

Squeeze the juice from the grapefruit – there should be about 1¼ cups – into a bowl. Stir the syrup into the juice and pour into a container. Cover and freeze until just becoming firm around the edges. Beat well in a bowl.

In another bowl, whip the egg white until stiff but not dry. Fold it into the juice. Return to the container, cover and freeze until firm.

About 30 minutes before serving, transfer the sorbet to the refrigerator.

Serves 4

Flavor variation
Add approximately 2 tablespoons of chopped fresh mint.

Grapefruit Frost

1 tablespoon gelatin
¾ cup canned frozen concentrated grapefruit juice, defrosted
1¼ cups plain yogurt
Finely grated zest of 1 large grapefruit
2 egg whites
Fine strips of twisted grapefruit peel, for decoration

Dissolve the gelatin in 4 tablespoons water in a small bowl placed over a pan of hot water. Beat the grapefruit juice, yogurt and grapefruit zest together then gradually blend with the gelatin.

Pour the mixture into a container, cover and freeze until slushy. Beat well in a bowl.

Put the egg whites in a bowl and whip until stiff but not dry. Fold the egg whites into the grapefruit mixture. Return the mixture to the container, cover and freeze until firm.

About 40 minutes before serving, transfer the frost to the refrigerator. Decorate each portion with twists of grapefruit peel.

Serves 4

Flavor variation
Substitute frozen orange juice and the finely grated zest of 2 oranges for the grapefruit juice and zest.

Grapefruit Ice Cream

1 cup grapefruit juice
1½ cups confectioners' sugar
1¼ cups heavy cream, whipped

Put the juice and sugar into a bowl and stir until the sugar has dissolved. Fold the juice into the cream and pour into a container. Cover and freeze until firm, beating twice at hourly intervals.

About 30 minutes before serving, transfer the ice cream to the refrigerator.

Serves 4

Serving suggestion
Put scoops in small éclairs and cover with Hot Chocolate Sauce* or Bitter Chocolate Sauce*.

Dessert suggestion
Form into 4 balls with a tablespoon of Mint Sorbet (page 71) in the center of each one. Serve in Gingersnap Baskets* or Coupelles*. Surround with grapefruit segments, pith and membrane removed, sprinkled with crème de menthe.

Grapefruit and Vermouth Granita

¾ cup sugar
2 large juicy grapefruit
5 tablespoons dry vermouth
Fine strips of grapefruit peel, blanched, for decoration

In a heavy-based saucepan, dissolve the sugar in 1¼ cups water. Bring to the boil then simmer for 5 minutes. Leave to cool.

Peel the grapefruit, divide into segments and remove any seeds. Purée the grapefruit with the vermouth then mix in the sugar syrup. Pour this mixture into a shallow tray and place in the freezer. Stir occasionally from the outside to the middle until the mixture forms into a mass of small ice crystals. Serve immediately, decorated with grapefruit peel.

Serves 6

Flavor variation
Use gin instead of vermouth.

Pink Grapefruit Sorbet

⅓ cup sugar
4 pink grapefruit

Dissolve the sugar in 3 tablespoons water in a small heavy-based saucepan. Bring to the boil and boil for 5 minutes. Leave to cool.

Squeeze the grapefruit and strain the juice into the syrup. Pour into a container, cover and freeze until firm, beating 3 times at 45-minute intervals.

About 30 minutes before serving, transfer the sorbet to the refrigerator.

Serves 4–5

Serving suggestion
Serve in chilled grapefruit shells decorated with swirls of whipped cream.

Dessert suggestion
Line a mold or pan with fingers of Genoise Cake* followed by a layer of Rhubarb Ice Cream (page 111) to which enough red food coloring has been added to color it a light red. Fill the center with the sorbet. Decorate the turned-out dessert with whipped cream tinted a delicate pink with very little food coloring, and small Meringues*.

Additional recipe using grapefruit: Grapefruit Crunch Sandwich (page 139).

To reduce your calorie intake
Tofu can be substituted for any soft cheese (see page 13); beat with the other ingredients until smooth. It has no cholesterol and is low in fat.

To reduce your sugar intake
Replace the sugar with half the quantity of **fructose** or with an **artificial sweetener**, provided the recipe does not call for a sugar syrup. Normally, 3–4 artificial sweeteners are the equivalent of 2 tablespoons sugar but always check that you have the right degree of sweetness. Artificial sweeteners must be added to custard-based ice creams after the custard has cooled.

Hazelnut

Hazelnuts can be used whole, chopped or ground and are especially flavorsome when they are toasted. Just heat them in a 350°F oven for 10–15 minutes or put them under a low broiler until the skin dries out and becomes flaky and easily removed when the nuts are rubbed in a dish towel. To grind hazelnuts, whizz them to a very fine paste in a coffee grinder or blender, or pound them in a mortar. A food processor does not produce the right consistency.

Simple Hazelnut Ice Cream
Add ½ cup chopped, lightly toasted hazelnuts to any of the Basic Recipes* or to a good-quality bought vanilla ice cream.

Hazelnut Ice Cream (with cottage cheese)

1½ cups cottage cheese, strained
1 cup confectioners' sugar
Few drops of vanilla extract
4 tablespoons light cream
¼ cup chopped hazelnuts
1 tablespoon sweet madeira or sherry
1 egg white
Small Chocolate Leaves or other shapes, for*
* decoration*

Put the cheese, sugar, vanilla extract and cream in a bowl and beat together until smooth and light. Fold in the nuts and madeira or sherry. In another bowl, whip the egg white until stiff but not dry and fold into the cream mixture. Pour the mixture into a container. Cover and freeze until firm.

About 30 minutes before serving, transfer the ice cream to the refrigerator. Decorate each portion with the small chocolate leaves or other shapes.

Serves 4

Serving suggestion
Serve as a sundae with sliced peaches and small Meringues. Top with Bitter Chocolate Sauce*.*

Rich Hazelnut Ice Cream

¾ cup sugar
5 egg yolks
2 cups cream, whipped
Few drops of vanilla extract
⅓ cup lightly toasted, ground hazelnuts

Melt the sugar in a heavy-based saucepan then cook to a light amber color. Immediately, but carefully, stir in ½ cup boiling water and continue stirring until the caramel has dissolved.

Beat the egg yolks in a bowl until very thick and pale. Pour in the caramel in a slow, steady stream, beating continuously, until the mixture is cool.

Fold in the cream, vanilla extract and hazelnuts. Pour the mixture into a container. Cover and freeze until firm.

About 30 minutes before serving, transfer the ice cream to the refrigerator.

Serves 6

Serving suggestion
Serve in individual dishes and accompany with Gingersnaps.*

Dessert suggestion
Make a bombe or freeze in a cake or loaf pan with an outer layer of Orange Ice Cream (page 85) and Butterscotch Parfait (page 38) in the center.

Smooth Hazelnut Ice Cream

¾ cup hazelnuts, lightly toasted
1½ cups milk
2 egg yolks
¼ cup sugar
Chocolate or coffee candies, for decoration

Grind the hazelnuts in a coffee grinder or a blender, or pound them in a mortar.

Heat the milk in a heavy-based saucepan over moderate heat to just below simmering point. Remove from the heat, stir in the ground nuts, cover and leave to cool completely. Strain the mixture through a strainer lined with a double thickness of cheesecloth, pressing it firmly to extract as much liquid as possible. Tie the ends of the cheesecloth over the hazelnut milk, compressing it tightly, and hang it over the strainer to drip. When it has finished dripping give it a final squeeze to press the last drop through. Return the hazelnut milk to the saucepan and bring to simmering point.

Beat the egg yolks and sugar together in a bowl until light and thick, then whisk in the milk. Return the mixture to the rinsed pan and cook over low heat, stirring constantly, until it thickens. Leave to cool, stirring occasionally. Pour into a container, cover and chill for 30 minutes. Then freeze until firm, beating twice at hourly intervals.

About 40 minutes before serving, transfer the ice cream to the refrigerator. Scatter 2 or 3 chocolate or coffee candies over each portion.

Serves 3–4

Dessert suggestion
Layer with chocolate chip cookies. Decorate the turned-out dessert with whipped cream, Chocolate Curls and chopped Caramelized* hazelnuts.*

Additional recipes using hazelnuts: Coffee and Hazelnut Ice Cream (page 52), Honey and Hazelnut Ice Cream (page 72), Pear and Hazelnut Yogurt Ice (page 92), Apricot and Hazelnut Meringue Cake (page 140), Chocolate Truffle and Hazelnut Ring (page 142).

Herbs, Flowers, Leaves

Some of the most unusual ices can be made with ingredients from your garden. Herbs impart a deliciously clean, fresh taste, while an infusion of leaves (including tea leaves) or flower petals adds a delicate, yet interesting, nuance of flavor and tantalizing perfume.

Geranium Leaf Sorbet

1/3 cup sugar
4 scented geranium leaves
Juice of 1 large lemon
1 egg white
Small geranium leaves and flowers, for decoration

In a heavy-based saucepan, dissolve the sugar in 1¼ cups water. Bring to the boil and boil for 3 minutes. Remove from the heat, stir in the geranium leaves, cover and leave for 35 minutes.

Stir the lemon juice into the syrup. Strain the syrup into a container. Cover and chill for 1 hour. Then freeze to the slushy stage. Beat well in a bowl.

Whip the egg white in a small bowl until stiff but not dry. Fold the egg white into the frozen syrup. Return to the container, cover and freeze until firm.

About 35 minutes before serving, transfer the sorbet to the refrigerator. Serve each portion decorated with small geranium leaves and flowers.

Serves 4

Serving suggestion
Serve in Coupelles* decorated with small, sweet geranium leaves and flowers.

Mint Ice Cream

1/2 cup sugar
Juice of 1/2 lemon
3 tablespoons finely chopped fresh mint leaves
2/3 cup sour cream
5 ounces soft/ricotta cheese
Mint sprigs, for decoration

In a heavy-based saucepan, dissolve the sugar in 2/3 cup water. Bring to the boil and boil for 5 minutes. Stir in the lemon juice and mint leaves and leave to infuse off the heat for about 30 minutes.

Beat the sour cream and cheese together in a bowl until evenly blended and smooth. Strain the syrup and gradually beat it into the cream mixture.

Pour the mixture into a container. Cover and freeze until firm, beating twice at hourly intervals.

About 20 minutes before serving, transfer the ice cream to the refrigerator. Serve with the mint sprigs.

Serves 4

Dessert suggestion
Layer with chocolate chip cookies. Decorate the turned-out dessert with whipped cream and Chocolate Curls*.

Thyme Sorbet

1¹/8 cups sugar
1 bunch fresh thyme
1 egg white

In a heavy-based saucepan, dissolve the sugar in 2¼ cups water. Bring to the boil and boil for about 1 minute. Remove from the heat, stir in the thyme, cover and leave to infuse for 15 minutes. Remove the thyme, cool then chill the syrup. When very cold pour the syrup into a container. Cover and freeze until becoming slushy. Beat well in a bowl.

Whip the egg white in a small bowl until stiff but not dry. Fold into the frozen syrup. Return to the container, cover and freeze until firm.

About 30 minutes before serving, transfer the sorbet to the refrigerator.

Serves 8

Serving suggestion
Scoop into Meringue Baskets* and serve with Sponge Fingers*.

Flavor variation
Use 8 fresh bay leaves instead of the thyme.

Rose Petal Sorbet

3/4 cup sugar
Juice of 1 small lime or lemon
1 cup rose petals
Pink food coloring
Rosewater, to taste
2 egg whites
Rose petals, for decoration

In a heavy-based saucepan, dissolve the sugar in 2 cups water. Add the lime juice and bring to the boil then simmer for about 10 minutes. Pour the hot syrup over the petals and leave to cool completely.

Put the rose petals and syrup in a blender and process. Then pass through a coarse strainer. Add a few drops of coloring and rosewater to taste.

Pour the mixture into a container, cover and freeze to the slushy stage. Beat well in a bowl.

Whip the egg whites in a bowl until stiff but not dry. Fold into the sorbet. Return to the container, cover and freeze until firm.

About 15 minutes before serving, transfer the sorbet to the refrigerator. Serve each portion decorated with a few rose petals.

Serves 6

Serving suggestion
Serve in Ice Cream Cones* arranged on a plate strewn with rose petals. Decorate with whipped cream, crystallized rose petals and small green leaves.

Black Currant Leaf Water Ice

1 cup sugar
Juice of 3 large lemons
4 large handfuls of black currant leaves, washed and
*   well dried*
2–3 drops green food coloring
1 egg white
4 bunches black currants, for decoration

In a heavy-based saucepan, dissolve the sugar in the lemon juice and 1 quart water. Bring to the boil and boil for 4 minutes. Reserve a few black currant leaves for decoration and add the remainder to the syrup, stirring them so they are well coated. Cover the pan and leave to infuse for 45 minutes.

Strain the syrup, pressing the leaves to extract as much flavor as possible. Add the coloring and pour into a container. Cover and chill. Freeze to the slushy stage. Beat well in a bowl.

Whip the egg white in a small bowl until it stands in soft peaks then gradually whip into the water ice. Return to the container, cover and freeze until firm.

About 45 minutes before serving, transfer the water ice to the refrigerator. Decorate each portion with black currant leaves and a bunch of black currants.

Serves 4

Serving suggestion
Put small scoops into frosted wine glasses, trickle a little crème de cassis over and decorate with Frosted* black currants. Serve with Sponge Fingers*.

Arrange scoops on plates, decorate with frosted black currants and surround with black currant leaves. Serve with Langues de Chat*.

Tea Ice Cream

2/3 cup very strong Earl Grey tea
2/3 cup milk
2/3 cup light cream
Long strip of lemon peel
3 egg yolks
1/2 cup sugar
2/3 cup cream, whipped

Put the tea, milk and light cream with the lemon peel into a heavy-based saucepan and bring to just below simmering point.

Beat the egg yolks and sugar together in a bowl until thick and light then whisk in the hot liquid. Remove the lemon peel. Return the mixture to the rinsed pan and cook over a low heat, stirring constantly, until the custard thickens. Return the lemon peel to the pan and leave to cool, stirring occasionally.

Remove the lemon peel. Pour the mixture into a container. Cover and freeze until just becoming firm. Turn into a bowl, beat, then fold in the whipped cream. Return the mixture to the container, cover and freeze until firm.

About 30 minutes before serving, transfer the ice cream to the refrigerator.

Serves 6

Serving suggestion
Place in Coupelles* containing finely chopped almonds, and sprinkle with shapes cut from orange peel or fine twisted strands of orange peel. Serve with Burnt Honey Sauce* or Orange Flower Sauce*.

Mint Sorbet

2 cups sugar
20 mint leaves
Juice of 1 lemon
6 tablespoons crème de menthe
2 large egg whites
8 small mint sprigs, for decoration

In a heavy-based saucepan, dissolve the sugar in 5 cups water over a gentle heat. Bring to the boil and boil rapidly for 8 minutes. Add the mint leaves and boil for a further 2 minutes. Remove from the heat, stir in the lemon juice and leave to infuse for 30 minutes.

Strain the syrup into a container. Cover and freeze to the slushy stage. In a bowl, whip the frozen mixture vigorously with a wire whisk to break down any ice particles. Whip in the crème de menthe until evenly blended. Whip the egg whites in a bowl until stiff but not dry. Whip them into the sorbet. Return the sorbet to the container, cover and freeze until firm.

About 30 minutes before serving, transfer the sorbet to the refrigerator. Serve in cold, frosted glasses and decorate with the mint sprigs.

Serves 8

Dessert suggestion
Form Grapefruit Ice Cream (page 67) into 4 balls with a tablespoon of the sorbet in the center of each one. Serve in Coupelles*. Surround with grapefruit segments, pith and membrane removed, sprinkled with crème de menthe.

Additional recipes using herbs, flowers and leaves: Apple and Elderflower Ice Cream (page 20), Blackberry Rose Ice Cream (page 30), Gooseberry and Geranium Leaf Yogurt Ice (page 62), Orange and Rosemary Sorbet (page 85), Raspberry Rose Water Ice (page 104), Strawberry and Elderflower Ice Cream (page 119), Strawberry Rose Ice (page 119), Elderberry Water Ice (page 135), Quince Ice Cream (page 134), Crystallized Violet Ice Cream (page 134), Crabapple Ice Cream (page 134), Black Currant, Rose Petal and Champagne Roll (page 136).

Honey

Honey comes in a whole range of blends and flavors. For more sophisticated ices, use a variety flavored with a single herb or flower, or make your own as in the 'Provençal' version on the right. Either thick or clear honey can be used, unless one or the other is specifically called for in a recipe.

Simple Honey Ice Cream
Ripple any of the Basic Recipes* with ¼ cup clear honey.

Honey and Hazelnut Ice Cream

4 tablespoons butter
½ cup thick honey
2 cups milk
½ cup lightly toasted, ground hazelnuts
3 egg yolks
¼ cup light brown sugar
1 tablespoon gelatin
1¼ cups cream, whipped
3 tablespoons brandy

For decoration
Whipped cream
Chocolate-covered hazelnuts
Fresh peaches, apricots or orange segments, for serving

In a heavy-based saucepan, melt the butter and honey in the milk. Bring to the boil, add the nuts, cover and leave to cool for 10 minutes.

Beat the egg yolks with the sugar in a bowl. Gradually stir in the flavored milk. Return to the rinsed pan and cook over a gentle heat, stirring constantly, until the custard thickens, but do not allow it to boil.

Dissolve the gelatin in 3 tablespoons water in a small bowl set over a pan of hot water. Stir the gelatin into the custard. Leave until cool but not completely cold then fold in the cream and brandy. Cover and freeze in a 1½ quart fluted ring mold until firm.

About 45 minutes before serving, turn the ice cream out onto a chilled plate and transfer to the refrigerator. Just before serving, decorate with whipped cream and chocolate-covered hazelnuts and fill the center with fresh fruits.

Serves 6

Dessert suggestion
Freeze in a mold lined with Sponge Fingers. Decorate the turned-out dessert with whipped cream, Chocolate Shapes* and shapes cut from orange peel.*

Flavor variation
Add 2 tablespoons good-quality instant coffee granules to the milk.

Provençal Honey Ice Cream

⅔ cup honey
1 large fresh rosemary or thyme sprig
6 egg yolks
1¼ cups milk or light cream
⅔ cup crème fraîche, heavy or whipping cream

Heat the honey and rosemary or thyme in a saucepan to just below boiling point. Remove from the heat, cover and leave to infuse for 30 minutes.

Beat the egg yolks in a bowl until light. Uncover the honey and reheat to just below boiling point, remove the herbs and gradually pour the honey onto the egg yolks, beating continuously.

In a heavy-based saucepan, bring the milk or cream to just below boiling point then whip into the egg yolk mixture. Return the mixture to the rinsed pan and cook over a low heat, stirring, until the mixture thickens, but do not allow it to boil. Leave to cool.

Whip the crème fraîche or cream until soft peaks form. Fold the cream into the honey custard. Pour into a container, cover and freeze until firm, beating once, when the mixture is just becoming firm.

About 15 minutes before serving, transfer the ice cream to the refrigerator.

Serves 6

Serving suggestion
Intermingle scoops of the ice cream with scoops of Passion Fruit Sorbet (page 128) and serve with Almond Tuiles.*

Honey Ice Cream

1 cup clear honey
5 egg yolks
2 cups cream, whipped
Lemon juice, to taste

In a heavy-based saucepan, heat the honey with 4 tablespoons water to just below boiling point. Beat the egg yolks in a bowl until thick and light then stir in the hot honey. Return the mixture to the rinsed pan and cook gently over low heat, whisking until the mixture thickens. Remove from the heat and continue to whisk until the mixture is cold.

Fold the cream into the honey mixture and add lemon juice to taste. Pour into a container, cover and freeze until firm. About 20 minutes before serving, transfer to the refrigerator.

Serves 5

Serving suggestion
Make into a sundae with layers of whipped cream and Bitter Chocolate Sauce. Finish with a scoop of ice cream decorated with a candied cherry.*

Honey and Fig Sorbet

1³/₄ pound can of green figs in syrup
²/₃ cup clear honey
4 tablespoons lemon juice
White rum, for serving
Whipped cream, for decoration

Drain the figs and reserve the syrup and 4 of the figs. Purée the remaining figs with the reserved syrup, honey and lemon juice.

Pour the mixture into a container. Cover and freeze until firm, beating twice at hourly intervals.

About 30 minutes before serving, transfer the sorbet to the refrigerator. Pour a teaspoon of white rum over each portion and decorate with a swirl of cream and the reserved figs.

Serves 4

Serving suggestion
Serve on a plate surrounded by sliced figs.

Honey and Soybean Milk Ice Cream

2 cups unsweetened soybean milk
¹/₄ cup honey
Few drops of vanilla extract
3 tablespoons oil

Blend all the ingredients together until smooth. Pour into a container, cover and freeze until firm, beating twice at 45-minute intervals. About 30 minutes before serving transfer to the refrigerator.

Serves 4

Additional recipe using honey: Banana and Honey Ice Cream (page 29).

KIRSCH: see WINES, LIQUEURS
KIWI FRUIT: see WARM CLIMATE
                    FRUITS
KUMQUAT: see ORANGE, ETC

Lemon, Lime

Juicy, thin-skinned lemons make the best ices. To soften one that feels hard, and to improve its yield of juice, steep the whole lemon in boiling water before squeezing it. When sugar lumps are rubbed over the skin they absorb its essential oils and impart an extra-tangy lemon flavor to the iced mixture.

Limes may look like green lemons, but have a sweeter, more subtle flavor and character of their own – which is in no way reproduced in bottled lime drinks. If fresh lime juice is not available, use bottled unsweetened lime juice instead.

Lemon Sorbet

5 large sugar lumps
3 large thin-skinned lemons
1 cup confectioners' sugar

Rub the sugar lumps over the lemon skins until they are soaked with oil. Put the sugar lumps with the confectioners' sugar into a bowl with 5 tablespoons water. Squeeze the lemons and strain the juice into the bowl. Stir to make sure the sugar has dissolved.

Pour the mixture into a container. Cover and freeze until firm, beating twice at 45-minute intervals.

About 20 minutes before serving, transfer the sorbet to the refrigerator.

Serves 2–3

Serving suggestion
Put small scoops into tall, thin-stemmed wine glasses and decorate with strips of lime peel.

Lime Sorbet

1 cup sugar
Zest and juice of 3 large or 4 small limes
1 tablespoon gelatin
½ an egg white
White rum to serve

In a saucepan, dissolve the sugar in 1 quart water with the lime zest. Bring to the boil and simmer for 5 minutes. Remove from the heat, add the lime juice, cover and leave to cool.

Strain the syrup. Dissolve the gelatin in a little of the strained syrup then stir it into the rest of the syrup.

Pour the mixture into a container. Cover and freeze until just becoming slushy. Beat well.

Whip the egg white in a small bowl until stiff but not dry and fold into the lime mixture. Cover and freeze until firm.

About 40 minutes before serving, transfer the sorbet to the refrigerator. Spoon a little white rum over each portion.

Serves 4–6

Dessert suggestion
Ripple with Avocado Ice Cream (page 27) and serve with Cigars Russe*.

Lime Cream Ice

Grated zest and juice of 3 large juicy limes
¾ cup sugar
1 egg white
2 tablespoons heavy cream

Put the lime zest and juice, sugar and 2½ cups water in a saucepan and heat gently until the sugar has dissolved. Bring to the boil and simmer gently for 12 minutes. Remove from the heat, cover and leave to cool.

Pour the mixture into a container. Cover and refrigerate for about an hour. Freeze until just becoming firm.

Remove from the freezer and gradually whip in the egg white followed by the cream. Freeze until firm.

About 40 minutes before serving, transfer the ice to the refrigerator.

Serves 6

Serving suggestion
Intermingle scoops of the cream ice with scoops of Ginger Wine Sorbet (page 60). Top with whiskey-flavored whipped cream sprinkled with chopped cashew nuts.

Dessert suggestion
Freeze in a mold or cake pan lined with Mincemeat Ice Cream (page 141). Decorate the turned-out dessert with whipped cream and shapes cut from lime peel. Serve with Langues de Chat*.

Lemon-Lime Ice Cream

3 large eggs, separated
½ cup sugar
Grated zest of 1 lemon
Grated zest of 1 lime
3 tablespoons lime juice
⅔ cup cream, whipped
Thin strips lemon and lime peel, to decorate

Beat the egg yolks and half the sugar in a bowl until thick and light. Stir in the lemon and lime zests and juice. Fold in the cream. In another bowl, whip the egg whites until stiff but not dry. Fold the egg whites into the lemon-lime cream.

Pour the mixture into a container. Cover and freeze until firm.

About 30 minutes before serving, transfer the ice cream to the refrigerator. Serve decorated with knots of lemon and lime peel.

Serves 6

Serving suggestion
Serve as a sundae with Apple Cream Ice (page 21), bananas tossed in lime juice, and walnuts. Top with Butterscotch Sauce* or Burnt Honey Sauce*.

Sweet Lime Ice Cream

4 eggs, separated
2/3 cup whipping cream
2/3 cup sour cream
1 cup lime pie filling
1/4 cup confectioners' sugar

For decoration
Lime slices
Mint leaves

Beat the egg yolks in a bowl until thick and light. Whip the creams together until soft peaks are formed. Whip the creams into the egg yolks followed by the pie filling.

In another bowl, whip the egg whites until stiff but not dry. Gradually whip in the sugar. Fold the egg whites into the lime mixture and spoon into a container. Cover and freeze until firm.

About 20 minutes before serving, transfer the ice cream to the refrigerator. Serve decorated with lime slices and mint leaves.

Serves 6

Dessert suggestion
Layer with Lemon Sorbet (page 74) or White Peach Sorbet (page 88), merging the layers into each other. Serve in a coconut-flavored Meringue Basket*. Decorate with lime-slice cones containing whipped cream, and long strands of shredded coconut.

Lime and Avocado Ice Cream

2 avocados
Juice of 2 large limes
1/4 cup confectioners' sugar
2/3 cup heavy cream, whipped

Remove the flesh from the avocados and purée with the lime juice and sugar into a bowl. Fold in the cream.

Spoon the mixture into a container. Cover and freeze until firm, beating once after an hour.

About 20 minutes before serving, transfer the ice cream to the refrigerator.

Serves 4

Serving suggestion
Serve with Sponge Fingers*.

Dessert suggestion
Freeze in large lime shells with scalloped edges, mounding the ice cream slightly to form a dome. Decorate with pieces of lemon segments, pith and membrane removed, and shapes cut from lime peel.

Lemon Frost

2/3 cup lemon juice
1/3 cup clear honey, preferably clover or a flower type
1 1/4 cups plain yogurt, chilled
2 egg whites

For decoration
Toasted almond slivers
Frosted* short strips of lemon peel

Put the lemon juice, honey and yogurt in a bowl and beat until smooth. Pour the mixture into a container, cover and freeze to the slushy stage. Turn into a bowl and beat well. Whip the egg whites until stiff but not dry, then fold the egg whites into the yogurt mixture.

Spoon the mixture back into the container. Cover and freeze until firm.

About 45 minutes before serving, transfer the lemon frost to the refrigerator. Serve decorated with the almond slivers and strips of lemon peel.

Serves 3–4

Serving suggestion
Freeze in lemon shells with scalloped edges. Decorate with lightly toasted slivered almonds and 'corkscrews' of fine lemon peel.

Low calorie version
Use fructose or a low calorie or artificial sweetener instead of honey.

Lime Ice Cream

3 eggs, separated
1/2 cup sugar
Grated zest and juice of 3 limes
2/3 cup sour cream, beaten
1 1/4 cups cream, whipped
Twisted lime slices, for decoration

Put the egg yolks, sugar and lime juice in a bowl and beat until very thick and light. Beat in the sour cream. Fold in the whipped cream and lime zest.

In another bowl, whip the egg whites until stiff but not dry. Fold the egg whites into the lime mixture.

Pour the mixture into a container. Cover and freeze until firm.

About 30 minutes before serving, transfer the ice cream to the refrigerator. Serve each portion decorated with a twisted lime slice.

Serves 4–6

Dessert suggestion
Form into 4–6 balls and coat in semi-sweet Chocolate*.

Soft Lemon Ice Cream

1³/₄ cups evaporated milk, chilled
³/₄ cup confectioners' sugar
¹/₄ pound full fat cream cheese, softened
Finely grated zest and juice of 2 lemons

For decoration
Lemon slices
Fresh mint sprigs

Put the evaporated milk into a bowl and whip until very light. Whip in the sugar. Fold in the cheese followed by the lemon zest and juice. Spoon into a container. Cover and freeze until firm.

About 20 minutes before serving, transfer the ice cream to the refrigerator. Serve decorated with lemon slices and mint sprigs.

Serves 4–6

Dessert suggestion
Ripple with Clove Sorbet (page 115).

Sweet Lemon Ice Cream

4 eggs, separated
1 cup lemon pie filling
1¹/₄ cups heavy cream, whipped
¹/₂ cup confectioners' sugar
Frosted* mint leaves, for decoration

Put the egg yolks in a bowl and beat until pale and thick. Beat in the pie filling. Fold in the whipped cream.

In another bowl, whip the egg whites until stiff but not dry then gradually whip in the sugar. Carefully fold into the lemon cream until evenly mixed. Pour the mixture into a container. Cover and freeze until firm.

About 15 minutes before serving, transfer the ice cream to the refrigerator. Decorate with mint.

Serves 6

Iced Lemon Mousse

1 quart plain yogurt
1 cup sugar
Juice and finely grated zest of 2 lemons
2 egg whites
¹/₂ cup cream, whipped

For decoration
Candied lemon slices
Pistachio nuts

Put the yogurt into a bowl and beat in ¹/₂ cup of the sugar. Stir in the lemon zest and juice.

In another bowl, whip the egg whites until soft peaks form. Gradually whip in the remaining sugar and continue whipping until the mixture is very stiff. Fold the egg whites into the yogurt mixture followed by the cream.

Tie waxpaper collars around freezer-proof custard cups or similar small dishes. Spoon the ice cream mixture into the dishes – it should come well above the level of the dishes. Put the dishes into a plastic bag taking care that it does not touch the tops, secure and freeze until firm.

About 30 minutes before serving, transfer the dishes to the refrigerator. Take out of the plastic bag and remove the collars. Serve decorated with lemon slices and pistachio nuts.

Serves 6–8

Serving suggestion
Serve as a sundae with Banana and Honey Ice Cream (page 29) and chopped hazelnuts, with Hot Fudge Sauce* poured over.

Additional recipes using lemon and lime:
Coconut and Lime Ice Cream (page 49), Ginger and Lime Granita (page 61), Melon-Lime Ice (page 83), Iced Lemon Soufflé Surprise (page 143), Lemon Icicle (page 142).

LITCHI: see WARM CLIMATE FRUITS
LIQUEURS: see WINES, LIQUEURS
LOGANBERRY: see BLACKBERRY,
*   LOGANBERRY*
MANDARIN: see ORANGE, ETC

Mango

Mangoes can make some of the most delicious of ices – but they must be fully ripe. The skin of a ripe mango will yield under slight pressure – any signs of hardness indicate that the fruit is not at its glorious best. To separate the flesh from the skin and pit, first peel the mango with a sharp knife. Then cut the flesh away from the pit, slicing down one side then the other. Finally, trim off any remaining flesh. Canned mangoes can be used. Always strain both fresh and canned fruit after puréeing to remove any fibers that might spoil the texture of the ice.

Simple Mango Ice Cream
Add 1¼ cups mango purée to any of the Basic Recipes*. Use 1 large or 2 small fresh mangoes, or a 1 pound can of mangoes (drained). Sweeten with confectioners' sugar if necessary.

Fresh Mango Ice Cream

⅓ cup thick plain yogurt
⅓ cup sour cream
1 large or 2 small very ripe mangoes, peeled and pitted
2 egg whites
¼ cup sugar
4 teaspoons lime or orange juice

Put the yogurt and sour cream in a bowl and beat together.

Purée the mango flesh and pass through a nylon strainer to remove any shreds. Beat the purée into the yogurt/cream mixture. Spoon into a container, cover and freeze to the slushy stage. Turn into a bowl and beat well.

In another bowl, whip the egg whites until very stiff. Gradually whip in the sugar and continue whipping until stiff again. Fold into the mango mixture with the lime or orange juice.

Spoon the mixture back into the container. Cover and freeze until firm.

About 30 minutes before serving, transfer the ice cream to the refrigerator.

Serves 4

Serving suggestion
Serve in Ice Cream Cones or Gingersnap Cones* or on a bed of mango slices. Accompany with cream, delicately flavored with orange liqueur.*

Place chopped mango in the base of hollowed-out brioche, spoon in the ice cream, trickle orange-liqueur-flavored cream over and replace the brioche tops.

Mango Sorbet

½ cup sugar
1 cup puréed, strained mango flesh
Juice of 1 lime

Put the sugar and ¼ cup water in a saucepan and stir over low heat to dissolve. Bring to the boil, remove from the heat and leave to cool.

Blend the syrup into the mango flesh with the strained lime juice.

Pour the mixture into a container. Cover and freeze until firm, beating 3 times at 45-minute intervals.

About 30 minutes before serving, transfer the sorbet to the refrigerator.

Serves 4

Serving suggestion
Serve small scoops in mango shells. Decorate with small rosettes of whipped cream and fine strips of orange peel.

Dessert suggestion
*Freeze in a can and coat in Candied Fruit Ice Cream (page 57). Decorate with Chocolate Shapes**

Mango Yogurt Ice

½ cup sugar
Flesh of 1 large mango, puréed and strained
2 tablespoons orange juice
⅔ cup thick plain yogurt
2 egg whites

In a heavy-based saucepan, dissolve the sugar in 1¼ cups water over low heat. Bring to the boil and boil until the temperature reaches 230°–234°F. Set aside to cool.

Beat the mango purée, orange juice and yogurt into the syrup. Pour the mixture into a container, cover and freeze to the slushy stage. Turn into a bowl and beat well. Whip the egg whites in a bowl until stiff but not dry and fold into the mango mixture.

Spoon the mixture back into the container. Cover and freeze until firm.

About 30 minutes before serving, transfer the ice to the refrigerator.

Serves 4

Serving suggestion
Serve with fresh mango slices and Low Calorie Topping.*

Low calorie version
Use fructose or a low calorie or artificial sweetener instead of sugar.

Iced Mango Mousse

3 egg yolks
³/₄ cup confectioners' sugar
1 very large ripe mango or 2 smaller ones, peeled and
*   pitted*
Lemon juice
²/₃ cup sour cream, beaten

Beat the egg yolks and confectioners' sugar in a bowl set over a pan of hot water until thick, light and lukewarm. Remove the bowl from the hot water and continue beating until the mixture is cold.

Strain the mango flesh into a bowl. Sharpen it with a little lemon juice then beat in the sour cream. Fold into the egg yolk mixture.

Pour the mixture into a container. Cover and freeze until firm.

About 30 minutes before serving, transfer the mousse to the refrigerator.

Serves 5–6

Serving suggestion
Use lime juice instead of lemon juice and spoon into large lime shells with scalloped edges. Decorate with rosettes of whipped cream delicately flavored with melon liqueur or brandy and a scattering of mint leaves.

Quick Mango Ice Cream

Approximately 1 pound can mangoes, drained
1¼ cups heavy cream, whipped
Approximately 2 tablespoons lemon juice

Purée the mango flesh then strain, if necessary, to remove any fibers. Gradually whip the purée into the cream and add lemon juice to taste.

Pour the mixture into a container. Cover and freeze until firm, beating well once after 1 hour.

About 30 minutes before serving, transfer the ice cream to the refrigerator.

Serves 4

Serving suggestion
Form into 4 balls, make an indentation in the top of each and fill with Southern Comfort. Serve with Langues de Chat.*

Mango Sherbet

³/₄ cup sugar
1 tablespoon lemon juice
Flesh of 2 large mangoes, puréed and strained
1 large egg white
3 tablespoons cream, whipped

Put the sugar and 1¼ cups water in a heavy-based saucepan and stir to dissolve. Bring to the boil and boil for 5 minutes. Remove from the heat, stir in the lemon juice and leave to cool.

Stir the mango purée into the syrup and pour into a shallow metal container. Chill the mixture for 30 minutes then cover and freeze to the slushy stage.

Turn the semi-frozen mixture into a bowl and beat well. Return the mixture to the container, cover and freeze until just becoming slushy again. Turn out into the bowl and beat well.

In a separate bowl, whip the egg white until stiff but not dry. Fold the cream and then the egg white into the mango mixture, spoon back into the container, cover and freeze until firm.

About 30 minutes before serving, transfer the sherbet to the refrigerator.

Serves 4–6

Mango and Coconut Ice Cream

2 eggs, separated
¹/₃ cup sugar
¹/₄ cup light cream
2 medium, ripe mangoes, peeled and pitted
3 tablespoons coconut liqueur
1 cup cream, whipped
¹/₄ cup flaked coconut

In a bowl, beat the egg yolks, sugar and light cream together. Place the bowl over a pan of hot water and cook, stirring constantly, until the sauce thickens. Remove from the heat and leave to cool.

Purée the flesh from the mangoes and pass through a strainer. Blend the purée with the liqueur and fold it into the egg yolk mixture. Put the egg whites in a bowl and whip until stiff but not dry. Fold the egg whites, whipped cream and flaked coconut into the mixture. Spoon into a shallow container, cover and freeze until firm.

About 30 minutes before serving, transfer the ice cream to the refrigerator.

Serves 6

Maple

Rich and sweet, with a distinctive taste, maple syrup is high on the list of popular ice cream flavors. Always check the contents on the label to make sure you get pure maple syrup. Some maple-flavored syrups are blended with other ingredients and taste rather bland as a result.

Simple Maple Syrup Ice Cream

Ripple ½ cup maple syrup through any of the Basic Recipes* or through a good-quality bought vanilla ice cream.

Maple and Walnut Ice Cream

1¼ cups sugar
1 cup walnut halves
½ cup maple syrup
2¼ cups milk
4 egg yolks
1 cup cream, whipped

To make the praline, heat half of the sugar in a heavy-based saucepan with just enough water to moisten. Boil the syrup to 248°F. Add the nuts, remove from the heat and stir until the nuts are coated in the syrup. Return to the heat, stirring constantly, until the sugar caramelizes. Turn onto a lightly oiled cold surface and leave to cool. Reserve half of the praline for decoration and reduce the remainder to a powder in a blender or food processor.

In a heavy-based saucepan, bring the maple syrup and milk to just simmering point. Beat the remaining sugar and egg yolks together in a bowl and stir in the flavored milk. Pour into the rinsed pan and cook gently, stirring constantly, until the mixture thickens. Do not allow to boil. Remove from the heat and leave to cool. Pour into a container, cover and freeze until just becoming firm. Turn into a bowl and beat well. Fold in the cream and praline powder. Spoon the mixture back into the container, cover and freeze until firm.

About 30 minutes before serving, transfer the ice cream to the refrigerator. Serve decorated with the reserved walnut praline.

Serves 6

Dessert suggestion

Layer with split chocolate brownies. Spoon Coffee Sauce* over the turned-out dessert.

Maple Mousse

1 egg white
3/4 cup maple syrup, heated
1 cup cream, whipped
8–12 pecan or walnut halves

Whip the egg white in a bowl until stiff but not dry. Slowly pour in the hot maple syrup, whipping constantly, and continue to whip until a thick meringue is formed. Carefully fold in the whipped cream and chill.

Pour the mixture into a freezer-proof dish. Cover and freeze until the top is just beginning to harden. Arrange the nuts over the surface, cover and freeze the mousse until firm.

About 40 minutes before serving, transfer the mousse to the refrigerator.

Serves 4–6

Serving suggestion
Freeze in individual dishes and decorate with the walnut halves just before serving.

Dessert suggestion
Ripple with Apricot Yogurt Ice (page 24).

Maple Granola Ice Cream

1/4 cup slivered almonds, toasted
1/3 cup shredded coconut, toasted
1 cup rolled oats, toasted
1/2 cup maple syrup
1 1/2 tablespoons oil
1/2 cup each raisins, chopped dates and prunes
1 1/2 tablespoons chopped dried apricots
2 1/2 cups cream, whipped

Mix the almonds, coconut and oats together in a bowl. Heat the maple syrup and oil together in a small saucepan and pour over the oat mixture. Toss well to coat it evenly. Spread the mixture out on a baking sheet and place under a medium hot broiler for about 10–15 minutes, turning frequently, until well toasted. Tip into a bowl and mix in the dried fruits. Leave to cool.

Stir the granola mixture into the cream. Pour into a container, cover and freeze until firm. About 15 minutes before serving, transfer the ice cream to the refrigerator.

Serves 5–6

Serving suggestions
Serve with orange segments, pith and membrane removed, sliced bananas sprinkled with lime juice (or Drambuie, Benedictine or Galliano) or poached apple slices. Spoon over 3 tablespoons plain yogurt beaten into 1/4 pound soft cheese and lightly sweetened with confectioners' sugar. Decorate with fine strips of orange peel.

Maple and Nut Ice Cream

1/3 cup raisins
1/4 cup whiskey or water
3 eggs, separated
3/4 cup maple syrup
1 cup sour cream
3 tablespoons melted butter
3 tablespoons each coarsely ground almonds and
    hazelnuts
1 egg white

Put the raisins and whiskey or water in a small saucepan and bring to simmering point. Remove from the heat and leave to cool.

Beat the egg yolks in a bowl until thick. Beat in the maple syrup, cream, butter and nuts.

In another bowl, whip the egg whites until stiff but not dry. Carefully fold the egg whites into the maple mixture with the raisins and their soaking liquor. Pour the mixture into a container. Cover and freeze until firm.

About 20 minutes before serving, transfer the ice cream to the refrigerator.

Serves 6

Dessert suggestion
Layer with Sponge Fingers. Press finely chopped walnuts over the turned-out dessert.*

Maple Ice Cream

3/4 cup maple syrup
3 eggs, separated
1 1/4 cups cream, whipped
Few drops of vanilla extract

Heat the maple syrup in a heavy-based saucepan to just below boiling point. Beat the egg yolks in a bowl until thick then beat in about 4 tablespoons of the maple syrup. Stir this mixture into the hot syrup and cook gently, stirring constantly, until the mixture thickens. Leave to cool, stirring occasionally. Fold the cream and vanilla into the custard. Pour the mixture into a container, cover and freeze until just becoming firm. Turn into a bowl and beat well.

Whip the egg whites until stiff but not dry. Fold into the custard. Spoon the mixture back into the container. Cover and freeze until firm.

About 30 minutes before serving, transfer the ice cream to the refrigerator.

Serves 6–8

Serving suggestion
Spoon onto hot waffles and trickle over Hot Chocolate Sauce or Bitter Chocolate Sauce*. Serve with fresh apricots.*

MARSALA: see WINES, LIQUEURS

Melon

At their best and ripest, melons are wonderfully fragrant with a deliciously aromatic flavor. Honeydew melons are especially suitable for ices, but Cantaloupes and other musk melons are almost as good. Watermelons have a distinctive sweetness and texture.

Melon Sorbet

1 large ripe melon weighing about 1½ pounds
3 tablespoons lemon juice
½ cup sugar or 1 cup confectioners' sugar

Peel the melon, discard the seeds and reduce the flesh to a purée with the lemon juice and sugar.

Pour the mixture into a container. Cover and freeze until firm, beating 3 times at 45-minute intervals.

About 30 minutes before serving, transfer the sorbet to the refrigerator.

Serves 4

Serving suggestion

Scoop into small balls and serve in a chilled melon shell intermingled with small wild strawberries or sliced strawberries.

Melon Ice Cream

2 ripe melons
Juice of 1/2 lemon
1/2 cup sugar
1 1/4 cups whipping or heavy cream
1 tablespoon Drambuie or Benedictine

Cut the melons in half, discard the seeds and scoop out the flesh taking care not to damage the shells. Put the shells in the freezer.

Purée the melon flesh with the lemon juice and 1/3 cup of the sugar. Put the cream in a bowl and whip with the remaining sugar and the liqueur until soft peaks form. Fold the cream into the purée.

Pour the mixture into a container. Cover and freeze until firm, beating twice at hourly intervals.

About 30 minutes before serving, scoop the ice cream into the shells and refrigerate until required.

Serves 4–6

Serving suggestion
Freeze in halved melon shells, then cut the shells into wedges. Decorate with Chocolate Shapes* and long, twisted strips of orange peel. Serve with Cigars Russe*.

Melon Ice Cream (with crème fraîche)

1 1/4 cups crème fraîche
4 egg yolks
1 cup sugar
2 small ripe melons to give about 1 pound flesh
Squeeze of orange juice

In a heavy-based saucepan, bring the crème fraîche to just below boiling point. Beat the egg yolks with the sugar in a bowl then beat in the hot crème. Return the mixture to the rinsed pan and cook gently, stirring constantly, until the custard thickens. Do not allow to boil. Leave to cool, stirring occasionally.

Remove the flesh from the melons, taking care not to include any hard flesh that may be near the rind. Purée the flesh then beat it into the custard, adding orange juice to taste.

Pour the mixture into a container. Cover and freeze until firm, beating twice at hourly intervals.

About 30 minutes before serving, transfer the ice cream to the refrigerator.

Serves 4–5

Serving suggestion
Serve in Coupelles* with a little crème de menthe-flavored whipped cream spooned over. Decorate with mint leaves and shapes cut from lime peel.

Form into balls and put into a chilled melon shell, its sides lined with orange or lemon slices. Decorate with sprigs of mint.

Watermelon Sorbet

1 1/2 pounds watermelon, weighed without seeds or skin
1 1/4 cups sugar
2 cinnamon sticks
2 tablespoons coriander seeds, crushed
3 tablespoons lemon juice

Reduce the watermelon flesh to a purée. In a heavy-based saucepan, dissolve the sugar in 2 cups water. Add the cinnamon sticks and coriander seeds and boil for 5 minutes. Cover and leave to infuse until cold.

Strain the syrup into the watermelon purée and stir in the lemon juice.

Pour the mixture into a container. Cover and freeze until firm, beating 3 times at 45-minute intervals.

About 30 minutes before serving, transfer the sorbet to the refrigerator.

Serves 8

Melon-Lime Ice

2/3 cup sugar
2/3 cup lime-flavored cordial
1 pound melon flesh, puréed
2 egg whites
Twisted fine strips of lime peel, for decoration

Put the sugar and lime-flavored cordial in a bowl and stir to dissolve the sugar. Stir into the melon flesh. Chill for about an hour. Pour into a container, cover and freeze to the slushy stage. Beat well in a bowl.

Whip the egg whites in a bowl until stiff but not dry. Fold the egg whites into the melon-lime mixture. Return to the container, cover and freeze until firm.

About 40 minutes before serving, transfer the ice to the refrigerator. Serve each portion decorated with twisted strips of lime peel.

Serves 6

Orange, etc

Oranges and their near relations tangerines and mandarins (which make one of the more delicious canned fruits) make sweet yet tangy ices. This section includes a recipe for kumquats. With their very thin skins, these small, oval fruits do not have to be peeled before use.

Simple Orange Ice Cream
Add the chopped flesh (pith and membrane removed) of 3 oranges to any of the Basic Recipes* or to a good-quality bought vanilla ice cream.

Orange Water Ice

1 1/2 cups sugar
2 cups orange juice
2/3 cup lemon juice
Finely grated zest of 2 oranges
Finely grated zest of 1 lemon
Thin orange slices, for decoration

Dissolve the sugar in 1 quart water in a heavy-based saucepan. Bring to the boil and boil for 10 minutes. Leave to cool completely.

Stir in the fruit juice and zests and pour into a container. Cover and freeze until firm, beating 3 times at 45-minute intervals.

About 1 hour before serving, transfer the ice to the refrigerator. Decorate each portion with a thin twist of orange.

Serves 6

Serving suggestion
Place small scoops in chilled orange shells. Serve with Almond Tuiles.*

Mandarin Cream Ice

6 ounces full fat cream cheese, softened
2/3 cup plain yogurt
3 cups canned mandarins, puréed
2 egg whites
3 tablespoons slivered almonds, toasted
Mandarin liqueur, for serving

Put the cheese in a bowl and gradually beat in the yogurt. Beat in the mandarin purée. Spoon into a container, cover and freeze to the slushy stage. Turn into a bowl and beat well.

In another bowl, whip the egg whites until stiff but not dry and fold into the mandarin mixture.

Spoon the mixture back into the container, sprinkle the almonds over the top, cover and freeze until firm.

About 30 minutes before serving, transfer the cream ice to the refrigerator. Pour a spoonful of mandarin liqueur over each portion as it is served.

Serves 4

Orange Sorbet de Luxe

1/2 cup sugar
1/4 cup lemon juice
2 cups frozen concentrated orange juice, defrosted but not diluted
1/2 cup chunky marmalade
1/4 cup Cointreau

Dissolve the sugar in 1/2 cup water in a saucepan. Bring to the boil and boil for 1 minute. Remove from the heat and stir in the remaining ingredients. Cool completely then chill for 30 minutes.

Pour the mixture into a container. Cover and freeze, beating twice at hourly intervals, until just softly frozen. Serve immediately.

If the sorbet is made in advance and becomes hard, transfer it to the refrigerator 45–60 minutes before serving.

Serves 6–8

Dessert suggestion
Encase in Muesli Ice Cream (page 37). Decorate with whipped cream and fine strips of orange peel. Serve with white Wine Sauce.*

Tangerine Ice Cream

12 tangerines
1/2 cup sugar
2 1/2 cups heavy cream

For decoration
Shapes cut from tangerine peel
Any small shiny leaves from the garden or fresh bay leaves

Finely grate the zest from 6 of the tangerines. Mix the zest with the sugar and half of the cream in a saucepan. Heat gently to dissolve the sugar then leave to cool.

Squeeze the juice from all the tangerines and mix with the sweetened cream. Whip the remaining cream in a bowl until soft peaks form and fold into the sweetened, flavored cream.

Pour the mixture into a container and freeze until firm, beating twice at hourly intervals.

About 30 minutes before serving, transfer the ice cream to the refrigerator. Serve decorated with the tangerine peel shapes and the leaves.

Serves 4–5

Dessert suggestion
Freeze in a container lined with Coconut Cake. Spread a thin layer of mandarin-liqueur-flavored whipped cream over the turned-out dessert and cover with finely chopped hazelnuts. Arrange tangerine segments around the base and serve with Langues de Chat*.*

Orange and Rosemary Sorbet

1/2 cup sugar
Large rosemary sprig
2 cups fresh orange juice
Grated zest of 3 large oranges

For decoration
Shapes cut from orange peel
Small rosemary sprigs, with flowers if possible

In a saucepan, dissolve the sugar in 1/2 cup water and bring to the boil. Add the rosemary, remove from the heat, cover and leave to infuse for 30 minutes. Strain the syrup and blend with the strained orange juice and the zest.

Pour the mixture into a container. Cover and freeze until firm, beating well at 45-minute intervals.

About 40 minutes before serving, transfer the sorbet to the refrigerator. Decorate each portion with orange peel shapes and rosemary sprigs.

Serves 4–5

Serving suggestion
Serve in Coupelles*. Decorate with orange segments, pith and membrane removed, and sprigs of fresh rosemary, preferably in bloom.

Mandarin Ice Cream

1 cup milk
1/2 cup sugar
3 egg yolks
1 teaspoon vanilla extract
2 cups cream, whipped
1/3 cup roughly crumbled brandysnaps
Approximately 1 pound can mandarins, drained and chopped
3 tablespoons brandy, optional

In a heavy-based saucepan, gently heat the milk to just below boiling point. Beat the egg yolks with the sugar in a bowl until very thick and light. Stir in the milk. Return the mixture to the rinsed pan and cook over a low heat, stirring constantly, until thickened. Remove from the heat, stir in the vanilla extract and cool, stirring occasionally.

Fold the cream, brandysnaps, mandarins and brandy, if you are using it, into the custard.

Pour the mixture into a container. Cover and freeze until firm.

About 30 minutes before serving, transfer the ice cream to the refrigerator.

Serves 6–8

Serving suggestion
Freeze in a loaf pan. Serve in slices, surrounded with Bitter Chocolate Sauce*.

Orange Ice Cream

3 eggs, separated
1/2 cup sugar
2 cups heavy cream, whipped
Finely grated zest and juice of 2 large oranges

Put the egg yolks in a bowl. Beat, gradually adding the sugar, until very thick and light.

In another bowl, whip the egg whites until stiff. Fold the cream, orange juice and zest into the egg yolks followed by the egg whites.

Pour the mixture into a container. Cover and freeze until firm.

About 20 minutes before serving, transfer the ice cream to the refrigerator.

Serves 6

Serving suggestion
Spoon into small Choux* pastry shells, pile into a pyramid and pour over Hot Chocolate Sauce* flavored with Grand Marnier.

Dessert suggestion
Form into 6 balls with a tablespoon of Nougat Glace à l'Orange (page 57), in the center of each one. Coat with very lightly toasted slivered almonds. Serve with orange segments, pith and membrane removed.

Iced Orange-Almond Mousse

3 eggs, separated
1/3 cup sugar
Finely grated zest of 1 orange
3 tablespoons orange juice
1/4 cup ground almonds
2/3 cup heavy cream, whipped
Slices of candied or fresh orange, for decoration

Put the egg yolks, sugar, orange zest and juice in a bowl and beat until very thick and light. Fold in the ground almonds. In another bowl, whip the egg whites until stiff but not dry and fold into the orange-almond mixture with the cream.

Pour into a container. Cover and freeze until firm.

About 20 minutes before serving, transfer the mousse to the refrigerator. Serve decorated with the orange slices.

Serves 6

Dessert suggestion
Layer with Chocolate Ice Cream (page 44). Decorate the turned-out dessert with orange-liqueur-flavored whipped cream, slivered almonds and slices of candied orange.

Valencia Orange Sorbet

2¼ pounds Valencia oranges
2½ cups sugar cubes
¼ cup sugar
Juice of ½ lemon
1 cup orange juice

To serve
Fresh orange segments
Orange caramel sauce
Caramelized* orange strips

Rub the skins of the oranges with the sugar cubes to extract as much of the essential oil as possible. Put the sugar cubes in a saucepan with the sugar, ¼ cup water and the lemon juice. Heat gently to dissolve the sugar. Squeeze the juice from the oranges and add to the pan, off the heat, with the cup of orange juice. Cool completely.

Pour the mixture into a container. Cover and freeze until firm, beating 3 times at 45-minute intervals.

About 30 minutes before serving, transfer the sorbet to the refrigerator. Serve topped by orange segments, a little orange caramel sauce and caramelized orange strips.

Serves 8

Serving suggestion
Serve in wine glasses. Pour a little crème fraîche over each serving and sprinkle with chopped preserved ginger.

Orange Cream Ice

3 oranges
1¼ cups milk
⅓ cup sugar
5 egg yolks
⅔ cup cream, whipped
Candied orange slices, for decoration

Peel the oranges very thinly and put the zest in a heavy-based saucepan with the milk and sugar. Stir to dissolve the sugar over low heat. Then boil for 10 minutes.

Put the egg yolks in a bowl and beat until light. Stir in the milk and return to the rinsed pan. Cook over a low heat, stirring constantly, until the custard thickens. Do not allow to boil. Strain through a fine strainer and cool, stirring occasionally.

Squeeze the oranges and stir the juice into the custard. Fold in the cream.

Pour the mixture into a container. Cover and freeze until firm, beating twice at hourly intervals.

About 40 minutes before serving, transfer the ice to the refrigerator. Serve decorated with candied orange slices.

Serves 4–5

Serving suggestion
Scoop into individual dishes and serve with round Langues de Chat.*

Dessert suggestion
Freeze in a pie plate or cake pan lined with crushed ginger cookies held with melted butter. Cover with the cream ice. Decorate the turned-out dessert with brandy-flavored whipped cream, shapes cut from orange peel and chocolate-coated peanuts.

Kumquat Ice Cream

¾ pound kumquats, thinly sliced and seeds removed
¾ cup sugar
1¼ cups heavy cream, whipped
1 piece of candied ginger, finely chopped, optional
Twisted fine strips of orange peel, for decoration

Put the kumquats, 1 cup water and the sugar in a saucepan and simmer gently until the fruit is soft. This may take 30 minutes but check occasionally.

Purée the fruit with the liquid and leave to cool.

Fold the cream into the purée with the ginger, if used. Pour into a container, cover and freeze until firm, beating twice at hourly intervals.

About 30 minutes before serving, transfer the ice cream to the refrigerator. Serve decorated with twisted strips of orange peel.

Serves 4

Serving suggestion
Serve in Coupelles. Decorate with Caramelized* strips of orange peel.*

Dessert suggestion
Freeze in small boxes made from Chocolate Squares. Decorate the tops with small swirls of whipped cream, and pieces of candied orange slices or fine strips of orange peel twisted together.*

Additional recipes using oranges: Orange Sorbet in a Chocolate Case (page 143), Blackberry and Orange Layer Cake (page 139).

PAPAYA: see WARM CLIMATE FRUITS
PASSION FRUIT: see WARM CLIMATE
FRUITS

Peach, Nectarine

Peaches and nectarines can be substituted for each other in recipes, but nectarines have a slightly richer, more scented yet more tangy flavor. White-fleshed varieties of both fruits are the best to use. To peel peaches and nectarines, pour boiling water over them and leave for 15 seconds if they are very ripe, a little longer if they are slightly hard. The skin should come easily away from the flesh. Never leave the fruit in the water until the skin falls away of its own accord as this will affect both taste and texture. Straining the puréed flesh gives a smoother ice, but is not always essential.

Simple Peach Ice Cream
Purée and strain the flesh of 1 pound white peaches and add to any of the Basic Recipes*.

Peach Ice Cream

4 large ripe peaches
1/2 cup sugar
3 egg yolks
2/3 cup whipping cream, whipped
Squeeze of lemon juice

Peel the peaches, remove the pits and reduce the flesh to a purée.

Put the sugar and 2/3 cup water in a saucepan and stir to dissolve over low heat. Bring to the boil.

Meanwhile, in a bowl, beat the egg yolks until thick. Pour the boiling syrup onto the egg yolks, beating all the time. Set the bowl over a pan of barely simmering water and continue to beat until the mixture thickens. Remove from the heat and continue to beat until the mixture cools.

Stir the peach purée into the egg yolk mixture. Fold in the cream and add lemon juice to taste.

Pour the mixture into a container. Cover and freeze until firm.

About 30 minutes before serving, transfer the ice cream to the refrigerator.

Serves 4

Dessert suggestion
Freeze in a pie plate or cake pan lined with a crust of ground, toasted pecans or walnuts mixed with brown sugar to taste and held together with melted butter. To serve, brush the surface of the ice cream with a glaze made from melted, strained apricot jam flavored with lemon juice, and decorate with peach slices and mint sprigs.

Peach Sorbet

1 1/4 pounds ripe peaches
2 ripe apricots
1 1/3 cups sugar
2 tablespoons lemon juice

Peel and pit the peaches and apricots and reduce to a purée. Make up the purée to 1 quart with cold water. Add the sugar and stir or blend until it has dissolved. Strain through a fine strainer. Stir in the lemon juice. Pour the mixture into a container, cover and freeze until firm, beating 3 times at 45-minute intervals.

About 30 minutes before serving, transfer the sorbet to the refrigerator.

Serves 6–8

Serving suggestion
Poach halved, pitted peaches in wine. Enlarge the cavities if necessary, fill with scoops of sorbet and top with a teaspoonful of crème fraîche. Serve with Macaroons.*

Flavor variation
Replace the water in the recipe with a full-bodied dry white wine.

White Peach Sorbet

Approximately 1 pound can of white peaches
Juices of 2 lemons
1 egg white

Purée the peaches and the juice with the lemon juice then pass through a strainer.

Pour the mixture into a container. Cover and freeze to the slushy stage. Beat well in a bowl.

Whip the egg white in a small bowl until stiff but not dry. Fold the egg white into the peach mixture. Return to the container, cover and freeze until firm.

About 30 minutes before serving, transfer the sorbet to the refrigerator.

Serves 4

Serving suggestion
Serve in tall, elegant glasses with a few brandy-soaked Macaroons in the base of each. Just before serving pour wine over the sorbets.*

Flavor variation
Use canned yellow peaches instead of white ones and add 2 or 3 tablespoons of white rum to the purée.

Iced Peach Yogurt

4 large ripe peaches
Finely grated zest and juice of 2 oranges
1¼ cups plain yogurt
2 tablespoons confectioners' sugar
2 egg whites, stiffly whipped

Peel and pit the peaches. Purée the flesh with the orange zest and juice, the yogurt and confectioners' sugar. Fold in the egg whites.

Pour the mixture into individual dishes or molds, cover and freeze until firm.

About 20 minutes before serving, transfer the ices to the refrigerator.

Serves 4

Serving suggestion
Freeze in individual ring molds. Fill the centers with diced peaches, topped with Low Calorie Topping* and a sprinkling of chopped almonds or hazelnuts if liked.

Low calorie version
Use fructose or a low calorie or artificial sweetener instead of sugar.

Iced Nectarine Mousse

½ cup sugar
4 large egg whites
1 pound ripe nectarines, puréed and strained
Squeeze of orange, lime or lemon juice
1¼ cups cream, whipped

In a heavy-based saucepan, dissolve the sugar in 5 tablespoons water over low heat. Bring to the boil and boil until a temperature of 239°F is reached.

Meanwhile, in a bowl, whip the egg whites until very stiff. Gradually pour on the hot syrup, whipping constantly, and continue to whip until the meringue is very thick and cold.

Fold the nectarine purée, sharpened with a little orange, lime or lemon juice, into the meringue. Fold in the cream.

Pour the mixture into a container. Cover and freeze until firm.

About 30 minutes before serving, transfer the mousse to the refrigerator.

Serves 4

Dessert suggestion
Freeze in hollowed-out nectarine shells. Decorate with kirsch-flavored whipped cream, small Chocolate Shapes* and a fine sprinkling of chopped hazelnuts. Serve with a sauce of strained, puréed nectarines 'lifted' with a squeeze of orange juice, and Langues de Chat*.

Lightly Spiced Peach Ice Cream

2 cups dried peaches, soaked overnight in 2 cups hot water and ⅔ cup white wine
3 egg yolks
⅓ cup light brown sugar
¼ teaspoon ground cinnamon
Large pinch grated nutmeg
1¼ cups milk
⅔ cup cream, whipped
Long strip lemon peel

Drain the peaches, reserving the liquid. Put the egg yolks in a bowl with the sugar and spices and whip together until thick. In a heavy-based saucepan, bring the milk to just below boiling point. Pour the hot milk onto the egg yolks, stirring. Return the mixture to the rinsed pan and cook over a low heat, stirring until thick. Cool, stirring occasionally, then pour into a container, cover and freeze until firm. Beat well in a bowl.

Finely chop half the peaches and fold into the custard with the cream. Spoon back into the container, cover and freeze until firm.

Simmer the remaining peaches in a saucepan with the lemon peel and the reserved liquid for about 5 minutes. Cool and store, covered, in the refrigerator.

About 30 minutes before serving, transfer the ice cream to the refrigerator. Gently warm the peaches and liquid and spoon a little over each portion as it is served.

Serves 6

Serving suggestion
Spoon into hollowed-out brioche. Add the warmed peaches, and spoon the liquid over each portion as it is served.

Additional recipe using peaches: Iced Peach Charlotte (page 140).

Recipes for cakes, sauces, etc., asterisked in the dessert and serving suggestions, are given on pages 145 to 152. For directions on layering, lining and other techniques involved in creating desserts, see pages 152 to 155. Basic recipes are on pages 16 and 17.

Peanut

Peanut ices can be made with ground or chopped nuts, smooth or crunchy peanut butter, peanut brittle or dry-roasted or plain unsalted nuts. It is possible to buy roasted, unsalted peanuts, but if they are not available prepare your own by heating shelled, skinned nuts in a 350°F oven for about 30–45 minutes, taking care they do not become too brown. To prevent peanuts from becoming oily when you grind them, chop the nuts by hand before processing small batches, briefly, in a coffee grinder, blender or food processor.

Simple Peanut Ice Cream
Add ⅔ cup chopped unsalted peanuts to any of the Basic Recipes* or to a good-quality bought vanilla ice cream.

Peanut Swirl

3 eggs, separated
⅓ cup light brown sugar
2¼ cups milk
Few drops of vanilla extract
1¼ cups light cream
¾ cup smooth peanut butter

Beat the egg yolks with the sugar in a bowl. In a heavy-based saucepan, heat the milk to simmering point. Stir the hot milk into the egg yolks. Return to the rinsed pan and cook gently, stirring constantly, until slightly thickened. Remove from the heat and leave to cool, stirring frequently.

Beat the vanilla extract and ½ cup of the cream into the custard. Put in the refrigerator to chill.

Pour the mixture into a container. Cover and freeze until just becoming firm.

Beat the remaining cream with the peanut butter in a bowl. In another bowl, whip the egg whites until stiff but not dry. Fold the egg whites into the ice cream and when just evenly blended fold the peanut cream through the mixture to give a swirled, marbled effect. Return to the container, cover and freeze until firm.

About 45 minutes before serving, transfer the ice cream to the refrigerator.

Serves 6

Dessert suggestion
Freeze in a can then coat the turned-out ice in crushed Macaroons. Serve in slices, surrounded by a sauce of puréed orange flesh.*

To reduce your calorie intake
Tofu can be substituted for any soft cheese (see page 13); beat with the other ingredients until smooth. It has no cholesterol and is low in fat.

Ground Peanut Ice Cream

1¼ pounds fromage blanc or strained cottage cheese
⅔ cup unsalted dry-roasted peanuts, ground
⅔ cup sugar
¾ cup golden raisins
Finely grated zest of 1 lemon
1¼ cups crème fraîche or ⅔ cup light cream and
  ⅔ cup sour cream, mixed together
Twists of lemon peel, to decorate

Leave the fromage blanc or cottage cheese to drain into a bowl for 3–4 hours through a strainer lined with cheesecloth.

Mix the nuts and sugar together and stir into the drained cheese with the golden raisins and lemon zest. Fold in the crème fraîche or light and sour creams mixed together.

Pour the mixture into a container. Cover and freeze until firm.

About 30 minutes before serving, transfer the ice cream to the refrigerator. Serve decorated with twists of lemon peel.

Serves 6

Serving suggestion
Form into 6 balls and arrange on a serving dish, with Gingersnaps and piped whipped cream. Decorate with chocolate vermicelli and chocolate flakes.*

Peanut Ice Cream

4 tablespoons milk or light cream
¾ pound soft cheese/ricotta, beaten
1 cup confectioners' sugar
Few drops of vanilla extract
⅔ cup unsalted peanuts, chopped
2 egg whites

Gradually beat the milk or cream into the soft cheese then beat in the sugar and vanilla extract. Stir in the nuts.

In another bowl, whip the egg whites until stiff but not dry then fold into the peanut mixture. Cover and freeze in individual dishes until firm.

About 30 minutes before serving, transfer the ice cream to the refrigerator.

Serves 4

Serving suggestion
Freeze in a ring mold. Fill the center with small scoops of Apricot Sorbet (page 23) or Pineapple Sorbet (page 98) and surround the turned-out dessert with apricot quarters or pineapple chunks.

Peanut Brittle Ice Cream

⅔ cup unsalted dry-roasted peanuts
½ cup sugar
3 egg yolks
½ cup confectioners' sugar
1 cup milk
½ cup heavy cream

To make the brittle, spread the peanuts on a non-stick cookie sheet or one lined with foil. Dissolve the sugar in 4 tablespoons water in a small, heavy-based pan. Bring to the boil and boil rapidly until the syrup caramelizes and turns an even, deep golden brown. Immediately pour the caramel over the peanuts and quickly stir them around so they are evenly coated. Leave to cool. Put the brittle into a heavy plastic bag and bang it firmly with a rolling pin until it is broken into small pieces – some will be powdered.

Beat the egg yolks and confectioners' sugar together in a bowl until thick and pale. Whip the milk and cream together, then whip into the egg yolks. Chill well.

Fold the peanut brittle and the fine powdery pieces into the cream mixture.

Pour the mixture into a container. Cover and freeze until firm.

About 30 minutes before serving, transfer the ice cream to the refrigerator.

Serves 4

Dessert suggestion
Layer with Banana Ice Cream (page 28) and Chocolate Ice Cream (page 44), gently swirling each layer into the one below. Decorate with chocolate-coated peanuts or Chocolate Curls* and chopped peanut brittle.

Additional recipe using peanuts: Peanut Chocolate Fudge Ice Cream (page 38).

Pear

The best-flavored ices are made from dessert pears, such as Bosc, Bartlett or Cornice. You can also use dried pears, soaked and puréed. Whichever type you use, make sure it is ripe but not 'sleepy', that is, soft, mushy and often discolored. Canned pears can make good ices.

Simple Pear Ice Cream
Drain and chop the contents of a 1 pound can pears and add to any of the Basic Recipes*.

Pear and Hazelnut Yogurt Ice

Approximately 1 pound can pears, in natural juice
2 teaspoons honey
1 tablespoon lemon juice
1 cup plain yogurt
¼ cup chopped hazelnuts
Lemon balm leaves, for decoration

Drain and chop the pears finely and set aside. Pour the juice into a saucepan. Add the honey and lemon juice and heat gently, stirring until evenly mixed. Cool. Stir in the yogurt and chill for about 30 minutes.

Pour the mixture into a container. Cover and freeze until slushy. Beat well in a bowl. Fold the chopped pears and hazelnuts into the yogurt mixture. Return to the container, cover and freeze until firm.

About 1 hour before serving, transfer the ice to the refrigerator. Serve decorated with lemon balm leaves.

Serves 4

Low calorie version
Add fructose or a low calorie or artificial sweetener instead of honey when the yogurt is stirred in. Freeze in individual containers. Serve with Low Calorie Topping.*

Pear and Red Wine Sorbet

4 medium-sized ripe dessert pears, peeled and cored
½ bottle of medium-quality red wine
¼ of an orange
¼ of a lemon
½ a cinnamon stick
1 cup sugar
3 tablespoons pear liqueur, optional

In a saucepan, poach the pears in the wine with the orange, lemon, cinnamon, sugar and ¼ cup water until tender. Remove the pears and put in a bowl. Strain the liquor over the pears and leave to cool. Purée the pears and liquor, adding the pear liqueur, if using.

Pour the mixture into a container. Cover and freeze until firm, beating well 3 times at 45-minute intervals.

About 30 minutes before serving, transfer the sorbet to the refrigerator.

Serves 4–5

Serving suggestion
Serve with poached pears and cinnamon-flavored Cigars Russe.*

Dessert suggestion
Encase in Pear Ice Cream (below) and surround with Langues de Chat. Decorate with whipped cream and finely chopped hazelnuts.*

Pear Ice Cream

1 pound dessert pears, peeled, cored and chopped
4 tablespoons sweet butter
¼ cup sugar
1 tablespoon orange flower water, or to taste
Strip of lemon peel
2 egg yolks
1¼ cups crème fraîche or 50/50 blend heavy and sour creams
Crystallized violets, for decoration

Gently poach the pears with the butter, sugar, orange flower water, lemon peel, and 4 tablespoons water in an uncovered saucepan, until very soft. Remove the peel and purée the fruit and the liquid (this should have reduced by about half).

Return the purée to the pan and beat in the egg yolks. Cook over a low heat, stirring constantly, until the mixture thickens, but do not allow it to boil. Leave to cool, stirring occasionally. Pour the mixture into a container, cover and freeze until just becoming firm. Turn into a bowl and beat well.

Whip the crème fraîche or creams in a bowl until soft peaks form. Fold into the pear mixture.

Spoon the mixture back into the container. Cover and freeze until firm.

About 30 minutes before serving, transfer the ice cream to the refrigerator. Serve each portion decorated with crystallized violets.

Serves 4

Serving suggestion
Serve in lightly spiced Coupelles or Gingersnap Baskets*. Arrange small thin slices of poached pears over the mounds of ice cream and sprinkle them with Poire Williams, pear liqueur or kirsch. Decorate each serving with long fine strips of orange peel.*

Dessert suggestion
Make a bombe or freeze in a loaf or cake pan with the ice cream encased in a layer of Raspberry Ice Cream (page 104) followed by a layer of Pistachio Frozen Custard (page 101). Surround the turned-out dessert with poached, sliced pears strewn with long, fine strips of orange peel.

Pear Sorbet

3 large, ripe dessert pears
2/3 cup white wine
1/3 cup sugar
Long strip of lemon peel

For decoration
Poached pear slices
Maraschino cherries

Peel, core and slice the pears. Poach the pears with the wine, sugar and lemon peel for about 5 minutes until the slices are tender. Remove the pan from the heat and leave to cool. Remove the lemon peel and purée the cold mixture.

Pour the mixture into a container. Cover and freeze until firm, beating well at 45-minute intervals.

About 15 minutes before serving transfer the sorbet to the refrigerator. Serve decorated with poached pear slices and maraschino cherries.

Serves 4

Dessert suggestion
Make into a bombe with a center of Ginger Crush (page 61).

Pear Ice Cream (with kirsch)

2 large ripe dessert pears
3 tablespoons lemon juice
1/2 cup sugar
2 egg whites
1/2 cup heavy cream
1/4 cup confectioners' sugar
1/4 cup pear liqueur, eau-de-vie or good-quality kirsch

Peel and core the pears then purée with the lemon juice. Chill. Dissolve the sugar in 3 tablespoons water in a small heavy-based saucepan. Bring to the boil and boil for 2 minutes until the syrup runs off the spoon in a slightly sticky stream.

In a bowl, whip the egg whites, preferably using an electric beater, until soft peaks form. Pour in the boiling syrup in a steady stream, whipping constantly for 2–3 minutes until the mixture is stiff, shiny and cool. Chill.

In another bowl, whip the cream with the confectioners' sugar and liqueur or kirsch until soft peaks form. Carefully fold in the pear purée then the meringue.

Spoon the mixture into a container. Cover and freeze until firm.

About 20 minutes before serving, transfer the ice cream to the refrigerator.

Serves 4

Serving suggestion
Serve in scooped-out pear shells or chocolate-covered Meringue Baskets*. Decorate with small rosettes of whipped cream, and crystallized violets or roses. Serve with Langues de Chat*.

Pear Ice Cream (with cream cheese)

1 1/4 pounds ripe pears, cored
1/3 cup apple juice
1/2 cup brown sugar
1/4 teaspoon ground cinnamon
2 eggs, separated
2/3 cup full-fat cream cheese, beaten

Gently poach the pears in the apple juice with the sugar and cinnamon in a covered pan until tender. Purée the pears with the cooking liquid then pass through a fine strainer. Return the mixture to the rinsed pan, stir in the egg yolks and heat gently until slightly thickened. Set aside to cool.

Beat the cheese into the pear mixture. Pour into a container, cover and freeze until just becoming firm. Turn into a bowl and beat well. Whip the egg whites in a bowl until stiff but not dry then fold into the cold mixture.

Spoon the mixture back into the container. Cover and freeze until firm.

About 30 minutes before serving, transfer the ice cream to the refrigerator.

Serves 4

Serving suggestion
Serve with Milky Way Sauce* or Hot Chocolate Sauce* and Langues de Chat*.

Dessert suggestion
Layer with crushed Macaroons*. Decorate the turned-out dessert with slices of candied orange and grated chocolate. Serve with white Wine Sauce*.

To reduce your calorie intake
Tofu can be substituted for any soft cheese (see page 13); beat with the other ingredients until smooth. It has no cholesterol and is low in fat.

PECAN: see WALNUT, PECAN
PEPPER (RED): see SAVORY

Peppermint

Ices can be flavored with the fresh, clean taste of peppermint in a number of ways – with oil or essence, with crushed peppermint or mint candies, or with crème de menthe for an extra 'kick'. Peppermint is well known for the beneficial effect it has on the digestion, and a peppermint ice must surely be the most enjoyable way to ward off, or cure, an attack of indigestion.

Simple Peppermint Ice Cream
Add ½ cup crushed peppermint candy to any of the Basic Recipes* or to a good-quality bought vanilla ice cream.

Peppermint Ice Cream

½ cup sugar
Juice of ½ lemon
3–4 drops peppermint oil
1 tablespoon finely chopped fresh mint
1¼ cups cream, whipped

For decoration
Créme de menthe
Mint leaves
Bitter Chocolate Sauce*, for serving

In a saucepan, dissolve the sugar in ⅔ cup water. Bring to the boil and remove from the heat. Strain in the lemon juice and leave to cool.

Mix the peppermint oil into the syrup. Fold the syrup and then the chopped mint into the cream.

Pour the mixture into a container. Cover and freeze until firm, beating well after 1 hour.

About 30 minutes before serving, transfer the ice cream to the refrigerator. Spoon a little crème de menthe over each portion and decorate with mint leaves. Serve with bitter chocolate sauce.

Serves 4

Serving suggestion
Freeze in small Chocolate Cases* and serve as petits fours.

Dessert suggestion
Layer with Black Currant Ice Cream (page 32).

Flavor variation
Use crème de menthe instead of peppermint oil.

Recipes for cakes, sauces, etc., asterisked in the dessert and serving suggestions, are given on pages 145 to 152. For directions on layering, lining and other techniques involved in creating desserts, see pages 152 to 155. Basic recipes are on pages 16 and 17.

Mint and Chocolate Ice Cream

¼ cup sugar
3 large egg yolks
1¼ cups light cream
1¼ cups heavy cream
6 tablespoons crème de menthe
4 squares bitter chocolate, coarsely chopped

In a heavy-based saucepan, dissolve the sugar in ½ cup water. Bring to the boil and boil until a temperature of 215°F is reached.

Beat the egg yolks in a bowl. Slowly pour in the syrup, beating constantly. Continue beating until the mixture becomes thick and light.

In another bowl, whip the creams together until soft peaks form. Fold the cream into the egg yolks with the crème de menthe and chocolate.

Pour the mixture into a container, cover and freeze until firm.

About 30 minutes before serving, transfer the ice cream to the refrigerator.

Serves 6

Dessert suggestion
Freeze in a 'box' of Genoise Cake* or use to fill a Jelly Roll*. Decorate the outside lavishly with crème de menthe-flavored whipped cream, Frosted* mint leaves and Chocolate Shapes*.

Peppermint Rock Ice Cream

Approximately 1 pound can sweetened condensed milk
1 tablespoon vanilla extract
½ cup crushed peppermint
2 cups cream, whipped
Crumbled chocolate flake, to decorate

Put the condensed milk, 1 cup water and the vanilla extract in a bowl and whip until thick and light. Fold in the peppermint candy and the cream.

Pour the mixture into a container. Cover and freeze until firm.

About 20 minutes before serving, transfer the ice cream to the refrigerator. Serve decorated with crumbled chocolate flake.

Serves 6–8

Dessert suggestion
Use to fill a Chocolate Roll*. Sprinkle the outside with sifted confectioners' sugar, or decorate with piped cream and finely grated mint-flavored chocolate.

PERSIMMON: see WARM CLIMATE FRUITS

Pineapple

Although it is fashionable to serve pineapple with all manner of savory ingredients, it is probably most enjoyable as a dessert. Ices can be made with canned, crushed pineapple as well as the fresh fruit. There is no need to waste the shell with its crown of leaves – it makes a marvelous, natural container for iced mixtures. However, the hard core that runs down the center of the fruit cannot be used. Even puréeing and straining will not render it edible.

Simple Pineapple Ice Cream
Add 1 cup well-drained crushed pineapple to any of the Basic Recipes* or to a good-quality bought vanilla ice cream.

Pineapple Ice Cream (with yogurt)

1¼ cups milk
2 whole eggs
2 egg yolks
½ cup sugar
1¼ cups plain yogurt
1¼ cups puréed pineapple flesh

In a heavy-based saucepan bring the milk to boiling point. Whip the eggs and egg yolks together in a bowl then whip in the boiling milk. Return the mixture to the rinsed pan and cook slowly, stirring constantly, until the custard thickens. Do not allow to boil. Remove from the heat, stir in the sugar and leave to cool, stirring occasionally to prevent a skin forming.

Blend the yogurt and pineapple together then stir into the cold custard. Pour into a container. Cover and freeze, beating twice at hourly intervals.

About 30 minutes before serving, transfer the ice cream to the refrigerator.

Serves 6

Serving suggestion
Put into chilled pineapple shells and decorate with candied cherries. Serve with wafer biscuits.

Dessert suggestion
Form into 6 balls and roll in grated chocolate or shredded coconut. Serve with a sauce of strained puréed pineapple flesh.

Pineapple and Cardamom Ice Cream

Seeds from 6 cardamom pods, finely crushed
⅔ cup milk
¾ cup sugar
1 cup finely chopped pineapple flesh
3 egg yolks
1¼ cups heavy cream

Put the cardamom seeds, milk and 2 tablespoons of the sugar in a small saucepan and bring just to simmering point. Remove from the heat, cover and leave for 5–8 minutes.

Put the pineapple with the remaining sugar and ⅔ cup water in another saucepan and simmer until soft and slightly translucent. Leave to cool.

Meanwhile, in a bowl beat the egg yolks until thick. Stir in the flavored milk and the cream. Pour back into the rinsed pan and cook over a low heat, stirring constantly, until the mixture thickens. Do not allow to boil. Leave to cool, stirring occasionally.

Blend in the pineapple and pour into a container. Cover and freeze until firm.

About 20 minutes before serving, transfer the ice cream to the refrigerator.

Serves 4–5

Dessert suggestion
Use to line a 'box' of Genoise Cake, with a center of Apple Cream Ice (page 21) or Pear Ice Cream (page 92). Serve with red or white Wine Sauce* or Coffee Sauce*.*

Pineapple Mallow Ice Cream

1 cup marshmallows, cut into pieces
½ cup medium dry white wine or hard cider or unsweetened apple juice
1⅔ cups canned crushed pineapple, thoroughly drained, syrup reserved
1¼ cups cream, whipped
¼ cup drained maraschino cherries, roughly chopped

For decoration
Pineapple cubes
Maraschino cherries, halved
Frosted mint leaves*

Put the marshmallows, wine, hard cider or apple juice and pineapple syrup in a saucepan over low heat, stirring constantly, until the marshmallows have dissolved. Leave to cool.

Fold the cream into the cooled marshmallow mixture. Pour into a container, cover and freeze to the slushy stage. Beat well in a bowl.

Fold the crushed pineapple and cherries into the frozen mixture. Return to the container, cover and freeze until firm.

About 20 minutes before serving, transfer the ice cream to the refrigerator. Decorate each portion with pineapple cubes, maraschino cherry halves and frosted mint leaves.

Serves 4–6

Serving suggestion
Serve in individual sweet pastry cases, accompanied by Bitter Chocolate Sauce.*

Dessert suggestions
Ripple with Toasted Oat and Nut Ice Cream (page 36).

Freeze in individual Chocolate Cases. Just before serving, decorate with small pineapple pieces and maraschino cherries.*

Pineapple Buttermilk Sherbet

2 cups buttermilk
1/2 cup sugar
1 teaspoon grated lemon zest
1 1/4 cups well-drained canned crushed pineapple
1 egg white
1 teaspoon vanilla extract
Fresh mint sprigs, for decoration

Mix the buttermilk, sugar, lemon zest and pineapple together in a bowl and leave until the sugar has dissolved.

Pour the mixture into a container. Cover and freeze until just becoming firm. Beat well in a bowl.

Lightly whip the egg white and the vanilla in a bowl. Whip into the pineapple mixture until light and fluffy. Return to the container, cover and freeze until firm.

About 30 minutes before serving, transfer the sorbet to the refrigerator. Serve decorated with mint sprigs.

Serves 6

Serving suggestion
Freeze in individual ring molds and fill the centers with chopped pineapple or scoops of Simple Chestnut Ice Cream (page 42).

Pineapple Sorbet

1 large ripe pineapple
Juice of 1 lemon
1 cup confectioners' sugar

Cut the top, including the leaves, from the pineapple. Using a sharp knife, remove all the flesh from the pineapple, taking care not to pierce the shell and leaving a border of about 1/2 inch. Put the pineapple shell and top into the freezer.

Cut away the core and chop the pineapple flesh then reduce to a purée. Stir in the lemon juice and sugar. Pour the mixture into a container. Cover and freeze until firm, beating 3 times at 45-minute intervals.

About 20 minutes before serving, use a spoon dipped in hot water to spoon the sorbet into the pineapple shell then place the top back in position.

Serves 4

Serving suggestions
Alternate the spoonfuls of sorbet with scoops of Banana Ice Cream (page 28) flavored with brandy instead of orange juice, and halved strawberries and grapes.

Serve the sorbet on pineapple rings decorated with small rosettes of whipped cream and Chocolate Shapes*.

Pina Colada Ice Cream

1 very large ripe pineapple
1/3 cup coconut cream
1 1/4 cups confectioners' sugar
1/4 cup white rum
1 1/4 cups heavy cream, whipped

For decoration
Cocktail cherries
Pineapple cubes
Toasted coconut strands

Remove the flesh from the pineapple and purée with all but 4 tablespoons of the juice that will run out when you peel the fruit. Put the reserved juice in a small saucepan. Add the coconut cream and dissolve over low heat.

Blend in the pineapple purée, sugar and rum. Fold in the cream.

Pour the mixture into a container. Cover and freeze until firm.

About 35 minutes before serving, transfer the ice cream to the refrigerator. Serve in glasses with frosted rims and decorate each portion with cocktail cherries and pineapple cubes on cocktail sticks and sprinkle the coconut around the edge.

Serves 6

Serving suggestion
Spoon into Gingersnap Cones* and serve surrounded by cocktail cherries and pineapple chunks.

Rich Pineapple Ice Cream (with cream cheese)

3 eggs, separated
1/4 cup sugar
1 cup cottage cheese, strained
1/4 pound full fat cream cheese
2/3 cup sour cream
Finely grated zest and juice of 1 large lemon
2 cups canned crushed pineapple, well drained

Beat the egg yolks with the sugar in a bowl until very thick and light.

Mix the cottage cheese, cream cheese, sour cream and lemon zest and juice together in a blender. Stir the mixture into the egg yolks.

In another bowl, whip the egg whites until stiff but not dry. Fold into the egg yolks with the pineapple.

Pour the mixture into a container. Cover and freeze until firm.

About 30 minutes before serving, transfer the ice cream to the refrigerator.

Serves 6

Flavor variation
Add ¼ cup chopped preserved ginger when you fold in the pineapple and egg whites.

Pineapple Ice Cream

1 ripe pineapple
Juice of ½ a lemon
4 eggs, separated
½ cup sugar
⅛ cup confectioners' sugar
1¼ cups heavy cream, whipped

Cut the pineapple in half lengthwise and cut out the central hard core. Carefully scoop out the pineapple flesh, taking care not to pierce the shells. Put the shells in the freezer. Purée the pineapple flesh with the lemon juice.

Beat the egg yolks with the caster sugar in a bowl until thick and light. Whip the egg whites in another bowl until stiff. Whip in the confectioners' sugar and continue whipping until stiff again. Fold the cream into the egg yolks with the pineapple purée. Fold in the egg whites.

Pour the mixture into a container. Cover and freeze until firm.

About 5 minutes before serving, scoop the ice cream into the shells, using a spoon dipped briefly in hot water, and refrigerate until required.

Serves 6–8

Serving suggestion
Add candied fruits steeped in a liqueur to the ice cream in the shells. Cover with Meringue* and place under a hot broiler just long enough to brown the outside of the meringue. Serve immediately, with Sponge Fingers*.

Caribbean Sorbet

½ cup sugar
2 cups pineapple juice
Finely grated zest and juice of 1 lime
¼ cup coconut cream
2 egg whites

For decoration
Long, thin strips of lime peel
Pineapple cubes
Cocktail cherries

In a heavy-based saucepan, dissolve the sugar in the pineapple juice with the lime zest and juice. Bring to the boil and boil the syrup until the temperature reaches 230°F (soft ball stage). Stir in the coconut cream and leave to cool.

Pour the mixture into a container. Cover and freeze until slushy. Beat well in a bowl.

Whip the egg whites in a bowl until stiff but not dry. Fold into the pineapple mixture. Return to the container, cover and freeze until firm.

About 20 minutes before serving, transfer the sorbet to the refrigerator. Serve scoops of the sorbet in chilled glasses decorated with strips of lime peel and with pineapple cubes and cocktail cherries.

Serves 4–6

Pineapple Crush Ice Cream

¾ cup evaporated milk, chilled
¼ cup confectioners' sugar, sifted
2 bananas
Juice of 2 lemons
1⅔ cups crushed pineapple
6 ounce jar maraschino cherries, drained and halved with 2 tablespoons syrup reserved

Put the milk in a bowl and whip until thick and frothy. Whip in the sugar.

Mash the bananas with the lemon juice. Stir them into the milk with the pineapple and its syrup.

Reserve a few cherries for decoration and stir the remainder into the milk with the reserved syrup.

Pour the mixture into a container. Cover and freeze until firm, beating well after 1½ hours.

About 30 minutes before serving, transfer the ice to the refrigerator. Serve in scoops decorated with the reserved cherries.

Serves 4–6

Dessert suggestion
Freeze in a pie or cake pan lined with crushed amaretti biscuits. Decorate the turned-out dessert with swirls of kirsch-flavored whipped cream and the reserved cherries.

Additional recipe using pineapple: Pineapple and Coconut Macaroon Cake (page 137).

Pistachio

The pale green pistachio has a delicate yet discernible flavor. Nuts for cooking are normally available as unsalted kernels. If you do have to skin them, simply soak them in boiling water for a few minutes, then cool quickly in cold water and rub off the skins.

Simple Pistachio Ice Cream
Add ½ cup chopped pistachio nuts to any of the Basic Recipes* or to a good-quality bought vanilla ice cream.

Iced Pistachio Nougat

3 cups light cream
5 egg yolks
1 cup honey
2 tablespoons orange flower water
1½ cups cream, whipped
3 egg whites
1 cup pistachio nuts
½ cup halved almonds

In a heavy-based saucepan, gently heat the cream to just below simmering point.

Beat the egg yolks in a bowl. Pour the hot cream onto the egg yolks in a slow steady stream beating continually. Return to the rinsed pan and cook over a low heat, stirring constantly, until the custard thickens. Stir in the honey. Add half the orange flower water and leave to cool, stirring occasionally. Pour into a container, cover and freeze until just becoming firm. Turn into a bowl and beat well. Fold in the cream. Whip the egg whites in a bowl until stiff but not dry. Fold into the mixture with the nuts.

Spoon the mixture back into the container. Cover and freeze until firm.

About 30 minutes before serving, transfer the iced nougat to the refrigerator.

Serves 6–8

Serving suggestion
Freeze in a loaf or cake pan and decorate the turned-out dessert with candied fruits. Serve with Orange Flower Sauce*.

Smooth Pistachio
Ice Cream

1¼ cups pistachio nuts
2 cups milk
4 egg yolks
½ cup sugar
Few drops of green food coloring, optional
1 cup drained fromage frais or low fat soft cheese/
  ricotta, beaten

Put the nuts in a bowl. Pour in boiling water and blanch for 1 minute. Drain and peel the nuts. Pound the nuts in a mortar or put them in a food processor with 2 tablespoons of the milk and process to a smooth paste.

Blend the paste with the remaining milk in a heavy-based saucepan and bring to simmering point. Remove from the heat, cover and leave for 20 minutes.

Beat the egg yolks with the sugar in a bowl until thick. Heat the flavored milk to boiling point again and pour onto the egg yolks, stirring. Return the mixture to the rinsed pan and cook gently, stirring constantly, until thickened, but do not allow the mixture to boil. Stir in the coloring, if you are using it, and leave to cool. Beat the fromage frais or cheese into the custard and leave to become completely cold.

Pour the mixture into a container. Cover and freeze until firm, beating twice at hourly intervals.

About 30 minutes before serving, transfer the ice cream to the refrigerator.

Serves 5–6

Serving suggestion
For each serving, swirl Bitter Chocolate Sauce* around the base of a wine glass, then fill with scoops of ice cream. Top with a wafer biscuit.

Rich Pistachio
Ice Cream

⅔ cup sugar
2½ cups whipping, heavy or 50/50 heavy/light cream
⅔ cup chopped pistachio nuts

Put the sugar and ⅔ cup of the cream in a saucepan. Stir over low heat to dissolve the sugar. Remove from the heat and leave to cool. Fold in the nuts. Put the sweetened cream in a bowl with the rest of the cream and whip until soft peaks form.

Pour the mixture into a container, cover and freeze until firm, beating well after 1½ hours.

About 20 minutes before serving, transfer the ice cream to the refrigerator.

Serves 4

Serving suggestion
Scoop into small Choux* balls, form these into a pyramid and pour over Bitter Chocolate Sauce*.

Pistachio and Green
Chartreuse Ice Cream

4 egg yolks
½ cup sugar
¾ cup finely chopped pistachio nuts
1¼ cups cream, whipped
2–3 tablespoons Green Chartreuse
Green food coloring, optional

Beat the egg yolks in a bowl until very thick and light. In a heavy-based saucepan dissolve the sugar in 5 tablespoons water. Bring to the boil and while it is still bubbling trickle it onto the egg yolks, stirring constantly. Continue to stir until thickened and cold. Fold in the nuts, whipped cream, Green Chartreuse and coloring, if using.

Pour the mixture into a container, cover and freeze until firm. About 20 minutes before serving, transfer the ice cream to the refrigerator.

Serves 6

Pistachio Frozen Custard

1 vanilla pod
2 cups milk
3 eggs, separated
½ cup sugar
⅔ cup cream, whipped
¼ cup chopped pistachio nuts

In a heavy-based saucepan, gently heat the vanilla pod in the milk and bring to boiling point. Remove from the heat, cover and leave for 20 minutes. Remove the vanilla pod and bring the milk to boiling point again.

Meanwhile, beat the egg yolks with the sugar in a bowl until thick and light. Stir in the hot milk. Return the mixture to the rinsed pan and cook over a low heat, stirring constantly, until the custard thickens. Do not allow to boil. Allow to cool, stirring frequently. Pour into a container, cover and freeze until just becoming firm. Turn into a bowl and beat well.

Fold the cream and nuts into the custard. Whip the egg whites in a bowl until stiff but not dry. Fold into the mixture and spoon back into the container. Cover and freeze until firm. About 30 minutes before serving, transfer to the refrigerator.

Dessert suggestion
To make a Baked Alaska, place a large circle of Jelly Roll* on a cookie sheet, sprinkle with pear liqueur or brandy and cover with the ice cream. Enclose with Meringue* and place under a hot broiler until browned. Serve immediately.

Additional recipe using pistachio: Cranberry and Pistachio Ripple (page 55).

Plum, Prune

Plums come in many hues – rich purple, glowing golden, ruby, crimson – plus the yellow-green of greengages and the intense blue of damsons. However, the flavor of an ice is more important than its color, so use only dessert varieties (except in the case of damsons) and taste the mixture to make sure it is sweet enough. Recipes for prunes – dried plums – are included in this section. Pie filling can be used for easy-to-make ices.

Simple Plum Ice Cream
Add the contents of a ½ pound can of plum pie filling to any of the Basic Recipes* or to a good-quality bought vanilla ice cream.

Plum Ice Cream (with pie filling)

½ pound soft cheese/ricotta
⅔ cup light cream
½ pound can plum pie filling
Lemon juice, to taste

Put the cheese in a bowl and beat until soft. Gradually beat in the cream taking care to keep the mixture smooth. Fold in the pie filling and add lemon juice to taste. Spoon the mixture into a container. Cover and freeze until firm, beating well after 1½ hours.

About 20–30 minutes before serving, transfer the ice cream to the refrigerator.

Serves 4

Serving suggestion
Serve in individual Meringue Baskets. Top with a spoonful of crème fraîche or yogurt and a sprinkling of slivered almonds.*

Damson Ice Cream

1¼ pounds damsons
¾ cup sugar
2 large egg whites
Juice and finely grated zest of 1 small orange
1¼ cups cream, whipped

Wash the damsons and put them, still wet, in a heavy-based saucepan with ¼ cup of the sugar. Cover the pan and cook gently until very soft. Pass the fruit through a strainer and remove the pits.

Dissolve the remaining sugar in ⅔ cup water in another saucepan. Bring to the boil and boil for 5 minutes.

Meanwhile, whip the egg whites until stiff. Pour the boiling syrup in a slow steady stream onto the egg whites, whipping constantly, until the meringue is very stiff.

Stir the orange juice and zest into the damson purée. Fold the mixture into the cream. Gently fold the flavored cream into the meringue.

Spoon the mixture into a container. Cover and freeze until firm.

About 30 minutes before serving, transfer the ice cream to the refrigerator.

Serves 6

Dessert suggestion
Freeze between individual Meringues flavored with orange flower water. To serve, surround each portion with a sauce of puréed, strained damsons. Accompany with Langues de Chat*.*

Plum Ice Cream (with red wine)

2¼ pounds ripe plums, preferably Victorias
⅔ cup red wine
⅓ cup sugar
4 egg yolks
2 cups light cream
Few drops of red food coloring, optional
2 tablespoons lemon juice
Large pinch of ground mace
slivered almonds, for decoration

In a saucepan, poach the plums in the wine with ¼ cup of the sugar for about 10 minutes until tender. Strain and reserve 1⅔ cups of the liquid. Remove the pits from the plums and purée the flesh then pass through a strainer.

Beat the egg yolks and remaining sugar in a bowl until thick and light. In a heavy-based saucepan, bring the cream to simmering point. Pour the hot cream onto the egg yolks beating continuously. Return the mixture to the rinsed pan and cook over low heat until thickened, stirring constantly and taking care not to let the custard boil. Leave to cool slightly then stir in the coloring, if you are using it, the lemon juice and mace. Blend with the plum purée. Leave to cool completely.

Pour the mixture into a container. Cover and freeze until firm, beating twice at hourly intervals.

Put the reserved juice into a saucepan and boil until reduced to ¾–1 cup. Leave to cool.

About 45 minutes before serving, turn out the ice cream and transfer it to the refrigerator. Serve coated in plum sauce with a few almonds sprinkled over.

Serves 6

Serving suggestion
Spoon into small Crêpes and deep fry briefly. Sprinkle with confectioners' sugar and serve with plum sauce.*

Plum Ice Cream

1 pound dark red plums
2 eggs, separated
½ cup sugar
1 cup cottage cheese, strained
⅔ cup cream, whipped

Remove the pits from the plums then purée the flesh.

Beat the egg yolks and sugar together in a bowl until thick and light then beat in the cheese. In another

bowl, whip the egg whites until stiff. Fold the plum purée into the egg yolk mixture, then the cream followed by the egg whites.

Pour into a container. Cover and freeze until firm.

About 30 minutes before serving, transfer the ice cream to the refrigerator.

Serves 4

Dessert suggestion
Layer with Smooth Coconut Ice Cream (page 49), in a loaf or cake pan lined with Langues de Chat*. Gently swirl each layer into the one below. Decorate the turned-out dessert with slivovitz-flavored whipped cream, long toasted strands of shredded coconut and twists of lime.

Prune Sorbet

3 cups prunes, soaked overnight in tea
Grated zest and juice of 1 lemon
2/3 cup red wine
2/3 cup sugar
Long, thin strips of lemon peel twisted into loose
    corkscrews, for decoration

Drain the excess liquid from the prunes and remove the pits. Mix the prunes with the lemon zest and juice, the red wine and sugar in a saucepan. Place over moderate heat and stir until the sugar has dissolved. Reduce the prunes to a pureé with the liquid and leave to cool.

Pour the mixture into a container. Cover and freeze until firm, beating 3 times at 45-minute intervals.

About 20 minutes before serving, transfer the sorbet to the refrigerator. Serve decorated with the corkscrews of lemon peel.

Serves 4–6

Dessert suggestion
Encase in Sweet Mixed Spice Ice Cream (page 115). Serve with Sponge Fingers*.

Prune Custard Ice

2 1/4 cups prunes, soaked in hot water overnight
1/3 cup sugar
Long strip of orange peel
Approximately 1 pound can dairy custard
Plain yogurt, for serving

In a saucepan, cook the prunes in the minimum amount of water with the sugar and orange peel until tender. Remove the orange peel and the pits and purée the prunes with the cooking liquid. Cool.

Whip the prune purée into the custard. Pour the mixture into a container. Cover and freeze until firm, beating twice at hourly intervals.

About 30 minutes before serving, transfer the ice to the refrigerator. Serve each portion topped by a spoonful of yogurt.

Serves 4

Dessert suggestion
Form into 4 balls, each enclosing a tablespoon of Clove Sorbet (page 115). Serve with Coffee Sauce*, Caramel Sauce*, Burnt Honey Sauce* or Hot Chocolate Sauce*.

Victoria Ice Cream

1 pound ripe Victoria plums, halved and pitted
3 tablespoons clear honey
Grated zest and juice of 1 lemon
1/3 cup light brown sugar
1 1/2 cups cottage cheese, strained
2/3 cup sour cream
2 egg whites

Cook the plums in a saucepan with the honey, lemon zest and juice and sugar until they are soft. Reduce to a purée or pass through a nylon strainer.

Beat the cheese and sour cream together in a bowl then gradually beat in the plum purée. Cool completely then chill.

Pour the mixture into a container. Cover and freeze until just becoming firm. Beat well in a bowl.

In another bowl, whip the egg whites until stiff but not dry. Fold into the frozen plum mixture. Return to the container, cover and freeze until firm.

About 45 minutes before serving, transfer the ice cream to the refrigerator.

Serves 4

Serving suggestion
Halve and pit large, ripe plums and spoon the ice cream into the hollows. Arrange in groups on individual plates. Serve surrounded by a sauce of strained, puréed plums, accompanied by large Macaroons*.

Flavor variation
Fold baby Meringues* into the plum mixture with the egg whites.

Additional recipes using prunes: Prune Ice Cream with Brandy (page 116). Prune Ice Cream with Wine and Brandy (page 130).

Raspberry, Mulberry

Raspberries have a rich, intense flavor that lends itself beautifully to all manner of iced mixtures: tangy, yogurt-based ones, ices rich in cream and refreshing sorbets. The berries are easily reduced to a purée, which should be strained to remove the seeds. One pound raspberries will make about 1¼ cups purée, depending on the juiciness of the fruit. Canned raspberries can be used. Mulberries can be substituted for raspberries; always check whether the mixture is sweet enough.

Simple Raspberry Ice Cream

Ripple any of the Basic Recipes* or a good-quality bought vanilla ice cream with 1¼ cups strained raspberry purée, sweetened with a little confectioners' sugar if necessary.

Raspberry Rose Water Ice

⅔ cup sugar
2 cups rosé wine
1¾ cups puréed and strained raspberries
¼ cup lime juice

Dissolve the sugar in the wine in a saucepan over low heat. Leave to cool. Stir in the raspberry purée and lime juice and chill for an hour.

Pour the mixture into a container. Cover and freeze until firm, beating 3 times at 45-minute intervals.

About 40 minutes before serving, transfer to the refrigerator.

Serves 5–6

Serving suggestion
Scoop into individual Meringue Baskets* flavored with rosewater and decorate with crystallized violets.

Raspberry Sorbet

1 pound raspberries
1 cup confectioners' sugar
Juice of 1 lemon

For decoration
Whole raspberries
Frosted* raspberry or mint leaves

Purée the raspberries and pass through a strainer into a bowl. Stir in the confectioners' sugar (more or less, to taste) and lemon juice. Pour the mixture into a container. Cover and freeze until firm, beating 3 times at 45-minute intervals.

About 30 minutes before serving, transfer the sorbet to the refrigerator. Decorate each portion with whole raspberries and frosted raspberry or mint leaves.

Serves 4

Serving suggestion
Freeze in individual ring molds and fill the centers with fresh raspberries. Trickle cream over the sorbet and decorate with Frosted* raspberry or mint leaves.

Raspberry Ice Cream

1¼ cups puréed and strained raspberries
¾ cup confectioners' sugar
Squeeze of lemon juice
⅓ cup sugar
3 egg yolks
1¼ cups cream, whipped

For decoration
Fresh raspberries
Lightly toasted slivered almonds

Put the raspberries in a bowl with the confectioners' sugar and 'lift' the flavor with a squeeze of lemon juice.

In a heavy-based saucepan, dissolve the sugar in ½ cup water. Then bring to the boil and boil until the temperature reaches 234°F.

Beat the egg yolks in another bowl until thick. Beat in the boiling syrup in a slow steady stream and continue beating until the mixture is cold and very light and thick. Fold in the raspberry purée and cream.

Spoon the mixture into a container. Cover and freeze until firm.

About 30 minutes before serving, transfer the ice cream to the refrigerator. Serve each portion decorated with raspberries and almonds.

Serves 4–6

Serving suggestion
Hollow out a large brioche and sprinkle with strawberry eau-de-vie fraise. Alternate scoops of the ice cream with Pomegranate Sorbet (page 129) or Pear Sorbet (page 93) and a light sprinkling of finely chopped hazelnuts. Pour over a little more eau-de-vie.

Raspberry Ice Cream
(with meringues)

1 pound raspberries
4 tablespoons confectioners' sugar
1¼ cups heavy cream
1¼ cups light cream
½ cup roughly broken Meringues*

Place the raspberries in a large bowl, sprinkle the sugar over and stir lightly to mix. Cover and leave in a cool place until the juices run. Purée the raspberries then pass through a strainer.

Whip the creams together in a bowl until soft peaks form. Fold in the meringues and the raspberry purée to give a marbled effect.

Pour into individual dishes or molds. Cover and freeze until firm.

About 15 minutes before serving, transfer the ice cream to the refrigerator.

Serves 4

Serving suggestion
Serve as a sundae with a base of raspberries sprinkled with Galliano, topped by scoops of the ice cream and scoops of Liqueur Sorbet (page 131), preferably made with Grand Marnier or Cointreau, or White Wine Sorbet (page 130).

Raspberry Ice Cream
(with sour cream)

⅔ cup sour cream
⅔ cup heavy cream
1 pound can raspberries, puréed and strained
1 egg white

Whip the creams together in a bowl until soft peaks form. Fold in the raspberry purée.

Pour the mixture into a container. Cover and freeze until just becoming firm. Beat well in a bowl.

Whip the egg white in a small bowl until stiff but not dry. Fold into the raspberry cream. Return to the container, cover and freeze until firm.

About 30 minutes before serving, transfer the ice cream to the refrigerator.

Serves 4–5

Raspberry Yogurt Ice

1¼ cups puréed and strained raspberries
⅔ cup plain yogurt
1–1¼ cups confectioners' sugar
2 tablespoons lemon juice
⅔ cup cream, whipped
2 egg whites

For decoration
Whole raspberries
Mint sprigs

Mix the raspberries, yogurt, sugar and lemon juice together in a bowl. Stir until evenly blended then fold in the cream.

Pour into a container, cover and freeze until just becoming firm. Beat well in a bowl.

Whip the egg whites in a bowl until stiff but not dry. Fold the egg whites into the raspberry ice. Return to the container, cover and freeze until firm.

About 20 minutes before serving, transfer the ice to the refrigerator. Serve decorated with whole raspberries and mint sprigs.

Serves 4

Low calorie version
Use fructose or a low calorie or artificial sweetener instead of sugar, and substitute the same quantity of strained cottage or low fat soft cheese/ricotta for the cream. Freeze in individual containers and decorate with fresh raspberries and mint leaves. Serve with Low Calorie Topping*.

Mulberry Sorbet

1 pound mulberries
Approximately 2 cups confectioners' sugar
Squeeze of lemon juice
2 egg whites
Fresh mulberries, for decoration

Cook the mulberries very gently in a covered saucepan until the juices run. Strain through a fine strainer. Stir in the sugar and lemon juice to taste. Cool the mixture then chill for about an hour.

Pour the mixture into a container. Cover and freeze to the slushy stage. Beat well in a bowl.

Whip the egg whites in a bowl until stiff but not dry. Fold into the mulberry mixture. Return to the container, cover and freeze until firm.

About 40 minutes before serving, transfer the sorbet to the refrigerator. Decorate each portion with fresh mulberries.

Serves 4–6

Serving suggestion
Serve in Coupelles* intermingled with fresh mulberries. Accompany with a sauce of strained, puréed mulberries.

Raspberry Ice Cream (with cottage cheese)

1 cup heavy cream, whipped
1½ cups cottage cheese, strained
¾–1 cup confectioners' sugar or to taste
Rosewater
1¼ cups thick raspberry purée, strained (see introduction)
Frosted* whole raspberries, for decoration

Put the cream and cottage cheese in a bowl or blender together with the sugar and blend until smooth. Mix in a few drops of rosewater and the raspberries. Refrigerate for about an hour.

Pour the mixture into a container. Cover and freeze until firm, beating twice at hourly intervals.

About 40 minutes before serving, transfer the ice cream to the refrigerator.

Serves 4

Dessert suggestion
Line a cake or loaf pan, charlotte or similar round mold with crumbled flakes of chocolate and fill with the ice cream. Decorate the turned-out dessert with scrolls of whipped cream, Chocolate Shapes* and fresh raspberries.

Raspberry and Red Currant Sorbet

1 pound red currants
¾ pound raspberries
⅓ cup sugar
Lemon juice
1 egg white
Whole red currants or raspberries, for decoration

Purée the fruits together and strain. Put the sugar in a saucepan with ⅔ cup water. Stir to dissolve over low heat. Stir the syrup into the fruit purée, adjusting the sweetness and adding lemon juice to taste.

Pour the mixture into a container. Cover and freeze until becoming firm around the edges. Beat well in a bowl.

Whip the egg white in a small bowl until stiff but not dry. Fold into the frozen fruit mixture. Return to the container, cover and freeze until firm.

About 40 minutes before serving, transfer the sorbet to the refrigerator. Serve decorated with whole fruit.

Serves 4–6

Dessert suggestion
Ripple with Rhubarb Frost (page 110). Serve with Meringue* fingers.

Raspberry Cream Cloud

³/₄ pound fresh or frozen (without sugar) raspberries
¹/₂ cup sugar
2 cups raspberry yogurt
3 tablespoons lemon juice
²/₃ cup heavy cream
2 egg whites

Pureé the raspberries then pass through a strainer. Purée the fruit again with the sugar, yogurt and lemon juice. Pour the mixture into a container. Cover and freeze until almost firm.

Just before removing the mixture from the freezer, whip the cream to the soft peak stage. In another bowl, whip the egg whites until stiff but not dry.

Turn the raspberry mixture into a bowl and beat it to the consistency of snow. Fold in the cream and then the egg whites. Return to the container, cover and freeze until firm. About 1 hour before serving, transfer to the refrigerator.

Serves 5–6

Serving suggestion
Serve in Ice Cream Cones* coated in shredded coconut. Decorate with Frosted* mint leaves and small Chocolate Shapes* or Curls*. Serve with Bitter Chocolate Sauce*.

Raspberry Cream Ice

¹/₃ cup confectioners' sugar
Squeeze of lemon juice
1¹/₄ cups raspberry purée, strained (see introduction)
¹/₄ pound full fat cream cheese
2 egg whites
Plain yogurt, for serving
Fresh raspberries, for decoration

Stir the sugar and lemon juice into the raspberry purée, adjusting the levels to taste. Pour the mixture into a container. Cover and freeze to the slushy stage. Beat well in a bowl.

Beat the cheese in a bowl. Whip the egg whites in another bowl until stiff but not dry. Beat the cheese into the frozen raspberry purée then fold in the egg whites. Return to the container, cover and freeze until firm.

About 35–40 minutes before serving, transfer the ice to the refrigerator. Pour a spoonful of yogurt over each serving and top with a few fresh raspberries.

Serves 4

Dessert suggestion
Form into 4 balls with a small scoop of Raspberry Sorbet (page 104) in the center of each. Coat with finely chopped almonds. Serve with Sponge Fingers* and a sauce of puréed, strained raspberries.

Raspberry Spumoni

1¹/₄ cups sugar
Juice of 2 lemons and 1 orange
1 cup raspberry purée, strained
1 egg white
Approximately 2 tablespoons raspberry eau-de-vie (framboise)

In a heavy-based saucepan dissolve 1 cup of the sugar in 1 cup water. Bring to the boil and boil for about a minute. Cool completely then strain in the lemon and orange juices, add the raspberry purée and put through a strainer. Pour the mixture into a container. Cover and freeze to the slushy stage. Beat well in a bowl.

Meanwhile, in a heavy-based saucepan dissolve the remaining sugar in ¹/₄ cup water. Bring to the boil and boil until the temperature reaches 248°F, brushing down any sugar crystals that form on the side of the pan with a pastry brush.

Whip the egg white in a bowl until stiff then gradually pour in the very hot syrup in a slow, steady stream and continue whipping until the meringue is cold. Fold the eau-de-vie and meringue into the raspberry mixture.

Let it set. Return to the container, cover and freeze until just firm.

About 15 minutes before serving transfer the spumoni to the refrigerator.

Serves 6

To reduce your sugar intake
Replace the sugar with half the quantity of **fructose** or with an **artificial sweetener**, provided the recipe does not call for a sugar syrup. Normally, 3–4 artificial sweeteners are the equivalent of 2 tablespoons sugar but always check that you have the right degree of sweetness. Artificial sweeteners must be added to custard-based ice creams after the custard has cooled.

Recipes for cakes, sauces, etc., asterisked in the dessert and serving suggestions, are given on pages 145 to 152. For directions on layering, lining and other techniques involved in creating desserts, see pages 152 to 155. Basic recipes are on pages 16 and 17.

Red Currant

Although red currants do not have the same intensity of flavor as black currants, the fully ripe fruit has a refreshing sweetness that blends enticingly with light, creamy mixtures. Always strain red currants after puréeing to remove the seeds. The fresh fruit is not easy to find, but juice, and sometimes red currant jelly, is available – and makes an exceptionally delicious sorbet.

Iced Red Currant Soufflé

4 egg whites
1¼ cups sugar
1 pound red currants, puréed and strained
1¼ cups heavy cream, whipped

Put the egg whites in a bowl and whip until stiff. Gradually add the sugar, whipping well after each addition. Continue whipping until a stiff meringue is formed. Lightly fold in the red currant purée and then the cream.

Pour the mixture into a container. Cover and freeze until firm.

About 30 minutes before serving, transfer the soufflé to the refrigerator.

Serves 4–6

Dessert suggestion
Make a bombe or freeze in a cake or loaf pan with an outer layer of Pear Ice Cream (page 92). Decorate the turned-out dessert with kirsch-flavored whipped cream and chocolate flakes.

Red Currant Sorbet

1 cup sugar
2½ cups red currant juice
Juice of 1 lemon
1 egg white
Pairs of Frosted* red currants joined by their stalks, for decoration

In a heavy-based saucepan, dissolve the sugar in the red currant juice. Bring to the boil and boil for 5 minutes. Leave to cool. Stir in the lemon juice.

Pour the mixture into a container. Cover and freeze until just becoming firm. Beat well in a bowl.

Whip the egg white in a small bowl until stiff but not dry. Fold into the red currant mixture. Return to the container, cover and freeze until firm.

About 35 minutes before serving, transfer the sorbet to the refrigerator. Serve decorated with pairs of frosted red currants.

Serves 4

Dessert suggestion
Form into 8 balls and surround with Litchi Ice Cream (page 127). Serve with fresh red currants and quartered litchis.

Red Currant Ice Cream (with cheese and yogurt)

1 pound red currants
Juice of 1 lemon
½ cup sugar
⅔ cup full fat cream cheese
¾ cup plain yogurt

Purée the red currants with the lemon juice and strain through a fine strainer into a bowl. Stir in the sugar.

In another bowl, beat the cream cheese with the yogurt. Fold in the red currant purée.

Spoon the mixture into a container. Cover and freeze until firm, beating twice at hourly intervals.

About 40 minutes before serving, transfer the ice cream to the refrigerator.

Serves 4

Dessert suggestion
Cover a Jelly Roll* filled with Rose Petal Sorbet (page 70) with the ice cream. Decorate with fresh or crystallized rose petals and Frosted* mint leaves.

Red Currant Ice Cream

1 pound red currants
⅔ cup sugar
1¼ cups cream, whipped
Squeeze of lemon juice

Purée the red currants and pass through a fine strainer into a bowl.

In a heavy-based saucepan, dissolve the sugar in ⅔ cup water. Bring to the boil and boil for 3 minutes. Stir the syrup into the red currant purée. Set aside to cool. Fold the red currant purée into the cream, adding lemon juice to taste.

Pour the mixture into a container. Cover and freeze until firm, beating once when the mixture becomes firm around the edges. About 30 minutes before serving, transfer to the refrigerator.

Serves 4

Serving suggestion
Serve in wine glasses, decorated with red currants and red currant leaves threaded onto toothpicks.

Additional recipes using red currants: Raspberry and Red Currant Sorbet (page 106), Double Berry Cream Ice (page 120).

Rhubarb

Tender, young, pink rhubarb stalks yield the best flavor and color and almost melt when cooked. Forced rhubarb is tender but all too often lacks flavor, while thicker, older stalks can be stringy and coarse tasting. Wash the stalks well and trim if necessary before use, removing all trace of the leaves which contain poisonous oxalic acid. One pound trimmed rhubarb will make about 1¼ cups of purée.

Rhubarb Sorbet

1 pound young rhubarb
½ cup sugar
2 teaspoons lemon juice
Pink food coloring, optional
2 large egg whites

Reserve about one-third of a stick of rhubarb and chop the remainder. Put the chopped rhubarb in a saucepan with 1 tablespoon water and cook gently until soft. Then reduce to a purée.

In a heavy-based saucepan, dissolve the sugar in 1¼ cups water. Bring to the boil and boil for 10 minutes. Leave to cool.

Add the rhubarb purée to the syrup with the lemon juice, and pink coloring if you are using it.

Pour the mixture into a container. Cover and freeze until just becoming firm around the edges. Beat well in a bowl.

Whip the egg whites in a bowl until stiff but not dry. Fold into the rhubarb mixture. Return to the container, cover and freeze until firm.

About 40 minutes before serving, transfer the sorbet to the refrigerator.

Serves 6

Rhubarb Frost

⅔ cup drained fromage frais or strained cottage cheese
⅔ cup plain yogurt
1¼ cups thick rhubarb purée
¾ cup confectioners' sugar or to taste
Few drops rosewater or orange flower water, optional
1 tablespoon gelatin dissolved in 4 tablespoons hot water
2 egg whites, whipped

Put the cheese into a bowl and gradually beat in the yogurt to form a smooth 'cream'. Beat in the rhubarb, confectioners' sugar (the amount depends on the sharpness of the rhubarb) and rosewater or orange flower water, if you are using it. Gradually stir in the dissolved gelatin. Fold in the egg whites. Chill in the refrigerator for 1 hour.

Pour the mixture into a container. Cover and freeze until firm.

About 40 minutes before serving, transfer the frost to the refrigerator.

Serves 4

Rhubarb Mousse

1½ pounds young rhubarb, sliced
¾ cup sugar
⅓ cup red wine
2 cups heavy cream

Cook the rhubarb with the sugar and wine over gentle heat in a covered pan until soft. Cool completely then strain off as much liquid as possible. Reserve this liquid and use for making rhubarb sauce. Pour the rhubarb into a container, cover and freeze to the slushy stage. Turn into a bowl and beat well.

Whip the cream until soft peaks form then fold into the rhubarb. Turn into a cold, 1 quart fluted metal mold. Cover and freeze until firm.

About 30 minutes before serving, turn out onto a cold plate and leave in the refrigerator. Serve with rhubarb sauce made by boiling down the reserved rhubarb juice.

Serves 8

Serving suggestion
Serve in Gingersnap Baskets* surrounded with the sauce. Decorate each serving with small shapes cut from orange peel.

Rhubarb and Ginger Wine Ice Cream

1½ pounds young rhubarb, chopped
½ cup sugar
⅔ cup ginger wine
1¼ cups heavy cream, whipped
2 egg whites

Poach the rhubarb with the sugar and 2 tablespoons water in a covered saucepan for about 7 minutes until just tender. Strain off the surplus juice and boil it until reduced and syrupy. Purée the rhubarb and pass through a fine strainer. Stir in the reduced juices and ginger wine and leave to cool.

Pour the mixture into a shallow container and chill for 30 minutes. Cover the container and freeze to the slushy stage.

Tip the rhubarb mixture into a bowl and beat well. Fold in the cream. Whip the egg whites until stiff but not dry, then fold into the rhubarb cream. Spoon the mixture back into the container, cover and freeze until firm.

About 35 minutes before serving, transfer the ice cream to the refrigerator.

Serves 4–6

> Rhubarb is often available canned or frozen. Drain and use as fresh; if it is sweetened, adjust recipe to taste.

Rhubarb Ice Cream

1 1/4 pounds young rhubarb, cut into 1 inch lengths
1/2 cup sugar
2 eggs, separated
1 cup cottage cheese, strained
3/4 cup sour cream

Poach the rhubarb with the sugar and 1 tablespoon water in a covered pan until soft. Reduce the rhubarb to a purée. Beat in the egg yolks and return to the heat. Cook gently, stirring constantly, until the mixture thickens, but do not allow it to boil. Leave to cool.

Whip the cottage cheese and sour cream together in a bowl and fold into the rhubarb custard. Spoon into a container, cover and freeze until just becoming firm. Turn into a bowl and beat well. In another bowl, whip the egg whites until stiff but not dry. Fold into the rhubarb.

Spoon the mixture back into the container. Cover and freeze until firm. About 40 minutes before serving, transfer to the refrigerator.

Serves 4

Dessert suggestion
Freeze in a mold or cake or loaf pan surrounded by a layer of Kulfi (page 18) and an outer jacket of Sponge Fingers. Decorate the turned-out dessert with pistachio nuts. Serve with red or white Wine Sauce*.*

Rhubarb and Strawberry Ice Cream

3/4 pound young rhubarb
2/3 cup sugar
1/2 pound strawberries
1 1/4 cups cream, whipped
Few drops red food coloring, optional

In a covered heavy-based saucepan, poach the rhubarb with the sugar and 1 tablespoon water until soft. Reduce to a purée with the strawberries, pass through a strainer and leave to cool completely.

Fold in the cream and the coloring, if used. Spoon the mixture into a shallow metal container, cover and freeze until just becoming firm.

Tip the semi-frozen mixture into a bowl and beat well. Spoon back into the container, cover and return to the freezer. Repeat once more, then leave to freeze until firm.

About 30 minutes before serving, transfer the ice cream to the refrigerator.

Serves 4

Serving suggestion
Serve with white Wine Sauce and Sponge Fingers*.*

Rhubarb Custard Ice

1 pound tender young rhubarb, cut into
*   1 inch lengths*
Juice of 1 orange
1/3 cup brown sugar
2 tablespoons sweet butter
1 cup light cream
3 egg yolks

Put the rhubarb, orange juice, sugar and butter in a covered pan and cook gently for about 3 minutes until tender. Reduce to a purée.

In a heavy-based saucepan, bring the cream to just below boiling point. Beat the egg yolks in a bowl until thick. Pour the hot cream over the egg yolks beating continuously. Return to the rinsed pan and cook over a low heat, stirring constantly, until the custard thickens but do not allow it to boil. Leave the custard to cool, stirring occasionally.

Stir the rhubarb purée into the custard. When the mixture is cold, pour into a container, cover and refrigerate for an hour. Freeze until firm, beating twice at hourly intervals.

About 40 minutes before serving, transfer the custard ice to the refrigerator.

Serves 4

Dessert suggestion
Freeze in individual containers or a pie or cake pan lined with crushed ginger cookies held together with melted butter. Put orange segments, pith and membrane removed, or drained canned mandarins, on the surface of the frozen custard ice. Cover entirely with Meringue and place under a hot broiler just long enough to brown the meringue. Flambé with rum and serve immediately.*

To reduce your calorie intake
Tofu can be substituted for any soft cheese (see page 13); beat with the other ingredients until smooth. It has no cholesterol and is low in fat.

ROSE PETAL: see HERBS, FLOWERS,
*   LEAVES*
SAFFRON: see SPICES
SALMON, SMOKED: see SAVORY

Savory

A savory ice is an unusual first course – impressive and often surprisingly economical. Smoked Salmon Ice Cream, for example, provides a definite touch of luxury for a fraction of what it would cost to serve the fish in the traditional way.

Cucumber Granita

¼ cup sugar
1 lemon
1 large cucumber
2 crisp dessert apples, peeled, cored and chopped
1 teaspoon fresh dill or ½ teaspoon dried dill weed
Salt and freshly ground black pepper

For garnish
Fresh dill, mint or borage sprigs
Strips of lemon peel

In a heavy-based saucepan, dissolve the sugar in ⅔ cup water. Remove the peel from the lemon in long strips and add to the syrup. Bring to the boil then simmer for 2 minutes. Remove from the heat and add the juice from the lemon. Leave to cool then strain and chill for 10 minutes.

Peel half the cucumber but leave the peel on the other half for additional color. Roughly chop the cucumber then purée with the apple and strained lemon-flavored syrup. Add the dill and seasonings and chill for 30 minutes.

Pour into a container. Cover and freeze. As crystals begin to form around the edges draw them into the center with a fork and continue until the mixture is a mass of small crystals. Serve immediately with fresh dill, mint or borage sprigs and strips of lemon peel.

Serves 5–6

Serving suggestion
Serve in goblets with long twisted spirals of lemon peel hanging down the sides. Accompany with dill-flavored crackers made from an enriched pie dough with chopped fresh dill added, or sprinkle dill seeds over each serving.

Smoked Salmon Ice Cream

1/8 pound smoked salmon
2/3 cup sour cream
1/2 cup cream, whipped
Juice and grated zest of 1 large juicy lemon
Approximately 1 tablespoon finely chopped fresh chives
Melon, for serving

Purée the salmon with the sour cream and put in a bowl. Fold in the whipped cream with the lemon juice and zest, and the chives.

Spoon the mixture into a container. Cover and freeze until firm, beating 3 times at 45-minute intervals. Serve straight from the freezer with slices of the melon.

Serves 4

Serving suggestion
Serve with chilled melon and wholewheat or sesame seed-coated breadsticks for a delicious summer first course.

Iced Tomato Cream

1 pound ripe tomatoes, skinned
2/3 cup thick mayonnaise
2/3 cup sour cream
1/3 cup cream, whipped
2 teaspoons onion juice (put diced onion through a garlic press)
2 teaspoons finely chopped fresh basil
2 tablespoons lemon juice
Salt and freshly ground black pepper

Purée the tomatoes. Put the mayonnaise and sour cream in a bowl and whip together. Fold in the whipped cream, tomato purée and remaining ingredients.

Spoon the mixture into a container, cover and freeze until firm. Turn into a bowl, beat well then spoon back into the container or into a mold – a ring mold is a good idea then the center can be filled with a salad or shrimp when the cream is served. Cover and freeze until firm.

About 20 minutes before serving, transfer the cream to the refrigerator or turn it out first onto a cold plate.

Serves 6

Serving suggestions
Spoon into hollowed-out tomato shells.

Accompany with sliced raw mushrooms, or zucchini or red peppers lightly sprinkled with a lemon vinaigrette.

Freeze in a ring mold. Surround the base with slices of cucumber and decorate with piped softened cream cheese and sprigs of parsley.

Iced Red Pepper Mousse

1/3 cup red wine vinegar
2 tablespoons raspberry vinegar
1 1/4 cups skinned and diced red peppers
1 red pimento
Salt and freshly ground white pepper
1 teaspoon gelatin
1/2 cup whipping cream

For decoration
Fresh basil sprigs
Strips of red and yellow pepper

Put the vinegars in a saucepan and boil until reduced by two-thirds. Add the peppers and simmer until thick. Put into a blender with the pimento and plenty of seasoning and process until smooth. Pour back into the rinsed saucepan and heat gently.

Put the gelatin with a little water in a small bowl placed over a pan of hot water and stir to dissolve.

Stir into the purée in the saucepan and leave to cool.

Whip the cream in a bowl until soft peaks form then gently fold into the purée. Pour into a shallow container, cover and freeze until just firm. Decorate the mousse with sprigs of basil, and the plates with strips of red and yellow pepper.

Serves 4

Serving suggestions
Spoon onto artichoke hearts and garnish with fine strips of red and yellow pepper.

Serve with shrimp, crab or strips of smoked salmon accompanied by blinis and sour cream or fromage blanc.

Additional savory recipes: Savory Avocado Ice Cream (page 26), Bloody Mary Water Ice (page 117).

Spices

The warm tones of cinnamon, the exotic scent of cloves and saffron with its luxurious perfume are all intriguing flavors for ice creams and sorbets. This section also includes a recipe using pumpkin, which blends wonderfully well with spices.

Cinnamon Ice Cream

²/₃ cup milk
2 whole cinnamon sticks
4 eggs, separated
2 tablespoons confectioners' sugar
2 teaspoons ground cinnamon
¹/₂ cup clear honey
²/₃ cup sour cream
²/₃ cup strained cottage cheese

In a heavy-based saucepan, heat the milk with the cinnamon sticks to just below boiling point, remove from the heat, cover and leave for about 4 hours.

Beat the egg yolks in a bowl. Sift the confectioners' sugar and ground cinnamon together and beat into the yolks.

Remove the cinnamon sticks from the milk. Stir in the honey and bring to just below boiling point. Slowly pour onto the egg yolks, stirring constantly.

Beat the sour cream and cheese together and stir into the custard. Continue stirring until cold. Whip the egg whites in a bowl until stiff but not dry. Fold into the mixture.

Pour the mixture into a container. Cover and freeze until firm.

About 30 minutes before serving, transfer the ice cream to the refrigerator.

Serves 4–6

Serving suggestion
Serve in tall wine glasses, topped with a swirl of whipped cream and round Langues de Chat*.

Saffron Ice Cream

4 egg yolks
¹/₄ cup sugar
1¹/₄ cups milk
1 heaped teaspoon saffron strands
¹/₄ cup cream, whipped

Beat the egg yolks with the sugar in a bowl until thick and light. In a heavy-based saucepan, heat the milk to

just below simmering point then whip into the egg yolks. Return to the rinsed pan and cook over a low heat, stirring constantly, until the mixture thickens. Do not allow to boil. Remove from the heat, strain and stir in the saffron. Leave to cool, stirring occasionally. Pour into a container, cover and freeze until just becoming firm. Turn into a bowl and beat well.

Fold in the cream. Spoon back into the container, cover and freeze until firm.

About 20 minutes before serving, transfer the ice cream to the refrigerator.

Serves 4

Serving suggestion
Scoop into Meringue Baskets* and serve with Sponge Fingers*.

Sweet Mixed Spice Ice Cream

½ cup chopped marshmallows
1 pound can evaporated milk
2 teaspoons ground mixed spice
½ cup brown sugar
⅔ cup cream, whipped

For decoration
Finely grated orange zest
Chopped sugar-coated almonds

Melt the marshmallows with the evaporated milk, spice and sugar in a bowl set over a pan of hot water, beating constantly but lightly until smooth. Leave to cool, beating occasionally.

Fold the cream into the marshmallow mixture. Pour into a container, cover and freeze until firm.

About 30 minutes before serving, transfer the ice cream to the refrigerator and serve decorated with the orange zest and nuts.

Serves 6–8

Serving suggestion
Serve in Almond Tuiles* with slices of poached pear. Spoon over a little applesauce: substitute apple juice for wine in the Wine Sauce*.

Dessert suggestion
Freeze around a center of Prune Sorbet (page 103). Serve with Sponge Fingers*.

Clove Sorbet

1⅛ cups sugar
10–15 cloves
1 egg white

In a heavy-based saucepan, dissolve the sugar in 2¼ cups water. Bring to the boil and boil for 1 minute. Remove from the heat, add the cloves, cover the pan and leave to infuse for 10–15 minutes. Remove the cloves and cool before chilling.

Pour the syrup into a container, cover and freeze to the slushy stage. Beat well in a bowl.

Whip the egg white lightly in a small bowl. Whip into the frozen syrup. Return to the container, cover and freeze until firm.

About 40 minutes before serving, transfer the sorbet to the refrigerator.

Serves 6

Serving suggestion
Put small balls of the sorbet and of Rich Brown Bread Ice Cream (page 36) on thin slices of orange, peel and pith removed. Spoon over a little white Wine Sauce*.

Dessert suggestion
Encase in Sweet Lemon Ice Cream (page 77) and serve with Langues de Chat*.

Flavor variation
For a cinnamon sorbet substitute a 2 inch piece of cinnamon stick for the cloves.

Spiced Pumpkin Pie Ice Cream

⅔ cup milk
⅔ cup light cream
3 eggs, separated
½ cup light brown sugar
1½ teaspoons ground cinnamon
¼ teaspoon ground cloves
½ teaspoon ground ginger
1½ cups canned pumpkin
Pumpkin seeds, for decoration

In a heavy-based saucepan, bring the milk and cream to just below boiling point. Put the egg yolks and sugar in a bowl and beat until thick and light. Stir in the hot milk and cream. Return to the rinsed pan and cook over a low heat, stirring constantly, until the mixture thickens. Stir in the spices and leave to cool, stirring occasionally. Stir in the pumpkin.

In another bowl, whip the egg whites until stiff but not dry. Fold into the pumpkin custard.

Pour the mixture into a container. Cover and freeze until firm.

About 40 minutes before serving, transfer the ice cream to the refrigerator.

Serves 4

Dessert suggestion
Freeze in a can. Coat the turned-out ice cream with finely chopped walnuts or pecans.

Additional recipes using spices: Chestnut and Cinnamon Circle (page 43), Lightly Spiced Peach Ice Cream (page 89), Pineapple and Cardamom Ice Cream (page 96).

Liquors are added to give a boost to a variety of different flavored iced mixtures, but there are also many recipes in which they are the primary flavoring. This section includes a recipe using pumpkin as a base and another with prunes.

Iced Whiskey Syllabub

Finely grated zest and juice of 1 orange and 1 lemon
1/3 cup sugar
1/2 cup whiskey
1 1/4 cups heavy cream

For decoration
Finely chopped walnuts
Short twisted spirals of lemon peel
Macaroons*, for serving

Put all the ingredients in a bowl and whip vigorously until thick and light. Pour the mixture into a container. Cover and freeze until firm, beating well after 1 1/2 hours.

About 20 minutes before serving, transfer the syllabub to the refrigerator. Serve in tall glasses with frosted rims and decorate with chopped walnuts and lemon spirals. Serve with long spoons and accompany with macaroons.

Serves 4

Serving suggestion
For each serving, intermingle scoops of the syllabub with scoops of Kiwi Fruit Sorbet (page 127) finished with long, fine spirals of lemon peel. Serve with Cigars Russe*.

Dessert suggestion
Top with a layer of Pistachio Frozen Custard (page 101), lightly swirling the layers together, and enclosing them in a jacket of Langues de Chat*. Decorate the turned-out dessert with whiskey-flavored whipped cream, shapes cut from lemon peel and pistachio nuts.

Iced Daiquiri Mousse

5 eggs, separated
3/4 cup sugar
1/4 cup lime juice
1/4 cup lemon juice
Grated zest of 1 lime and 1 lemon
1 tablespoon gelatin
1/4 cup white rum
1 cup cream, whipped

For decoration
Candied lemon slices
Finely chopped pistachio nuts
Whipped cream

Beat the egg yolks in a bowl until light and fluffy. Gradually beat in half the sugar and continue beating until light. Beat in the lime and lemon juice and zests. Place the bowl over a pan of hot water and cook gently, stirring constantly, until the mixture thickens.

Soak the gelatin in the rum in a small bowl set over a pan of hot water. When the gelatin has dissolved stir it into the thickened egg mixture. Leave to cool.

Whip the egg whites in a bowl until stiff then gradually add the remaining sugar, whipping well after each addition. Fold the egg whites and cream into the egg mixture and leave to cool completely.

Spoon the mixture into a freezerproof dish and freeze until firm.

About 30 minutes before serving, transfer the mousse to the refrigerator. Decorate the top with candied lemon slices, chopped pistachio nuts and cream.

Serves 6–8

Serving suggestion
Scoop into chilled lime shells cut in half lengthwise. Decorate with small rosettes of coconut-liqueur-flavored whipped cream and long, fine strips of lemon and lime peel.

Dessert suggestion
Make a bombe or freeze in a cake or loaf pan with a jacket of Pineapple Ice Cream (page 99). Decorate the turned-out dessert with lime-flavored whipped cream and shapes cut from lime peel.

Prune Ice Cream (with brandy)

1 cup good-quality prunes, pitted
Finely grated zest and juice of 1 orange
1/2 cup armagnac or brandy
1 Earl Grey tea bag
1/2 cup sugar
1/2 cup fromage blanc or strained cottage cheese
1 cup whipping or heavy cream
2 tablespoons confectioners' sugar

Put the prunes in a bowl with the orange zest and juice, the armagnac or brandy and tea bag and enough water to cover and leave to soak overnight.

Next day, measure out 1 1/2 cups of the prunes and keep the rest for decoration. Strain the soaking liquid into a saucepan. Add the sugar and dissolve over low heat. Then bring to the boil and boil until very syrupy and just beginning to caramelize around the edges. Pour the syrup into a food processor with the cheese and prunes and mix until just evenly blended. Cool. Pour into a container, cover and freeze until just becoming firm. Turn into a bowl and beat well.

Whip the cream in a bowl with the confectioners' sugar. Fold into the prune mixture. Spoon back into the container. Cover and freeze until firm.

Freeze the reserved prunes separately, if not serving the ice cream within a day or so, otherwise, keep them, covered, in the refrigerator.

About 30 minutes before serving, transfer the ice cream to the refrigerator. Let the reserved prunes warm to room temperature if frozen – heat them slightly, if necessary. Serve each portion garnished with prunes and sprinkled with a little armagnac.

Serves 6

Dessert suggestion
Freeze in a pie or cake pan lined with crushed hazelnut Macaroons*. Decorate the turned-out dessert with orange-liqueur-flavored whipped cream and shapes cut from orange peel. Serve the reserved prunes separately.

Bloody Mary Water Ice

1¼ cups tomato juice
⅓ cup vodka
Juice of 2 lemons
4–6 drops Worcestershire sauce
6 ice cubes, crushed
½ green pepper, finely diced
4 celery leaves, chopped
Celery salt and freshly ground black pepper

For decoration
6 × 4 inch cucumber sticks
6 mint, basil, borage or watercress sprigs

Put the tomato juice, vodka, lemon juice, Worcestershire sauce and crushed ice together in a blender and mix at high speed. Add the green pepper, celery leaves and seasoning to taste and blend again until smooth.

Pour into a container. Cover and freeze until firm, beating 3 times at 45-minute intervals.

About 30 minutes before serving, transfer the water ice to the refrigerator. Spoon the water ice into small chilled goblets, add a cucumber stick to look like a straw and garnish with the mint, basil, borage or watercress sprigs.

Serves 6

Dessert suggestion
Freeze in a mold and surround the base of the turned-out water ice with celery leaves and crowns formed from cucumber slices with mayonnaise piped into the centers, finished with a fine sprinkling of fresh fennel or dill leaves.

Recipes for cakes, sauces, etc., asterisked in the dessert and serving suggestions, are given on pages 145 to 152. For directions on layering, lining and other techniques involved in creating desserts, see pages 152 to 155. Basic recipes are on pages 16 and 17.

Eggnog Ice Cream

¾ cup condensed milk, chilled
3 eggs
½ cup rum
¼–½ teaspoon freshly grated nutmeg
1½ cups cream, whipped

Put the milk, eggs, rum and nutmeg in a bowl and whip until very light and thick. Fold in the cream.

Pour the mixture into a container. Cover and freeze until firm. About 20 minutes before serving, transfer to the refrigerator.

Serves 4–5

Serving suggestions
Serve as a sundae with Atholl Brose (page 37) with Chunky Marmalade Sauce* poured over and topped with slivered almonds.

Serve in individual glasses with Sponge Fingers*.

Dessert suggestion
Freeze in a pie or cake pan lined with crushed ginger cookies held together with melted butter, the top covered with more crushed ginger cookies. Decorate the turned-out dessert with whipped cream and candied lemon or orange slices.

Pumpkin Sorbet

⅓ cup sugar
1 lb fresh, peeled pumpkin, diced
3 tablespoons dark rum
2–3 tablespoons lemon juice
½ teaspoon ground cinnamon
1 large egg white
Sugared cranberries, for decoration

In a heavy-based saucepan, dissolve the sugar in 1¼ cups water. Bring to the boil and boil for 5 minutes. Leave to cool until lukewarm. Put the syrup and pumpkin in a blender and blend until smooth. Add the rum, lemon juice and cinnamon and blend again. Pass through a strainer into a large measuring cup. There should be 1¾ cups so add some water, if necessary. Leave to cool completely.

Pour the mixture into a container. Cover and freeze until slushy. Beat well in a bowl.

Whip the egg white in a small bowl until stiff but not dry. Fold it into the pumpkin ice. Return to the container, cover and freeze until firm.

About 1 hour before serving, transfer the sorbet to the refrigerator. Served decorated with sugared cranberries.

Serves 8

Additional recipes using spirits: Atholl Brose (page 37), Ginger Ice Cream (page 61).

Strawberry

The fresh, fragrant taste of ices made at home with fresh strawberries is totally different to the flavor of most commercial products. The berries also blend well with a number of other ingredients, such as raspberries, orange juice and even rosewater. Always remember to hull strawberries before puréeing and straining them.

Simple Strawberry Ice Cream
Add 1¼ cups strained strawberry purée to any of the Basic Recipes*.

Strawberry Rose Ice

1 pound strawberries, hulled
½ cup sugar
1 teaspoon rosewater
2 cups plain yogurt
1 egg white
Crystallized pink rose petals, for decoration

Purée the strawberries, sugar, rosewater and yogurt together. Strain through a fine strainer into a container. Cover and freeze until just becoming firm. Beat well in a bowl.

Whip the egg white in a small bowl until stiff but not dry and fold into the frozen strawberry mixture. Return to the container, cover and freeze until firm.

About 30 minutes before serving, transfer the ice to the refrigerator. Serve decorated with crystallized rose petals.

Serves 4–5

Serving suggestion
Freeze in small decorative molds. Surround with fresh or crystallized rose petals and decorate with Low Calorie Topping.*

Dessert suggestion
Freeze in individual "sandwiches" made from crushed graham crackers held together with melted butter. Decorate with whipped cream flavored with a good-quality strawberry syrup, and small pieces of strawberry.

Low calorie version
Use fructose or a low calorie or artificial sweetener instead of sugar.

Strawberry and Elderflower Ice Cream

⅔ cup sugar
Finely pared zest of 2 lemons
2 handfuls elderflowers
7 ounces full fat cream cheese, beaten
⅓ cup milk
1 pound strawberries, puréed and strained
1 egg white
Small elderflower sprigs, for decoration

In a heavy-based saucepan, dissolve the sugar in 2¼ cups water. Bring to the boil, add the lemon zest and boil for 7 minutes. Remove from the heat, stir in the elderflowers, cover and leave to cool completely.

Beat the cheese and milk together in a bowl until smooth and airy.

Strain the syrup and measure 1 cup into the strawberry purée. Stir to mix and fold into the cheese and milk mixture. Spoon into a container, cover and freeze until becoming firm. Turn into a bowl and beat well.

Whip the egg white in a small bowl until stiff but not dry. Fold the egg white into the strawberry mixture.

Spoon back into the container, cover and freeze until firm.

About 30 minutes before serving, transfer the ice cream to the refrigerator. Decorate each portion with a small sprig of elderflowers.

Serves 4–5

Serving suggestion
Arrange scoops on white plates and surround with a sauce of strained, puréed strawberries, perhaps 'lifted' with a little strawberry eau-de-vie (fraise). Decorate with sprigs of elderflowers or elderberries and serve with Sponge Fingers*.

> ### To reduce your sugar intake
> Replace the sugar with half the quantity of **fructose** or with an **artificial sweetener**, provided the recipe does not call for a sugar syrup. Normally, 3–4 artificial sweeteners are the equivalent of 2 tablespoons but always check that you have the right degree of sweetness. Artificial sweeteners must be added to custard-based ice creams after the custard has cooled.

Iced Strawberry Mousse

⅓ cup sugar
4 egg yolks
⅔ cup cream, whipped
1¼ cups puréed and strained strawberries
2 tablespoons orange liqueur or orange juice

In a heavy-based saucepan, dissolve the sugar in 4 tablespoons water. Bring to the boil and boil until the temperature reaches 234°F.

Meanwhile, beat the egg yolks in a bowl until very thick and light. Gradually beat in the boiling syrup and continue beating until well increased in volume.

Fold in the cream. Blend the strawberry purée and liqueur or orange juice together and fold into the egg yolk and cream mixture.

Pour into a container. Cover and freeze until firm.

About 20 minutes before serving, transfer the mousse to the refrigerator.

Serves 4–5

Serving suggestions
Spoon each serving into a mound on a circle of Genoise Cake* sprinkled with kirsch. Arrange sliced strawberries neatly over the sides. Surround with a sauce of strained, puréed strawberries and make a cobweb pattern with crème fraîche. Sprinkle a little confectioners' sugar carefully over the strawberries.

For each serving, put a few strawberries in the base of a tall wine glass, then fill the glass with scoops of iced mousse. Decorate with fresh strawberry leaves.

For each serving, make an indentation in the base of a large Meringue* and fill with the mousse. To serve, pour over a little Orange Flower Sauce*, Chocolate Sauce*, Bitter Chocolate Sauce* or Fudge Sauce*.

Iced Strawberry Soufflé

3/4 cup sugar
3 egg whites
1 1/4 cups cream, whipped
1 1/4 pounds strawberries, puréed and strained
Lemon juice
2 tablespoons kummel or kirsch, optional

For decoration
Whipped cream
Crystallized roses or violets

In a heavy-based saucepan, dissolve the sugar in 1/2 cup water. Bring to the boil and boil for 5 minutes.

Meanwhile, whip the egg whites in a bowl, set over warm water, until just stiff. Slowly pour the hot syrup onto the egg whites, whipping constantly. Remove the bowl from the warm water and continue to whip until the meringue is cold and very thick.

Fold in the cream and strawberry purée and 'lift' the flavor with lemon juice, adding the kummel or kirsch, if using.

Pour the mixture into a container. Cover and freeze until firm.

About 20 minutes before serving, transfer the soufflé to the refrigerator. Decorate with whipped cream and crystallized roses or violets.

Serves 6

Dessert suggestion
Freeze in a cake or loaf pan around a center of Rose Petal Sorbet (page 70) or Crystallized Rose Petal Ice Cream (see Crystallized Violet Ice Cream, pages 134-135). Decorate the turned-out dessert with rose petals, fresh or crystallized, leaves and piped whipped cream. Serve with Sponge Fingers.*

Strawberry Ice Cream (with strawberry yogurt)

3/4 pound strawberries, hulled
1/2 cup sugar
2 cups strawberry yogurt
3 tablespoons lemon juice
2/3 cup heavy or whipping cream
2 egg whites
Sliced strawberries, for decoration

Put the strawberries, sugar, yogurt and lemon juice together in a blender and process until smooth. Strain the mixture through a fine strainer into a container, cover and freeze to the slushy stage. Beat well in a bowl.

Whip the cream in a bowl until soft peaks form. In another bowl whip the egg whites until stiff but not dry. Fold the cream and then the egg whites into the frozen strawberry mixture. Return to the container, cover and freeze until firm.

About 45 minutes before serving, transfer the ice cream to the refrigerator. Serve each portion decorated with strawberry slices.

Serves 5

Dessert suggestion
Layer with fine sheets of almond Meringue. Decorate the turned-out dessert with whipped cream, lightly toasted almonds and strawberries.*

Iced Strawberry Crush

1/2 pound strawberries, puréed and strained
1 tablespoon lemon juice
4 teaspoons confectioners' sugar
*Approximately 1/2 cup roughly broken Meringues**
2/3 cup heavy cream, whipped
1 egg, separated
3 tablespoons sugar

Mix the strawberry purée, lemon juice and confectioners' sugar together in a bowl. Cover and leave in a cool place for 2 hours.

Fold the meringues into the cream. Beat the egg yolk with the sugar in a bowl until very thick and light. In another bowl, whip the egg white until stiff but not dry.

Fold the purée, cream and then the egg white into the egg yolk mixture. Spoon into a container, cover and freeze until firm.

About 30 minutes before serving, transfer the crush to the refrigerator.

Serves 4–5

Dessert suggestion
Freeze in a Chocolate Case. Decorate the top with crushed peppermint or mint candies and small Chocolate Curls*.*

Flavor variation
Make with Macaroons instead of meringues.*

Double Berry Cream Ice

2/3–3/4 cup sugar
1 pound strawberries, puréed and strained
2/3 cup red currant or cranberry juice
1 tablespoon lemon juice
1 1/4 cups cream, whipped
Sliced strawberries, for decoration

In a heavy-based saucepan, dissolve the sugar in 2/3 cup water. Bring to the boil and boil until the syrup reaches 234°F. Set aside to cool.

Blend the strawberry purée, red currant or cranberry juice and lemon juice with the syrup. Gradually pour the mixture into the cream and fold lightly together.

Pour the mixture into a container. Cover and freeze until firm, beating twice at hourly intervals.

About 30 minutes before serving, transfer the cream ice to the refrigerator. Serve decorated with sliced strawberries.

Serves 5–6

Dessert suggestion
Spoon into individual Meringue Baskets*. Decorate with sliced strawberries.

Strawberry Cream Ice

1/2 cup sugar
1 pound strawberries, puréed and strained
Squeeze of lemon juice
1 egg white
2/3 cup heavy cream, whipped
Sliced whole strawberries, for decoration

In a heavy-based saucepan, dissolve the sugar in 1¼ cups water. Bring to the boil and boil steadily for 10 minutes. Cool then blend with the strawberry purée and lemon juice.

Pour the mixture into a container. Cover and freeze to the slushy stage. Beat well in a bowl.

Whip the egg white in a bowl until stiff but not dry. Fold the cream and then the egg white into the frozen strawberry mixture. Return to the container, cover and freeze until firm.

About 40 minutes before serving, transfer the ice to the refrigerator. Serve each portion decorated with sliced strawberries.

Serves 4

Serving suggestions
Spoon into Ice Cream Cones* coated in shredded coconut.

Serve with Marshmallow Sauce* or Bitter Chocolate Sauce*.

Strawberry Ice Cream

1½ pounds strawberries, hulled
Juice of 1/2 an orange
3/4 cup sugar
2 cups heavy cream, whipped

Purée the strawberries with the juice then stir in the sugar. Strain through a fine strainer. Fold the cream into the purée.

Pour the mixture into a container. Cover and freeze until firm, beating twice at hourly intervals.

About 30 minutes before serving, transfer the ice cream to the refrigerator.

Serves 6–8

Serving suggestion
Freeze in individual fancy molds and serve on a bed of sliced strawberries, lightly sprinkled with framboise liqueur, if liked. Decorate with mint leaves.

Strawberry Tofu Ice Cream

1¼ cups tofu
1¼ cups puréed and strained strawberries
1 tablespoon fructose or to taste
Few drops of vanilla extract

Blend all the ingredients together until smooth. Pour into a container, cover and freeze until firm, beating twice at hourly intervals.

About 30 minutes before serving, transfer the ice cream to the refrigerator.

Serves 3–4

Strawberry Water Ice

2 pounds strawberries, hulled
2 tablespoons kirsch
2 tablespoons grenadine
Juice of 1 lemon

Purée then strain the strawberries into a bowl. Mix in all the other ingredients.

Pour the mixture into a container. Cover and freeze until firm, beating 3 times at 45-minute intervals.

About 35 minutes before serving, transfer the water ice to the refrigerator.

Serves 6

Additional recipes using strawberries: Rhubarb and Strawberry Ice Cream (page 111), Passion Fruit and Strawberry Ice Cream (page 128).

Recipes for cakes, sauces, etc., asterisked in the dessert and serving suggestions, are given on pages 145 to 152. For directions on layering, lining and other techniques involved in creating desserts, see pages 152 to 155. Basic recipes are on pages 16 and 17.

Vanilla, Custard

Vanilla is *the* traditional ice cream, and a firm favorite with many people. The best ices are flavored with a whole vanilla pod or bean steeped in warm cream or milk. Wash and dry the pod when you remove it and keep it for further use. If you store it in a jar of sugar, the vanilla flavor will permeate the sugar, which can then be used in a variety of desserts. For a more pronounced taste, split the pod open to release the seeds into the ice cream. Real vanilla essence, stronger than extract, can be used, with discretion, but try to avoid artificial flavorings. Recipes for custard ice creams, also traditional favorites, are included in this section.

Fresh Custard Ice Cream

Use the Basic Custard Ice Cream on page 16, or a good-quality bought dairy custard. Beat the bought version before putting it into the freezer and beat twice during freezing, at 45-minute intervals.

Philadelphia Ice Cream

2¼ cups heavy or whipping cream
⅓ cup confectioners' sugar
Pinch of salt
Approximately ½ teaspoon finely grated vanilla seed
   (found inside a split vanilla pod)

Put all the ingredients in a bowl and whip together until thick. Pour the mixture into a container. Cover and freeze until firm, beating twice at hourly intervals.

About 20 minutes before serving transfer the ice cream to the refrigerator.

Serves 4–6

Dessert suggestion
Encase in Apricot Ice Cream (page 24). Decorate with whipped cream flavored with apricot brandy or brandy, lightly toasted slivered almonds and chocolate-covered almonds or Chocolate Shapes*. Serve with Cigars Russe*.

Vanilla Ice Cream

4 eggs, separated
1 cup confectioners' sugar, sifted
1 teaspoon vanilla extract
1¼ cups heavy cream, whipped

Whip the egg whites until stiff in a bowl. Add the confectioners' sugar a tablespoon at a time, whipping well after each addition. Whip in the egg yolks one at a time with the vanilla extract. Carefully fold in the cream.

Pour the mixture into a large container or 8 small dishes. Cover and freeze until firm.

If frozen in a large container, transfer to the refrigerator about 15 minutes before serving.

Serves 8

Serving suggestion
Make into a sundae with sliced strawberries, topped with whole berries and a sauce made from strained, puréed ripe strawberries.

Dessert suggestion
Serve in a checkerboard with one of the following ice creams: Butterscotch Ice Cream (page 39), Caramel Ice Cream (page 39), Cherry Ice Cream (page 41), Chocolate Ice Cream (page 44), Raspberry Ice Cream (page 104), Strawberry Ice Cream (page 121), Walnut Ice Cream (page 124). Spread whipped cream, flavored with a liqueur if liked, over the turned-out dessert. Decorate with nuts, chocolate or fruit.

Rich Vanilla Ice Cream

⅓ cup sugar
2 cups whipping cream
½ vanilla pod, split
4 egg yolks
4 tablespoons sweet butter, diced

Dissolve the sugar in the cream in a heavy-based saucepan. Add the vanilla pod and bring to the boil. Remove from the heat, cover the pan and leave to infuse for 15 minutes.

Lightly beat the egg yolks in a bowl. Strain in the cream mixture, beating all the time, and continue to beat until the custard is light and frothy. Pour back into the pan and cook gently, stirring constantly, until the mixture thickens slightly. Do not allow to boil. Remove from the heat and stir in the butter.

Pour the mixture into a shallow container and cool completely. Cover and freeze until firm, beating well after about 1½ hours.

About 30 minutes before serving transfer the ice cream to the refrigerator.

Serves 4

Vanilla Yogurt Ice Cream

1 egg
⅓ cup sugar
¼ cup light corn syrup
¾ cup whipping or heavy cream
¾ cup plain yogurt
1½ teaspoons vanilla extract
Pinch of salt

Put all the ingredients in a bowl and thoroughly whip together until smooth and light. Pour the mixture into a container. Cover and freeze until firm, beating twice at hourly intervals. About 30 minutes before serving, transfer the ice cream to the refrigerator.

Serves 6

Custard Ice Cream

1 large egg, separated
¼ cup sugar
1 tablespoon cornstarch
2½ cups milk
½ teaspoon vanilla extract
Approximately 1½ tablespoons dessert topping

Blend the egg yolk, sugar and cornstarch together in a bowl with ⅔ cup of the milk. In a heavy-based saucepan, bring 1¼ cups of the milk to boiling point and stir into the blended mixture with the vanilla extract. Return to the rinsed pan and cook over a gentle heat, stirring constantly, until the custard has thickened. Do not allow to boil. Leave to cool, stirring occasionally to prevent a skin forming.

Make up the dessert topping mix with the remaining milk. Whip the egg white until stiff but not dry. Fold the dessert and the egg white into the cooled custard.

Pour the mixture into a container. Cover and freeze until firm.

About 30 minutes before serving, transfer the ice cream to the refrigerator.

Serves 4–5

Serving suggestion
For each serving, put the ice cream in the center of a rum baba, doughnut or waffle soaked in rum and top with Hot Fudge Sauce*, Butterscotch Sauce*, Hot Chocolate Sauce*, Caramel Sauce* or Milky Way Sauce*.

VIOLETS, CRYSTALLIZED: see OLD-FASHIONED FAVORITES
VODKA: see BLOODY MARY WATER ICE (page 117)

Walnut, Pecan

The purest-tasting walnut ices are made soon after the walnut season with fresh nuts removed from their shells just before use. Packaged nuts do not have the same quality of flavor, even when they are vacuum-sealed. To toast walnuts, heat the peeled nuts in a 350°F oven until golden brown. Chop walnuts by hand before grinding them, briefly in small batches, in a coffee grinder or food processor.

Pecans have a higher fat content than walnuts, and lose their freshness even more quickly. They can be substituted for walnuts in recipes and have a delectable flavor of their own.

Simple Walnut or Pecan Ice Cream
Add ½ cup finely chopped nuts to any of the Basic Recipes*.

Iced Pecan Mousse

3 cups sugar
¾ cup coarsely chopped pecans
4 egg whites
2 cups cream, whipped
Whole strawberries or pecan halves, for decoration

Heat half the sugar gently in a heavy-based saucepan until it melts and caramelizes. Stir in the pecans and continue to heat, stirring, until a rich golden brown. Pour immediately onto an oiled surface and leave to become cold and hard. Put the caramel in a thick plastic bag or dish-towel and hit with a rolling pin to break it into fairly coarse granules.

Dissolve the remaining sugar in ⅔ cup water in a heavy-based saucepan. Bring to the boil and boil to 234°F. Meanwhile, whip the egg whites in a bowl until stiff. Whip the boiling syrup into the egg whites and continue whipping until the meringue is cool and very stiff. Fold in the crushed caramel and the cream.

Pour the mixture into a freezerproof bowl or soufflé dish. Cover and freeze until firm.

About 15 minutes before serving, remove from the freezer. Decorate with the strawberries or pecan halves and place in the refrigerator.

Serves 6

Serving suggestion
Spoon into Ice Cream Cones and surround with Bitter Chocolate Sauce*.*

Dessert suggestion
Form into 6 balls and coat in finely grated semi-sweet chocolate or cocoa. Serve with orange slices steeped in a dessert wine, and Cigars Russe.*

Rich Walnut Ice Cream

4 egg yolks
½ cup sugar
1¼ cups milk
⅛ pound marzipan, chopped
½ cup ground walnuts
⅔ cup cream, whipped
Walnut halves, for decoration

Beat the egg yolks and sugar together in a bowl. Bring the milk to simmering point in a heavy-based saucepan. Remove from the heat and stir into the egg yolks. Stir in the marzipan and nuts. Leave to cool, stirring occasionally. Pour into a container, cover and freeze until becoming firm. Turn into a bowl and beat well. Fold in the cream.

Spoon the mixture back into the container. Cover and freeze until firm.

About 20 minutes before serving, transfer the ice cream to the refrigerator. Serve decorated with walnut halves.

Serves 5

Dessert suggestion
Layer with Applesauce Yogurt Ice (page 21). Decorate with whipped cream, chopped walnuts and short strips of orange peel.

Walnut Ice Cream

2 eggs, separated
¾ cup confectioners' sugar, sifted
½ pound cream cheese
2 tablespoons sweet madeira, optional
3 tablespoons very lightly toasted crushed walnuts

Put the egg yolks and the sugar in a bowl and beat until very light. Beat in the cheese and continue beating until the mixture is smooth.

In another bowl, whip the egg whites until stiff but not dry. Carefully fold the egg whites into the cheese mixture with the madeira, if using, and the walnuts.

Pour the mixture into a container. Cover and freeze until firm.

About 30 minutes before serving, transfer the ice cream to the refrigerator.

Serves 4

Dessert suggestion
Layer with Coffee Ice Cream (page 50) and Caramel Ice Cream (page 39). Serve in slices with thickish slices of apple lightly caramelized in butter, sugar and crushed coriander seeds. Accompany with Sponge Fingers.*

Fresh Walnut Ice Cream

¹/₃ cup peeled and roughly chopped fresh walnuts
2¹/₄ cups milk
4 egg yolks
¹/₂ cup clear honey
1 tablespoon walnut liqueur, optional

In a heavy-based saucepan, slowly bring the walnuts and the milk to boiling point. Remove from the heat, cover and leave to infuse for 15 minutes.

Beat the egg yolks with the honey in a bowl until very light and thick. Beat in the milk and walnuts. Return to the rinsed pan and cook over gentle heat until the custard thickens, but do not allow it to boil. Pour the custard into a bowl and leave to cool, stirring occasionally.

Put in the refrigerator to chill. Stir in the liqueur, if using, and pour into a container. Cover and freeze until firm, beating twice at hourly intervals.

About 30 minutes before serving, transfer the ice cream to the refrigerator.

Serves 4

Serving suggestion
Serve in Coupelles* with Orange Flower Sauce*.

Walnut Mocha Ice Cream

¹/₃ cup sugar
²/₃ cup walnut halves
10 ounces semi-sweet chocolate, chopped
²/₃ cup freshly made strong black coffee
Finely grated zest and juice of 1 orange
2 cups cream, whipped

For decoration
Chopped walnuts lightly Caramelized* with sugar
Finely grated orange zest

In a heavy-based saucepan, melt the sugar over low heat until it begins to caramelize. Stir in the walnuts and continue to stir until the mixture is a deep golden brown. Pour onto a cold oiled surface and leave to cool. Put the praline into a thick plastic bag and break into small pieces with a rolling pin.

Melt the chocolate with the coffee and orange juice in a bowl placed over a pan of hot water. Leave to cool. Mix in the orange zest and walnut praline. Fold in the cream.

Pour the mixture into individual molds and leave until completely cold. Cover the molds and freeze until firm.

About 20 minutes before serving, turn out the molds and transfer to the refrigerator. Decorate with caramelized walnuts and orange zest.

Serves 6

Spicy Nut Tofu Cream

¹/₂ cup chopped walnuts
¹/₃ cup brown sugar
1¹/₄ cups tofu
Very large pinch of ground cinnamon
Large pinch of grated nutmeg
2 tablespoons chopped candied ginger, optional

Put the nuts and 1 cup water in a saucepan and simmer for 10 minutes. Purée the nuts and liquid in a blender until smooth and pass through a strainer. While still warm, mix with the sugar and then with the tofu, spices and ginger, if using.

Pour into a container. Cover and freeze until firm, beating twice at hourly intervals.

About 30 minutes before serving, transfer the ice cream to the refrigerator.

Serves 4

Butter Pecan Ice Cream

³/₄ cup light brown sugar
2 eggs, beaten
2 tablespoons sweet butter
1 cup milk
Few drops of vanilla extract
3 tablespoons medium-dry sherry
1 cup whipping cream, whipped
¹/₂ cup chopped toasted pecan nuts

Put the sugar and ½ cup water in a heavy-based saucepan and stir to dissolve. Bring to the boil and boil for 2 minutes. Allow to cool slightly then slowly pour onto the eggs, stirring constantly.

Pour the mixture into a bowl placed over a pan of hot water and cook, stirring constantly, until the mixture thickens. Remove from the heat and stir in the butter. Leave to cool slightly then stir in the milk, vanilla extract and sherry and leave to cool completely.

Pour the mixture into a shallow metal container and chill for 30 minutes then cover and freeze until just becoming firm.

Tip the semi-frozen mixture into a bowl and beat well. Fold in the cream and nuts then spoon back into the container, cover and freeze until firm.

About 35 minutes before serving, transfer the ice cream to the refrigerator.

Serves 6

Additional recipes using walnuts or pecans:
Apple and Walnut Ice Cream (page 20), Maple and Walnut Ice Cream (page 80), Pecan Pie Ice Cream (page 135).

Warm Climate Fruits

Exotic fruits – papaya, litchis, passion fruit and persimmons are just a few – make delicious and attractive ices that add a sense of occasion to any meal. Guavas, peeled and with the seeds scooped out, can be used in any of the papaya recipes.

Papaya Sorbet

1½ pounds papayas
½ cup sugar
1½ tablespoons lemon juice
2 teaspoons kirsch
1 small egg white

Peel the papayas, scrape out the seeds and purée the flesh. Put in a bowl and add the sugar, lemon juice and kirsch. In another bowl, whip the egg white until stiff but not dry and fold into the papaya mixture.

Pour the mixture into a container. Cover and freeze until firm, beating 3 times at 45-minute intervals.

About 30 minutes before serving, transfer the sorbet to the refrigerator.

Serves 4

Serving suggestion
Serve in wine glasses and decorate each serving with peach and kiwi fruit slices and a candied cherry.

Kiwi Fruit Sorbet

¼ cup sugar
6 kiwi fruit
2 egg whites
Cointreau or other orange liqueur

Dissolve the sugar with ⅔ cup water in a small heavy-based saucepan. Bring to the boil and boil for 1–2 minutes. Leave to cool.

Halve the kiwi fruit and remove the skins. Then reduce the flesh to a purée and blend with the cooled syrup.

Whip the egg whites in a bowl until stiff but not dry. Carefully fold them into the kiwi fruit mixture.

Pour the mixture into a container. Cover and freeze until firm, beating 3 times at 45-minute intervals.

About 15 minutes before serving, transfer the sorbet to the refrigerator. Pour about 1 teaspoon Cointreau or other orange liqueur over each serving to bring out the flavor.

Serves 6

Dessert suggestion
Encase in Pistachio and Green Chartreuse Ice Cream (page 101). Decorate the turned-out dessert with brandy-flavored whipped cream and Chocolate Shapes*.

Litchi Ice Cream

½ cup sugar
1¼ cups milk
2½ cups heavy or whipping cream
1 vanilla pod, split
8 egg yolks
Approximately 1 pound can litchis, drained and very finely sliced
Preserved stem ginger in syrup, for serving

In a heavy-based saucepan, heat the sugar, milk, cream and vanilla pod to just below boiling point. Remove from the heat, cover and leave for 30 minutes.

Beat the egg yolks in a bowl. Strain in the milk mixture, stirring. Return to the rinsed pan and heat gently, stirring constantly, until the custard thickens. Do not allow to boil. Leave to cool, stirring occasionally. Chill for an hour.

Stir in the litchis and pour into a container. Cover and freeze until firm, beating twice at hourly intervals.

About 40 minutes before serving, transfer the ice cream to the refrigerator. Slice the ginger into fine strips and sprinkle over each portion as it is served together with a spoonful of the syrup.

Serves 6–8

Serving suggestion
Serve in Gingersnap Baskets* or Cones* intermingled with sliced fresh or canned litchis.

Dessert suggestion
Encase in a layer of Black Currant Ice Cream (page 32) followed by a jacket made with fingers of Genoise Cake*.

Papaya Ice Cream

1½ cups papaya flesh (from about 1¼ pounds papayas), puréed
Juice of 1 large juicy lemon
Juice of ½ a large juicy orange
Approximately 1½ cups confectioners' sugar
1¼ cups cream, whipped

In a bowl, blend the papaya flesh with the fruit juices and sweeten with the sugar. Fold in the cream. Taste and adjust the sugar level, if necessary, to make the mixture slightly oversweet.

Pour the mixture into a container. Cover and freeze until firm, beating twice at hourly intervals.

About 30 minutes before serving, transfer the ice cream to the refrigerator.

Serves 6

Serving suggestion
Freeze in a ring mold. Fill the center with Lime Ice Cream (page 75) and decorate with twisted lime slices and shapes cut from lemon peel. Serve with Almond Tuiles*.

Quick Litchi Sorbet

1¼ pounds canned litchis
2 tablespoons orange flower water
1 tablespoon kirsch, optional
2 egg whites

Purée the litchis with their juice, the orange flower water and kirsch, if you are using it.

Pour the mixture into a container. Cover and freeze to the slushy stage. Beat well in a bowl.

Whip the egg whites in a bowl until stiff but not dry. Fold into the sorbet. Return to the container, cover and freeze until firm.

About 10 minutes before serving, transfer the sorbet to the refrigerator.

Serves 6

Serving suggestions
Accompany with Chunky Marmalade Sauce* made with lime or ginger marmalade.

Serve with Almond Tuiles* flavored with orange flower water.

For each serving, arrange one or two scoops on a plate with a selection of different colored sorbets such as Apricot Sorbet (page 23), Blackberry Sorbet (page 30) and Rhubarb Sorbet (page 110).

Persimmon Ice Cream

3 large, sweet, very ripe persimmons
⅓ cup sugar
2 tablespoons lemon juice
2 cups whipping cream, whipped

Cut the persimmons in half, scoop out the flesh and pass through a nylon strainer into a bowl to remove the seeds. Stir in the sugar and lemon juice and fold in the cream.

Pour the mixture into a container. Cover and freeze until firm, beating twice at hourly intervals.

About 45 minutes before serving, transfer the ice cream to the refrigerator.

Serves 4–6

Dessert suggestion
Make a bombe or freeze in a cake or loaf pan enclosed in a layer of Candied Peel Ice Cream (page 59) with a jacket of Quick Brown Bread Ice Cream (page 36) flavored with ¼ cup orange liqueur (added when the ingredients are stirred together). Decorate the turned-out dessert with whipped cream and pour over a sauce made from puréed orange flesh.

Passion Fruit Sorbet

¾ cup sugar
Peel and juice of 1 lemon
1 pound passion fruit pulp (from about 1½ pounds fruit), strained
1 egg white

In a heavy-based saucepan, dissolve the sugar in 2 cups water. Add the lemon peel and bring to the boil. Boil for 5 minutes. Cool and strain the syrup. Stir in the passion fruit pulp and lemon juice. Chill for 30 minutes.

Pour the mixture into a container. Cover and freeze to the slushy stage. Beat well in a bowl.

Whip the egg white in a small bowl until stiff but not dry and fold into the passion fruit mixture. Return to the container, cover and freeze until firm, beating 3 times at 45-minute intervals.

About 40 minutes before serving, transfer to the refrigerator.

Serves 6

Passion Fruit and Strawberry Ice Cream

3 egg yolks
⅓ cup sugar
1¼ cups milk
Pulp and seeds of 6 passion fruit
⅔ cup strawberry purée (from about 1½ cups hulled strawberries)
Squeeze of orange juice
2 cups crème fraîche, beaten

For decoration
Whipped cream
Strawberries

Put the egg yolks and sugar in a bowl and beat until thick and light. In a heavy-based saucepan, heat the milk to just below boiling point. Pour the hot milk on to the egg yolks, beating continuously. Return the mixture to the rinsed pan and cook over a low heat, stirring constantly, until the mixture thickens. Do not allow to boil. Remove from the heat and beat until cool.

Mix half the custard with the pulp and seeds of the passion fruit and half with the strawberry purée. Add a squeeze of orange juice to each mixture then leave until cold.

Strain each mixture into a separate bowl. Fold half the crème fraîche into each one. Fold the two mixtures together to give a marbled effect. Pour the mixture into a container. Cover and freeze until firm.

About 30 minutes before serving, transfer the ice cream to the refrigerator. Serve each portion decorated with a swirl of cream and a sliced strawberry.

Serves 4–5

Passion Fruit Ice Cream

8 ripe passion fruit
1 teaspoon lemon juice
2 eggs, separated
½ cup sugar
1¼ cups cream, whipped

For decoration
Pulp and seeds of 1 passion fruit
Whipped cream

Cut the passion fruit in half and scoop the pulp out into a strainer placed over a bowl. Press through the strainer to extract as much juice as possible. Discard the seeds. Add the lemon juice.

Beat the egg yolks and half the sugar in a bowl until very thick and light. In another bowl, whip the egg whites until stiff but not dry. Gradually whip in the remaining sugar. Fold the egg yolks into the passion fruit mixture then the cream and egg whites. Freeze in a 1 quart loaf pan or mold until firm.

About 30 minutes before serving, unmold the ice cream onto a cold plate, spoon the passion fruit pulp and seeds down the center and finish with whipped cream.

Serves 6

Pomegranate Sorbet

1 cup sugar
2 cups pomegranate juice (from 6–8 fruit)
Juice of ½ lemon

In a heavy-based saucepan, dissolve the sugar in 1¼ cups water and bring to the boil. Cool then stir in the remaining ingredients. Chill for an hour.

Pour the mixture into a container. Cover and freeze until firm, beating 3 times at 45-minute intervals.

About 30 minutes before serving, transfer the sorbet to the refrigerator.

Serves 6–8

Dessert suggestion
Encase in Pear Ice Cream (with kirsch) (page 93).
Decorate the turned-out dessert with whipped cream,
flavored with kirsch or grenadine if liked, and
crystallized rose petals.

WATERMELON: see MELON
WHISKEY: see SPIRITS

At first sight ices made from wines or liqueurs may seem to be an extravagance. However, they need not be expensive. Wines can be bought in half bottles and most liqueurs are available in miniature sizes. Remember, though, that it is a false economy to use an inferior quality product as this will ruin the taste of the ice. You can use the end of a bottle of wine as long as it has not been opened too long.

Simple Liqueur Ice Cream
Add 3 tablespoons of any liqueur to any of the Basic Recipes*.

Red Wine Granita

1 cup sugar
1 bottle (75 cl) red wine, preferably St. Emilion or
*   Pomerol*
Juice of 1 orange
Juice of 1 lemon
Fresh mint leaves, for decoration

In a heavy-based saucepan, dissolve the sugar in 1 cup water. Bring to the boil and boil for 1 minute. Leave to cool completely. Stir the wine and fruit juices into the syrup. Chill for 30 minutes then strain into a container. Cover and freeze until lightly set and a mass of small, light crystals.

Stir the granita and spoon into 6 cold wine glasses, shaping it into a dome. Serve garnished with mint leaves.

Serves 6

Prune Ice Cream (with wine and brandy)

1½ cups prunes, pitted
⅞ cup good sweet wine
4 tablespoons armagnac or brandy
⅓ cup sugar
3 egg yolks
2 tablespoons all-purpose flour
1 cup milk infused with a vanilla pod
1 teaspoon sweet butter
Few drops of vanilla extract
1 cup heavy cream

Cut the prunes into 3 or 4 pieces and put in a bowl with the wine and armagnac or brandy. Cover and leave to soak in a cool place for several hours.

Beat the sugar, egg yolks and flour together in a bowl until very thick and pale. In a heavy stainless steel or enamel saucepan, slowly bring the milk and vanilla pod to just on boiling point. Gradually strain the milk onto the egg yolk mixture, beating all the time (keep the vanilla pod, washed and dried, for future use). Pour the custard back into the rinsed pan and bring to the boil over a moderate heat, beating all the time.

Simmer over a low heat for 2–3 minutes to cook the flour, still beating. Remove from the heat, beat in the butter and a few drops of vanilla extract. Pour into a bowl, cover closely with plastic wrap and leave to cool, then refrigerate.

Pour into a container, cover and freeze until becoming firm. Turn into a bowl and beat well. Whip the cream, adding a little of the unabsorbed syrup from the prunes, until soft peaks form. Fold the cream into the custard with half the soaked prunes.

Spoon the mixture back into the container. Cover and freeze until firm. Freeze the remaining fruit and syrup separately, unless serving the ice cream within a day or so. Otherwise keep covered in the refrigerator.

About 45 minutes before serving, transfer the ice cream to the refrigerator and let the fruit and syrup warm to room temperature. Spoon some of the fruit and syrup over each portion as it is served.

Serves 4–6

Dessert suggestion
Encase in Tea Ice Cream (page 71). To serve, spoon some of the reserved prunes and syrup over the top of the turned-out dessert, allowing the syrup to trickle over the surface and down the sides, and surround with the remaining prunes and syrup.

White Wine Sorbet

1 cup sugar
2 lemons
1 cup good-quality white wine
2 egg whites

In a heavy-based saucepan, dissolve the sugar in ¾ cup water. Bring to the boil and boil until the temperature reaches 225°F. Remove from the heat.

Thinly pare the peel from one of the lemons and add it to the syrup. Cover and leave for a few hours.

Remove the lemon peel from the syrup and stir in the wine and juice from both lemons. Pour the mixture into a container, cover and freeze until slushy. Beat well in a bowl.

Whip the egg whites in a bowl until stiff but not dry. Fold them into the frozen wine syrup. Return to the container, cover and freeze until firm, although it will not become really hard. Serve straight from the freezer.

Serves 5–6

Serving suggestions
Intermingle small scoops of the sorbet with small scoops of Melon Ice Cream (page 83) and Quick Mango Ice Cream (page 79) in a chilled melon half.

Serve small scoops of the sorbet with scoops of White Peach Sorbet (page 88) piled into Almond Tuiles.*

Dessert suggestion
Freeze in a cake or loaf pan around a center of Grape Ice Cream (page 64). Decorate the turned-out dessert with whipped cream and quartered black grapes.

Gewürztraminer Sorbet

2 cups sugar
½ bottle (35 cl) Gewürztraminer or similar wine
Juice of 1 orange
Juice of 1 lemon
3 egg whites

In a heavy-based saucepan, dissolve the sugar in 2½ cups water. Bring to the boil then simmer for 10 minutes. Set aside to cool.

Pour the wine and an equal amount of the sugar syrup into a bowl and mix in the strained fruit juices.

Pour the mixture into a container. Cover and freeze to the slushy stage. Beat well in a bowl.

Whip the egg whites in a bowl until stiff but not dry. Fold into the wine mixture. Return to the container, cover and freeze until firm.

Serve directly from the freezer.

Serves 6–8

Serving suggestion
For each serving, put sliced strawberries (wild, if possible) in the bottom of a tall, slim, frosted glass and sprinkle with strawberry eau-de-vie (fraise). Add scoops of the sorbet and top with more sliced strawberries. Sprinkle with eau-de-vie and pour over some good-quality sweet sparkling wine. Finish with a scattering of lightly toasted slivered almonds. Serve with long-handled spoons.

Liqueur Sorbet

¾ cup sugar
Finely grated zest and juice of 1 lemon
6 tablespoons liqueur, e.g. Grand Marnier, crème de cassis, apricot brandy
1 egg white
Bay leaves, for decoration

In a heavy-based saucepan, dissolve the sugar in 1½ cups water. Bring to the boil and boil for 5 minutes. Remove from the heat, stir in the lemon zest and juice and the liqueur. Leave to cool completely.

Strain the syrup and pour into a container. Cover and chill for 30 minutes. Place in the freezer and freeze to the slushy stage. Beat well in a bowl.

Whip the egg white in a small bowl until stiff but not dry. Fold into the sorbet. Return to the container, cover and freeze until firm.

About 30 minutes before serving, transfer the sorbet to the refrigerator. Decorate each portion with bay leaves.

Serves 4

Dessert suggestion
Encase in an appropriately flavored and colored ice cream. Maraschino with Vanilla Ice Cream (page 123) is a good combination.

Iced Kirsch Soufflé

1 cup sugar
4 egg whites
¼ cup good-quality kirsch
1¼ cups crème fraîche or heavy cream, whipped
Crystallized violets, for decoration

In a heavy-based saucepan, dissolve the sugar in ⅔ cup water. Bring to the boil and boil for 3–5 minutes or until the temperature reaches 234°F.

Whip the egg whites in a bowl until stiff. Gradually pour in the syrup, whipping well. Whip in the kirsch then carefully fold in the crème fraîche or heavy cream. Leave to cool then chill in the refrigerator.

Pour the mixture into a freezerproof soufflé dish and freeze until firm.

About 20 minutes before serving, transfer the soufflé to the refrigerator. Decorate with crystallized violets.

Serves 6

Serving suggestion
Put scoops into the centers of pineapple rings and decorate with small Macaroons.*

Dessert suggestion
To make a Bombe Aida encase in Strawberry Ice Cream (page 121) and decorate the turned-out dessert with whipped cream, halved black cherries and Chocolate Curls.*

Iced Zabaglione

4 egg yolks
⅔ cup marsala
3 tablespoons sugar
1¼ cups heavy cream
Macaroons, to serve*

Beat the egg yolks, marsala and sugar together in a bowl placed over a pan of hot water, until very thick and light. Put the bowl into a basin of iced or very cold water to prevent the mixture cooking further and beat until it is cold.

In another bowl, whip the cream until soft peaks form. Carefully fold the cream into the marsala mixture.

Pour the mixture into a container. Cover and freeze until firm.

About 20 minutes before serving, transfer the iced zabaglione to the refrigerator. Serve with macaroons.

Serves 4

Serving suggestion
Serve with Cigars Russe or Sponge Fingers*.*

Dessert suggestion
Freeze in a Chocolate Case around a center of Valencia Orange Sorbet (page 86).*

Champagne Ice Cream

1½ cups sugar
3 tablespoons orange juice
2 tablespoons brandy
1¾ cups champagne or good-quality dry sparkling
    wine
1 cup heavy cream
Strawberries marinated in slightly sweetened brandy,
    to serve

In a heavy-based saucepan, dissolve the sugar in
1¼ cups water. Bring to the boil and boil until the
temperature reaches 230–234°F. Leave to cool.

Stir the orange juice, brandy and champagne into
the syrup. Pour the mixture into a container. Cover
and freeze until just becoming firm. Beat well in a
bowl.

Whip the cream in a bowl until soft peaks form. Fold
the cream into the champagne ice. Return to the
container, cover and freeze until firm.

About 30 minutes before serving, transfer the ice
cream to the refrigerator. Serve with the marinated
strawberries.

Serves 6

Serving suggestion
*Freeze in a ring mold and fill the center with
strawberries steeped in brandy. Sprinkle lightly with
sugar.*

Dessert suggestion
*Encase in Iced Apricot Mousse (page 25). Decorate the
turned-out dessert with warmed apricot-brandy-
flavored whipped cream and slivered almonds.*

Liqueur Cream Ice

1 cup sugar
Juice of 1 lemon
⅓ cup any kind of liqueur
⅔ cup cream, whipped
Candied fruits soaked in cognac, to serve

In a heavy-based saucepan, dissolve the sugar in
2 cups water. Bring to the boil and boil until the
temperature reaches 234°F. Set aside to cool.

Stir the strained lemon juice into the syrup. Pour
into a container, cover and freeze to the slushy stage.

Stir the liqueur into the frozen mixture and fold in
the cream. Return to the freezer and freeze until firm.

About 40 minutes before serving, transfer the ice to
the refrigerator. Serve each portion topped by candied
fruits soaked in cognac.

Serves 4

Serving suggestion
Freeze in small Chocolate Cases and serve as petits
fours.*

Dessert suggestion
*Layer with a similar-flavored ice cream or sorbet, or
one with a complementary or contrasting flavor:
Cointreau with Orange Ice Cream (page 85), crème de
cacao with Mint Sorbet (page 71), Amaretto with
Apricot Ice Cream (page 24) or Chocolate Ice Cream
(page 44).*

Marsala and Chocolate Ice Cream

1¼ cups sugar
½ cup slivered almonds, toasted
5 squares bitter chocolate
⅓ cup marsala
3 egg whites
2 cups cream, whipped
Few drops of almond extract

In a heavy-based saucepan, dissolve ½ cup sugar in
2 tablespoons water. Bring to the boil and boil until
pale golden at the edges. Shake the pan until the syrup
is evenly browned then quickly stir in the almonds and
pour onto an oiled surface to cool. When the praline is
cold put it in a thick plastic bag and hit with a rolling
pin until broken into small pieces.

Melt the chocolate in the marsala in a bowl set over
a pan of hot water. Then leave to cool slightly.

Whip the egg whites in a bowl until stiff. Gradually
whip in the remaining sugar and continue whipping
until the meringue is stiff and glossy. Fold in the cream
with the almond extract and praline. Carefully fold in
the chocolate to give a marbled effect.

Pour the mixture into a container. Cover and freeze
until firm.

About 10 minutes before serving, transfer the ice
cream to the refrigerator.

Serves 8

Dessert suggestion
*Freeze in a cake or loaf pan lined with plain or
hazelnut Meringues* around a center of Raspberry
Sorbet (page 104). Serve with crème fraîche.*

Dessert Wine Granita

½ cup sugar
½ bottle (35 cl) good-quality dessert wine
Juice of ½ an orange
Juice of ½ a lemon
Mint leaves, for decoration

In a heavy-based saucepan, dissolve the sugar in
½ cup water. Bring to the boil and boil for 1 minute.
Leave to cool.

Stir the wine and fruit juices into the syrup. Pour the mixture into a container. Cover and freeze until just firm, occasionally forking through the mixture to form small granules. Serve straight from the freezer, decorating each portion with mint leaves.

Serves 5–6

Additional recipes using wines and liqueurs:
Apricot and Wine Ice Cream (page 23), 'Irish Coffee' Banana Ice Cream (page 28), Ginger Wine Sorbet (page 60), Grapefruit and Vermouth Granita (page 67), Pear Ice Cream (page 92), Pistachio and Green Chartreuse Ice Cream (page 101), Rhubarb and Ginger Wine Ice Cream (page 110), Black Currant, Rose Petal and Champagne Roll (page 136).

Old-Fashioned Favorites

The ices in this section are based on old-fashioned recipes, with ingredients like elderberries and quinces. They include cassata – a traditional favorite.

Crabapple Ice Cream

2 pounds crabapples
1½ cups sugar
Juice of 1 large juicy orange
1¼ cups cream, whipped

Cut the crabapples in half and remove the stalks. Put them in a large saucepan, just cover with water and simmer until soft, adding a little more water if necessary. Pass the crabapples through a strainer.

In a heavy-based saucepan, dissolve the sugar in ⅔ cup water. Bring to the boil and boil for 3 minutes. Set aside to cool.

Add the syrup to the crabapples with the orange juice – taste and adjust the level of sweetness and orange, if necessary.

Pour the mixture into a container. Cover and freeze to the slushy stage. Beat well in a bowl.

Fold the cream into the frozen mixture. Return to the container, cover and freeze until firm.

About 30 minutes before serving, transfer the ice cream to the refrigerator.

Serves 4–5

Serving suggestion
Serve in Gingersnap Baskets*. Decorate with ginger-wine-flavored cream and slivered almonds.

Quince Ice Cream

2 pounds quinces, peeled, cored and chopped
1½ cups sugar
Juice of 1 orange
1¼ cups whipping or heavy cream

Put the quinces, sugar and just enough water to cover in a saucepan and cook gently for about 40 minutes or until soft, adding more water if necessary. Pass the quinces through a strainer – there should be about 2½ cups purée.

Mix in the orange juice and pour into a container. Cover and freeze to the slushy stage. Beat well in a bowl. Whip the cream in a bowl until soft peaks form. Fold into the purée. Return to the container, cover and freeze until firm.

About 30 minutes before serving, transfer the ice cream to the refrigerator.

Serves 5–6

Dessert suggestion
Make a bombe or freeze in a cake or loaf pan with a jacket of finely chopped walnuts Caramelized* with sugar and orange zest, followed by a layer of the ice cream around a center of Iced Whiskey Syllabub (page 116).

Cider Sorbet

1 cup sugar
⅓ cup lemon juice
2¼ cups apple purée
⅔ cup hard cider
Mint leaves, for decoration

In a heavy-based saucepan, dissolve the sugar in 1 cup water. Bring to the boil and boil for about a minute or until the temperature reaches 215°F. Strain in the lemon juice and leave to cool.

Blend the apple purée and cider into the syrup. Pour the mixture into a container, cover and freeze until firm, beating well 3 times at 45-minute intervals.

About 40 minutes before serving, transfer the sorbet to the refrigerator. Decorate each portion with mint leaves.

Serves 6–8

Serving suggestion
Serve in Almond Tuiles* with slices of apple poached in calvados or brandy. Decorate with fine strips of orange peel.

Dessert suggestion
Encase in Apple Cream Ice (page 21). Decorate the top of the turned-out dessert with slices of red-skinned apples and surround the base with calvados-flavored whipped cream and chopped walnuts.

Crystallized Violet Ice Cream

⅓ cup sugar
4 egg yolks
2 tablespoons crystallized violet petals
2 cups cream, whipped
1–2 tablespoons strawberry eau-de-vie (fraise)

For decoration
Whipped cream
Crystallized violet petals

Dissolve the sugar in 4 tablespoons water in a heavy-based pan. Bring to the boil and boil until the syrup reaches 230°F.

Beat the egg yolks in a bowl until very light and thick. Gradually whisk in the hot syrup. Continue beating until cold.

Fold in the crystallized violet petals, cream and fraise.

Pour the mixture into a container. Cover and freeze until firm.

About 20 minutes before serving transfer the ice cream to the refrigerator. Decorate with whipped cream and crystallized violets.

Serves 4

Dessert suggestion
Freeze in a fancy mold. Pipe whipped cream around the base and top of the turned-out dessert and decorate with fresh or crystallized roses.

Flavor variation
Use 2 tablespoons crystallized rose petals instead of violet petals; garnish with crystallized rose petals.

Elderberry Water Ice

¾ cup sugar
1 pound elderberries
Squeeze of lemon juice
Sparkling sweet elderberry wine, for serving

In a heavy-based saucepan, dissolve the sugar in 1¼ cups water. Bring to the boil and boil for 5 minutes. Stir in the elderberries and simmer until tender.

Purée the elderberries and pass through a fine strainer into a bowl. Strain in the lemon juice to taste. Chill for 30 minutes. Pour into a container, cover and freeze until firm, beating 3 times at 45-minute intervals.

About 30 minutes before serving, transfer the water ice to the refrigerator. Pour some sparkling sweet elderberry wine over each portion as it is served.

Serves 4–6

Serving suggestion
Scoop into tall, slim, frosted glasses and trickle over a little elderberry wine. Serve with Meringue Fingers*.

Dessert suggestion
Ripple with Raspberry Ice Cream (page 104) and cover the sides and top of the turned-out dessert with Sponge Fingers*. Surround the base with decorative swirls of whipped cream and raspberries.

Pecan Pie Ice Cream

3 eggs, separated
⅓ cup sugar
4 tablespoons sweet butter, melted
⅔ cup milk
1 cup light corn syrup
1 cup roughly chopped pecans
Few drops of vanilla extract

Put the egg yolks and sugar in a bowl and beat together until light. Place the bowl over a pan of hot water and cook, stirring constantly, until the mixture thickens slightly. Do not allow to boil. Remove from the heat and beat in the butter.

Heat the milk and corn syrup in a saucepan until just beginning to bubble around the edges. Pour the milk and syrup onto the egg mixture, stirring constantly. Leave the mixture to cool, stirring occasionally.

Pour the mixture into a shallow container, cover and freeze until just becoming firm around the edges.

Tip the semi-frozen mixture into a bowl and beat well. In another bowl, whip the egg whites until stiff but not dry, then fold into the corn syrup mixture with the pecans and vanilla extract. Spoon back into the container, cover and freeze until firm.

About 30 minutes before serving, transfer the ice cream to the refrigerator.

Serves 4

Cassata

1¼ cups Vanilla Ice Cream (page 123), slightly softened
1¼ cups Strawberry Ice Cream (page 121) or Raspberry Ice Cream (page 104), slightly softened
2 cups Pistachio Frozen Custard (page 101), slightly softened
2 tablespoons chopped candied cherries
2 tablespoons chopped candied angelica
2 tablespoons slivered almonds
2 tablespoons chopped candied peel
Candied fruits, for decoration

Chill a 5 cup mold. Spoon in the vanilla ice cream and smooth it evenly over the base and sides. Cover and freeze until firm. Then smooth the strawberry or raspberry ice cream evenly over the base and sides of the frozen lining. Cover and freeze until firm.

Fold the cherries, angelica, almonds and candied peel into the pistachio frozen custard and spoon into the center of the mold. Cover and return to the freezer for at least 6 hours.

About 35–40 minutes before serving turn the cassata out onto a chilled plate and leave in the refrigerator. Serve decorated with candied fruits.

Serves 6

Special Occasions

Different-flavored ices can be combined with each other, and with a variety of ingredients, to make spectacular desserts – with the added advantage that, impressive as they are, most can be prepared well ahead of time.

I have included dessert suggestions as well as suggestions for serving with many of the recipes in the first part of the book. The ones that follow are rather more elaborate, and include some of my favorite desserts for special occasions.

Ginger Freezer Cake

1 × 1 pound loaf moist gingerbread
4 tablespoons ginger marmalade
1 tablespoon advocaat, optional
1¼ cups cream, whipped
Slices of candied fruits, for decoration

Cut the cake horizontally into 4 even slices. Fold the marmalade and advocaat, if using, into the cream then sandwich the cake back together with about half of the mixture. Place the cake on a freezer tray and spread the remaining cream mixture over the top and sides.

Freeze, then pack in a rigid container if storing for any length of time.

About 20 minutes before serving, place the cake on a cold plate. Decorate with the candied fruit to serve.

Serves 6–8

Coffee Ice Cream Slice

For the meringue
3 egg whites
¾ cup sugar
½ teaspoon ground cinnamon

For the ice cream
6 ounces full fat cream cheese
⅓ cup sugar
2 tablespoons coffee extract
1¼ cups milk
1 tablespoon lime juice

For decoration
Marrons glacés
Bitter Chocolate Sauce*

Make the meringue mixture according to the recipe on page 150, folding the cinnamon in at the end. Line cookie sheets with foil or waxpaper. Spread the meringue into 3 rectangles, 9 × 4 inches each, on the cookie sheets. Bake at 275°F for 2–3 hours until dry and crisp. Cool on a wire rack.

To make the ice cream, put the cream cheese, sugar and coffee extract in a bowl and blend until smooth. Gradually beat in the milk and lime juice. Pour the mixture into a container, cover and freeze until just becoming firm.

On a cookie sheet sandwich the meringue layers together with the ice cream and return to the freezer until firm. Wrap with foil or freezer paper, pack to protect the meringue and leave until required.

Just before serving, unwrap the meringue and decorate with the marrons glacés, whole or chopped as desired, and trickle a thin stream of chocolate sauce over the top.

Serves 6–8

Pineapple and Coconut Macaroon Cake

For the macaroons
½ cup creamed coconut
¾ cup ground almonds
½ cup sugar
2 egg whites

For the ice cream
1 medium-sized fresh pineapple
4 tablespoons kirsch
½ cup sugar
2 egg whites
1 cup heavy cream

For decoration
Fresh pineapple
Whipped cream
Toasted slivered almonds

To make the macaroons, beat the creamed coconut, almonds and sugar together in a bowl. Mix in the egg whites to form a stiff, sticky mixture. Line a cookie sheet with rice paper or waxpaper. Spread the mixture into four 6½ inch circles on the lined baking sheet. Put in the oven and bake at 375°F for about 12 minutes until lightly browned. Transfer the macaroons to a wire rack and leave to cool.

Peel the pineapple. Remove the core then reduce the flesh to 2 cups purée, adding a little water, if necessary. Add the kirsch and leave in a cool place to marinate for a few hours.

Dissolve the sugar in ¼ cup water and any juice leftover when the pineapple is peeled in a small heavy-based saucepan. Bring to the boil and boil for 5 minutes.

Whip the egg whites in a bowl to a stiff white foam then gradually whip in the hot syrup and continue whipping until cool.

In another bowl, whip the cream to a consistency similar to the meringue. Lightly fold the cream into the pineapple purée followed by the meringue.

Pour the mixture into a container. Cover and place briefly in the freezer.

Trim the 4 macaroons to fit into a loose-bottomed 6½ inch cake pan. Press one into the bottom of the tin and cover with one-third of the pineapple mixture. Continue with alternate layers of macaroons and pineapple mixture then cover and freeze until firm.

About 30–45 minutes before serving, push up the bottom of the cake pan – if necessary, run a knife around the inside of the pan – and when the whole cake is released remove it from the base with a knife and place on a cold plate. Decorate with pineapple, cream and almonds and leave in the refrigerator.

Serves 8–10

Chocolate-Coated Coffee Ice Cream Balls

1¼ cups milk
⅓ cup oatmeal, toasted
⅔ cup sour cream
¼ pound full fat cream cheese
½ cup sugar
3 egg yolks, lightly beaten
2 teaspoons instant coffee granules
1 tablespoon Irish cream liqueur
¼ pound semi-sweet chocolate

Put the milk and oatmeal in a saucepan and bring to the boil. Simmer gently for 4–5 minutes. Remove from the heat.

Blend the sour cream, cheese and sugar together in a bowl. Gradually stir in the oatmeal mixture. Beat in the egg yolks, coffee granules and liqueur. Leave to cool completely.

Pour the mixture into a container. Cover and freeze until firm.

Soften the ice cream for 10–15 minutes at room temperature then scoop out small balls onto a foil-lined cookie sheet. Return to the freezer for at least 4 hours or until hard.

Meanwhile, break the chocolate into a small bowl, add 5 tablespoons water and melt over a pan of simmering water until smooth. Leave to cool and thicken. Dip each ice cream ball into the melted chocolate, shake off any excess and return to the cookie sheet. Freeze for at least 30 minutes until set.

About 10 minutes before serving, transfer to the refrigerator.

Serves 4–6

Cranberry Snowballs

1 egg white
1¼ cups crème fraîche
2 tablespoons milk
1½ cups bought cranberry sauce or thick, sweetened homemade cranberry sauce
¾ cup confectioners' sugar
¼ cup fresh cranberries
2 teaspoons sugar
4 tablespoons brandy or whiskey, warmed
Cigars Russe*, for serving

Whip the egg white in a small bowl until stiff but not dry. In another bowl whip the crème fraîche with the milk until soft peaks form. Fold the cranberry sauce and confectioners' sugar into the cream followed by the egg white. Pour into a container, cover and freeze until just becoming firm.

Meanwhile, cook the cranberries in 4 tablespoons water by the method for Cranberry Ice Cream on page 55. After the second heating remove the cranberries from the liquid with a slotted spoon and put into a bowl with the sugar and brandy or whiskey. Cover and leave to cool.

Divide the cranberry cream into 4 pieces and roll each into a smooth ball inside a piece of freezerproof foil, enclosing a quarter of the marinated cranberries in the center. Place in the freezer until firm.

About 30 minutes before serving, transfer the balls to the refrigerator. Carefully peel away the foil and serve with Cigars Russe*.

Serves 4

Black Currant, Rose Petal and Champagne Roll

3 egg quantity Sponge Cake*
Sugar
Champagne Ice Cream (page 132)
Rose Petal Sorbet (page 70)
Black Currant Ice Cream (page 32) or Blueberry Ice Cream (page 35)

For decoration
Whipped cream
Rose petals
Frosted* black currants or blueberries
Frosted* black currant leaves

Spoon the whipped sponge into a greased and lined 9 × 13 inch shallow cake pan, smooth the surface and bake in an oven preheated to 375°F for about 8 minutes.

Meanwhile, place a sheet of waxpaper on a warmed, dampened dish-towel and sprinkle it liberally with sugar.

Turn the baked cake out onto the sugared paper, carefully peel away the lining paper and quickly roll up the cake leaving the sugared paper inside. Leave to cool.

Leave the champagne ice cream at room temperature for about 25 minutes, the sorbet for 10 minutes.

Unroll the cake and remove the waxpaper. Spread the cake with the sorbet. Spoon the champagne ice cream lengthwise down the center (if a batch is made for this dessert, any left over can be used for decoration) and roll the cake up. Place the roll in the freezer for 1 hour.

Leave the black currant or blueberry ice cream at room temperature for 35 minutes. Spread the black currant or blueberry ice cream over the roll and return it to the freezer for 30 minutes.

Decorate the roll with whipped cream, any remaining champagne ice cream, rose petals or crystallized roses, and frosted fruit and leaves.

Serves 6–8

Iced Plum Pudding

1 cup mixed golden raisins and raisins
½ cup currants
3 tablespoons each chopped mixed candied peel and
  candied cherries
4 tablespoons brandy
½ pound full fat cream cheese
⅓ cup sugar
½ teaspoon ground mixed spice
1¼ cups milk

For decoration
Whipped cream
Candied cherries

Soak the fruits and peel in the brandy for 4 hours or more.

Put the cheese in a bowl and beat until smooth. Beat in the sugar and spice. Gradually beat in the milk, taking care to keep the mixture smooth. Fold in the fruits and brandy. Spoon the mixture into a container. Cover and freeze until firm.

About 20 minutes before serving, transfer the ice cream to the refrigerator.

Serves 4–5

Grapefruit Crunch Sandwich

1 tablespoon gelatin
1 pound soft cheese/ricotta
¾ cup concentrated frozen grapefruit juice, defrosted
⅓ cup sugar
1¼ cups heavy cream, whipped
¼ cup crushed graham crackers
¼ cup crushed ginger cookies
4 tablespoons butter, melted
2 tablespoons light brown sugar

For decoration
Mint leaves
Knots tied with strips of grapefruit peel

Dissolve the gelatin in 3 tablespoons water in a bowl placed over a pan of hot water. Set aside to cool.

Put the cheese in a bowl and beat until smooth. Gradually beat in the grapefruit juice and sugar. Blend in the cooled gelatin. Fold the cream into the grapefruit mixture. Spoon half the mixture into a lightly oiled 8 inch cake pan, preferably a loose-bottomed one. Place this briefly in the freezer.

Mix the cookie crumbs with the melted butter and brown sugar and leave to cool. Press the crumbs evenly over the top of the grapefruit mixture in the pan and cover with the remaining grapefruit mixture.

Cover and freeze until firm.

About 30 minutes before serving turn the sandwich out onto a cold plate and leave in the refrigerator. Just before serving decorate with mint leaves and grapefruit peel knots.

Serves 8

Flavor variation
Use frozen concentrated orange juice instead of grapefruit juice.

Blackberry and Orange Layer Cake

For the blackberry ice
¾ cup sugar
2 tablespoons rosewater
1 pound blackberries
1 egg white

For the orange butter
½ cup sweet butter, softened
½ cup sugar
Finely grated zest of 2 oranges
Juice of 1 orange or 3 tablespoons orange liqueur
½ cup hazelnuts, toasted and finely ground
½ cup heavy cream
Butter
Approximately 24 Sponge Fingers*
Juice of 2 oranges
¼ cup roughly crushed Meringues*

To make the blackberry ice, boil the sugar in 1 cup water in a heavy-based saucepan for 10 minutes. Remove from the heat and stir in the rosewater. Leave to cool.

Strain the blackberries and add the fruit to the syrup. Pour into a container, cover and freeze until just becoming slushy. Beat well in a bowl.

Whip the egg white in a small bowl until stiff. Fold it into the blackberry mixture.

Meanwhile, make the orange butter: beat the butter and sugar in a bowl until fluffy. Beat in the orange zest, juice or liqueur and hazelnuts. Whip the cream until it stands in soft peaks and fold into the butter.

Thickly butter the side of a 5 cup charlotte mold or bowl. Dip the sponge fingers in the orange juice and arrange them around the sides and over the bottom of the mold. Cover the base with half the orange butter. Spoon half of the slushy blackberry ice over the orange butter and cover with the crushed meringues. Place in the freezer until the ice is firm.

Cover the ice with the remaining orange butter. Place in the freezer until firm, then spoon in the remaining blackberry ice. Cover and freeze overnight.

About 15 minutes before serving, trim the ends of the sponge fingers, invert the mold onto a cold plate and leave in the refrigerator.

Serves 6

Black Forest Bombe

For the chocolate ice cream
1/4 pound semi-sweet chocolate, broken into small
  pieces
6 ounces cream cheese, softened
1/2 cup sugar
1 cup milk
2/3 cup heavy cream

For the cherry ice cream
3 1/2 ounces cream cheese, softened
3 tablespoons sugar
1/4 cup milk
1/4 cup heavy cream
Approximately 1/2 pound can cherry pie filling

For the plain ice cream
3 1/2 ounces cream cheese, softened
3 tablespoons sugar
1/2 cup milk
2 tablespoons heavy cream

For decoration
Whipped cream
Black cherries, pitted
Chocolate Curls*

To make the chocolate ice cream, melt the chocolate in a bowl set over a pan of hot water. Leave to cool. Beat the cream cheese and sugar together in a bowl until smooth then beat in the cooled chocolate. Gradually beat in the milk until evenly blended. In another bowl, whip the cream until soft peaks form then fold into the chocolate mixture. Pour into a container, cover and freeze until just becoming firm.

To make the cherry ice cream, beat the cream cheese and sugar together in a bowl until smooth. Gradually beat in the milk. In another bowl, whip the cream until soft peaks form then fold into the cheese mixture. Lastly, fold in about half of the pie filling. Spoon into a container, cover and freeze until just becoming firm.

To make the plain ice cream, beat the cream cheese and sugar together in a bowl until smooth then gradually beat in the milk. In another bowl, whip the cream until soft peaks form then fold into the cheese mixture. Pour into a container, cover and freeze until just becoming firm.

Assemble the bombe by lining a cold 6–7 inch loose-bottomed cake pan with the chocolate ice cream, making sure there is an even layer over the base and sides. Cover and return to the freezer until firm then line with the cherry ice cream and return to the freezer. Fill the center with the plain ice cream swirled with the remaining pie filling. Cover and freeze until firm. About 20–30 minutes before serving, turn the bombe out onto a cold plate and leave in the refrigerator. Decorate with the cream, cherries and chocolate curls.

Serves 8

140

Iced Peach Charlotte

1/2 cup sugar
5 peaches, halved and pitted
3 tablespoons brandy
Approximately 20 Sponge Fingers*
Sherry
2 cups whipping or heavy cream
1/2 cup shredded coconut
2 tablespoons lightly toasted slivered almonds
Whipped cream, for decoration

In a heavy-based saucepan, dissolve the sugar in 1 1/4 cups water. Add the peaches and poach until tender. Remove the peaches with a slotted spoon and set aside on a plate. Return the pan to the heat and boil the syrup until reduced by two-thirds. Remove from the heat and stir in the brandy.

Line a charlotte mold with the sponge fingers and sprinkle them with sherry.

Put the cream and the brandy syrup in a bowl and whip until soft peaks form. Peel and chop the peaches and fold into the cream with the coconut and almonds.

Spoon the mixture into the mold, cover and freeze until firm. About 15 minutes before serving, unmold the charlotte onto a cold plate. Decorate with whipped cream.

Serves 6

Apricot and Hazelnut Meringue Cake

For the meringue
4 egg whites
1 1/8 cups sugar
2–3 drops vanilla extract
1/3 cup ground hazelnuts

For the filling
1/3 cup dried apricots soaked in 1 cup strained tea
Long strip lemon peel
1/4 cup sugar
1 1/4 cups crème fraîche (whipped) or whipped cream

For decoration
Whipped cream
Chocolate-covered almonds or Chocolate Curls*
Apricot Sauce*

Prepare the meringue according to the recipe on page 150, adding the nuts with the last of the sugar. Mark two 8 inch circles on waxpaper and place on a cookie sheet. Spread the meringue over the circles. Put the cookie sheet in the oven and bake at 275°F for 50 minutes.

Remove the cookie sheet from the oven. Peel away the paper and leave the meringues to cool on a rack.

To make the filling, put the apricots and their soaking liquid with the lemon peel in a saucepan and cook for about 15 minutes until tender. Remove the peel, and purée the apricots into a bowl. Stir in the sugar and leave to become cold. Fold the crème fraîche or cream into the apricot purée.

Place one of the meringues upsidedown on a freezerproof tray or plate and spread with the apricot cream. Cover with the other meringue and place in the freezer. When firm, cover to protect the meringue from being broken and return to the freezer.

About 10 minutes before serving, decorate with the whipped cream and chocolate-covered almonds or curls. Leave in the refrigerator. Serve the apricot sauce separately.

Serves 6

Mincemeat Ice Cream

1¹/₂ cups mincemeat
¹/₄ cup brandy
1¹/₄ cups cream, whipped
2 egg whites

Mix the mincemeat with the brandy in a bowl and fold into the cream. In another bowl, whip the egg whites until stiff but not dry. Carefully fold them into the mincemeat cream. Spoon the mixture into a container. Cover and freeze until firm.

About 20 minutes before serving, transfer the ice cream to the refrigerator.

Serves 4

Serving suggestion
Accompany each serving with a sprig of holly.

Lemon Icicle

Butter
¼ cup crushed ginger cookies
3 eggs, separated
½ cup sugar
1¼ cups heavy cream
Finely grated zest and juice of 2 lemons

For decoration
Twisted lemon slices
Whipped cream

Fairly thickly butter a 1½ quart loaf pan and sprinkle with the cookie crumbs to coat evenly.

Whip the egg whites in a bowl until very stiff. Gradually add the sugar, whipping well after each addition, until the mixture is very thick.

In another bowl, whip the cream with the egg yolks until thick and light. Carefully fold the egg yolk mixture into the egg whites with the lemon zest and juice. Pour into the crumb-lined pan, cover and freeze until firm.

About 10 minutes before serving the dessert turn out onto a cold plate and leave in the refrigerator. Decorate with twisted lemon slices and whipped cream just before serving.

Serves 6–8

Chocolate Truffle and Hazelnut Ring

3 cups light cream
1 cup sugar
7 egg yolks, beaten
1 cup cocoa
¾ cup whipping cream
6 ounces good-quality semi-sweet chocolate
¼ cup praline or other nut liqueur
2 tablespoons chopped, toasted hazelnuts
1 tablespoon Grand Marnier

For decoration
Whipped cream
Chocolate Curls*

In a heavy-based saucepan, gently heat the light cream and sugar until the sugar has dissolved. Bring to the boil, remove from the heat and leave to cool for 5 minutes. Pour the cream onto the egg yolks whipping constantly. Return the mixture to the rinsed pan and cook over a gentle heat, stirring constantly, until the custard thickens but do not allow it to boil. Remove from the heat and stir in the cocoa, leave to cool then chill well.

Pour the custard into a container. Cover and freeze until just becoming firm.

Warm the whipping cream in a saucepan. Add the chocolate and stir until it has melted. Mix in the nut liqueur, hazelnuts and Grand Marnier then cool completely.

Line the bottom of a 5 cup ring mold with three-quarters of the chocolate ice cream. With a small spoon push the ice cream up the sides of the mold leaving a deep groove in the center. If necessary, place in the freezer for a few minutes to firm up. Pour the cream and hazelnut mixture into the groove and spread the remaining ice cream over the top. Cover and freeze until firm.

About 30 minutes before serving, turn the ice cream out onto a cold plate and leave in the refrigerator. Decorate with whipped cream and chocolate curls just before serving.

Serves 8–10

Chestnut and Chocolate Bombe

2 cups Chocolate Ice Cream (page 44), slightly softened
⅔ cup chopped canned whole chestnuts in syrup, drained
½ cup canned, sweetened chestnut purée
1 tablespoon brandy
¾ cup heavy cream
1 small egg white

For decoration
Whipped cream
Candied orange or lemon peel, roughly chopped
Marrons glâcés, sliced

Spoon the chocolate ice cream into a cold 1 quart bombe mold or bowl, smoothing it into an even layer over the base and sides to a depth of about ¾ inch using the back of a metal spoon. Cover and freeze until firm.

Press the chopped chestnuts into the base and sides of the ice cream-lined mold, cover and return to the freezer.

Mix the chestnut purée and brandy together until well blended. Whip the cream in a bowl until it stands in soft peaks. Gently fold into the chestnut purée. Whip the egg white in a small bowl until stiff but not dry. Carefully fold it into the chestnut cream. Spoon the chestnut cream into the mold, cover and freeze until firm.

About 30 minutes before serving turn the bombe out onto a cold serving plate and leave in the coldest part of the refrigerator. Just before serving decorate with whipped cream, candied orange or lemon peel and slices of marrons glâcés.

Serves 5–6

Iced Lemon Soufflé Surprise

For the filling
¼ cup sugar
¼ cup lemon juice
3 tablespoons sweet butter
2 large egg yolks
1 tablespoon finely grated lemon zest

For the soufflé
5 egg yolks
⅔ cup sugar
⅓ cup lemon juice
1 tablespoon finely grated lemon zest
1¼ cups heavy cream

First make the filling. Put all the ingredients together in a bowl set over a pan of hot water. Beat for about 8 minutes until the mixture is thick enough to coat the back of a spoon but do not let it boil. Leave to cool before chilling until firm.

Tie strips of double thickness waxpaper or foil around 6 individual freezerproof soufflé dishes, so that they form collars over and above the tops of the dishes.

To make the soufflé, in a bowl beat the egg yolks briefly. Put the sugar, lemon juice and ⅓ cup water in a saucepan and stir to dissolve. Add the lemon zest and bring to the boil. Beat the hot syrup into the egg yolks. Put the bowl over a pan of hot water, beating constantly, until the mixture is very light and thickened. Leave to cool, stirring occasionally.

Whip 1 cup of the cream until soft peaks form. Fold into the cold soufflé. Divide half of this mixture between the prepared dishes.

Whip the remaining cream until soft peaks form. Reserve and keep chilled 2 tablespoons of the lemon filling. Fold the cream into the remaining filling and divide between the soufflés. Cover with the remaining soufflé mixture, then cover and freeze until firm.

Spoon the reserved filling into a piping bag fitted with a small star nozzle (freeze the mixture briefly if it is too runny to pipe). Pipe a star or rosette in the center of each soufflé (if these are frozen solid leave them in the refrigerator for 15 minutes first).

Serves 6

Orange Sorbet in a Chocolate Case

Oil
½ pound semi-sweet chocolate, chopped
1 cup sugar
Finely grated zest of 1 orange
1⅔ cups orange juice
4 tablespoons lemon juice
1 large egg white

For decoration
Strips of orange peel
Whipped cream

Liberally oil a 1 quart mold and leave it upsidedown to drain. Put the mold in the refrigerator to chill.

Melt the chocolate in a bowl set over a pan of hot water. As soon as it has melted pour it into the mold. Tip and rotate the mold to coat the inside evenly and completely. Put the mold in a bowl of crushed ice and tip and rotate it so that it remains evenly coated until it has set. Return the mold to the refrigerator.

In a heavy-based saucepan, dissolve the sugar in ⅔ cup water. Bring to the boil and boil for 5 minutes. Remove from the heat, stir in the orange zest and fruit juices and leave to cool.

Pour the mixture into a container. Cover and freeze until just becoming firm. Beat well in a bowl.

Lightly whip the egg white in a small bowl. Fold it into the frozen mixture. Spoon the sorbet into the chocolate-lined mold. Cover and freeze until firm. Just before serving turn the dessert out onto a cold plate and decorate with strips of orange peel and whipped cream.

Serves 4–6

To reduce your sugar intake
Replace the sugar with half the quantity of **fructose** or with an **artificial sweetener**, provided the recipe does not call for a sugar syrup. Normally, 3–4 artificial sweeteners are the equivalent of 2 tablespoons sugar but always check that you have the right degree of sweetness. Artificial sweeteners must be added to custard-based ice creams after the custard has cooled.

Creating Desserts

Delicious on its own, ice cream can be even more delectable if it is served with a flourish. Some serving ideas are simple – just sprinkle the ice with a topping of your choice. Others, using a specially made sauce or accompaniments like Cigars Russe* and Almond Tuiles* involve rather more preparation. And, of course, there are almost endless combinations of different-flavored ices, with cookies, meringues, cakes and so on, in plain or shaped containers.

This chapter includes the sauces, accompaniments and decorations called for in the serving and dessert suggestions that follow the main recipes, as well as basic recipes for meringues, crêpes, choux pastry, etc, plus a description of the techniques involved in creating iced cakes and desserts and suggestions for unusual containers.

Coupes and Sundaes

Among the simplest of ice cream desserts, these include a number of classic dishes:

Poire Belle Hèlene: vanilla ice cream, pears and hot chocolate sauce.

Pêche Melba: vanilla ice cream, peaches and raspberry sauce.

Pêche Cardinale: strawberry ice cream, peaches and red currant jelly.

Champagne Charlie: champagne ice cream, macaroons with champagne poured over.

Café Liègoise: coffee ice cream in a tall glass topped with a large swirl of whipped cream.

Alternatively, think up your own combinations to suit the ingredients you have and the occasion.

Simple Toppings

The following suggestions involve little or no preparation.

Chopped or slivered, plain or toasted nuts
Shredded coconut: color green or pink, if desired, by putting into a jar, adding some coloring and shaking vigorously, then leaving to dry before using
Chocolate toppings: grated semi-sweet chocolate; crumbled flake bars; chopped chocolate
Cocoa or plain or malted drink powders
Candied fruit, chopped or whole peanut brittle; peppermint; butterscotch or caramel
Crushed cookies: ginger cookies, macaroons, graham crackers
Crushed meringues
Fresh herbs, leaves and flowers
Crystallized roses and violets

Whipped cream: flavor to taste with liqueurs, orange flower water and so on. For a peppermint flavor, add peppermint oil or crème de menthe to taste

Fruit zests and peels: grated; cut into long, fine strips; cut into shapes with aspic cutters or the point of a sharp, small knife
Marrons glâcés, chopped or sliced
Chocolate or coffee-covered almonds, or any small, candy decorations

Sauces

The right sauce enhances and complements the flavor and texture of an ice. Spoon it over, to trickle down the sides, or arrange it around the ice like the frame of a picture. The sauce can be hot, warm or cold – but should never swamp the ice cream itself.

Butterscotch Sauce

4 tablespoons sweet butter, diced
1/4 cup light brown sugar
1/4 cup light corn syrup
2/3 cup milk
Squeeze of lemon juice, optional

Heat the butter, sugar and syrup in a heavy-based saucepan over low heat, stirring, until the sugar has dissolved. Bring to the boil and boil until the temperature reaches about 240°F. Cool slightly then stir in the milk and leave to cool completely. Add a squeeze of lemon juice to taste, if liked.

Serves 4–5

Nutty Butterscotch Sauce

Add 2 tablespoons chopped walnuts, almonds, hazelnuts or peanuts with the milk.

Black Cherry Sauce

1/2 cup black cherry jam
Knob of butter
1 tablespoon kirsch or brandy
Squeeze of lemon juice

Put the jam, butter and 1 1/4 cups hot water in a saucepan and heat until evenly mixed and syrupy. Remove from the heat and stir in the kirsch or brandy and a squeeze of lemon juice to taste. Serve as it is or purée in a blender or food processor for a smooth sauce.

Serves 4–6

Alcoholic Cherry Sauce

For a spectacular cherry sauce, warm the fruit from a 1 pound can of pitted black cherries with about half of the juice, pour 2 tablespoons brandy over and ignite. When the flames have subsided add 1 tablespoon kirsch and serve at once.

Bitter Chocolate Sauce

¼ pound good-quality semi-sweet chocolate, chopped
1 teaspoon sugar
6 tablespoons milk
2 tablespoons whipping cream
1½ tablespoons sweet butter

Melt the chocolate in a bowl set over a pan of hot water. Put the sugar, milk, cream and butter in a saucepan and stir to dissolve. Bring to the boil and stir it into the melted chocolate. Pour this mixture back into the pan and bring to the boil, stirring. Pour it back into the bowl and leave to cool, stirring occasionally.

Serves 4–6

Hot Chocolate Sauce

¼ pound semi-sweet chocolate, chopped
2 tablespoons confectioners' sugar
1 tablespoon sweet butter, chopped

Place all the ingredients in a bowl with ¼ cup hot water and place over a pan of hot water. Heat until the chocolate has melted, stir well and serve hot or warm.

Serves 4

Coffee Sauce

½ cup sugar
1¼ cups strong black coffee
2 tablespoons coffee liqueur, optional

Dissolve the sugar in 2 tablespoons water in a heavy-based saucepan. Bring to the boil and boil until the mixture becomes a light golden brown. Stir in the coffee to dissolve the caramel and simmer for a few minutes until it becomes slightly syrupy. Remove from the heat and stir in the liqueur, if using.

Serves 4

Hot Fudge Sauce

¾ cup whipping or heavy cream
4 tablespoons sweet butter, chopped
⅓ cup brown sugar

Heat the cream and butter in a heavy-based saucepan over low heat until the butter has melted, stirring constantly. Stir in the sugar and continue stirring until the sugar has dissolved and the mixture comes to the boil. Boil for 2 minutes until thick and glossy.

Serves 4–6

Burnt Honey Sauce

1 cup sugar
½ cup clear honey

In a heavy-based saucepan, dissolve the sugar in 4 tablespoons water. Bring to the boil and boil for 5 minutes or until it becomes a deep brown caramel. Off the heat stir in another 4 tablespoons water, taking care as the mixture will splatter. Cook for another 1–2 minutes until the temperature reaches 240°F. Stir in the honey and remove from the heat. Leave to cool.

Serves 6–8

Chunky Marmalade Sauce

3 tablespoons chunky marmalade
⅔ cup orange juice
Finely grated zest of 1 orange
Squeeze of lemon juice
2 tablespoons whiskey, optional

Gently warm the marmalade, orange juice and zest and lemon juice together in a saucepan until the marmalade has melted. Stir in the whiskey, if using. Serve warm.

Serves 4

Apricot Sauce

Substitute apricot jam for the marmalade. Brandy or rum could be substituted for the whiskey.

Fresh Fruit Sauces

Purée fresh fruit and sweeten to taste with confectioners' sugar. Spoon over the ice cream. Strain raspberries, blackberries, etc. to get rid of any seeds. This is unnecessary with fruits such as apricots unless you want a really smooth sauce. Always remember to remove the pith and membrane from oranges before puréeing.

For a really dramatic effect, warm a tablespoon of liqueur or liquor. Ignite it and pour it, still flaming, over the sauce after it has been spooned over the ice. The cool richness of the ice will mingle and contrast with the fresh warmth of the fruit sauce and the extra 'kick' of the liqueur.

Caramel Fruit Sauce

Heat and stir Caramelized* fruit zest in orange or other fruit juice.

Orange Flower Sauce

2 egg yolks
¼ cup sugar
1 cup light cream
1 tablespoon orange flower water

Beat the egg yolks and sugar together in a bowl until light. In a heavy-based saucepan, heat the cream to just below simmering point then beat into the egg yolks. Return the mixture to the rinsed pan and cook over a low heat, stirring constantly, until the mixture thickens. Remove from the heat and stir in the orange flower water. Leave to cool, beating occasionally.

Serves 6

Wine Sauce

1 cup dry red or white wine
2 cloves
½ cinnamon stick
Strip of lemon peel
Strip of orange peel
¼ cup sugar
1 tablespoon cornstarch
2 tablespoons red currant jelly or port

Put the wine, cloves, cinnamon, lemon and orange peel and sugar in a saucepan and gradually bring to just below simmering point. Cover the pan and leave over a very low heat for about 20 minutes.

Blend the cornstarch with 2 tablespoons water in a bowl. Strain in the spiced wine, stirring. Return to the pan and cook over a low heat, stirring, until the sauce thickens. Continue to cook for 1–2 minutes then stir in the red currant jelly or port. Taste and adjust the sweetness, adding more sugar if necessary.

Serves 6

Low Calorie Topping

½ cup dry nonfat milk
2 teaspoons lemon juice
Artificial sweetener, to taste
Few drops of vanilla extract, optional

Reconstitute the dry milk with ¾ cup very cold water and stir in the lemon juice and sweetener together with the vanilla extract, if using. Whip until the mixture has doubled in volume and is very thick. Leave in a cool place for 30 minutes.

Serves 4

Quick Sauces
(All serve 4)

Sweet and Sour Molasses Sauce

⅔ cup sour cream
1 teaspoon molasses
1 teaspoon sugar

Blend all the ingredients together. To serve hot, warm in a bowl set over a pan of hot water.

Marshmallow Sauce

1 cup miniature marshmallows
⅔ cup light cream

Beat the marshmallows with the cream in a bowl set over a pan of hot water.

Caramel Sauce

¼ pound caramel candies
⅔ cup light cream

Melt the caramels in the cream in a bowl set over a pan of hot water then beat until smooth.

Milky Way Sauce

1 Milky Way, chopped

Heat the Milky Way in a bowl set over a pan of hot water until smooth.

Praline

½ cup sugar
¾ cup shelled, unpeeled almonds or hazelnuts

In a heavy-based pan, dissolve the sugar in ⅓ cup water. Add the almonds or hazelnuts and boil for about 10 minutes until golden brown. Pour onto a cold, oiled surface and leave until set. Then place in a thick plastic bag or clean cloth and hit with a rolling pin until the praline has broken into small pieces.

Cakes, Cookies and Decorations

This section includes cookies and other extras to serve with ices. There are also recipes for ingredients called for in some of the dessert suggestions in the main part of the book, and directions on how to make decorations for party spectaculars.

Almond Tuiles

2 egg whites
3 tablespoons sweet butter, softened
1/4 teaspoon finely grated orange zest
1/3 cup sugar
Pinch of salt
3 tablespoons all-purpose flour
1 tablespoon cornstarch
2 tablespoons ground almonds
Few drops almond extract and vanilla extract
3 tablespoons slivered almonds

Lightly grease and flour 2 cookie sheets.

Put the egg whites in a bowl and beat very lightly with a fork. In another bowl, beat the butter, orange zest, sugar and salt together until fluffy and light. Gradually add the egg whites, beating well after each addition.

Sift together the flour and cornstarch, then fold into the beaten egg mixture with the ground almonds and extracts.

Drop spoonfuls of the mixture onto the cookie sheets, adjusting the size according to the size of tuile desired. Leave plenty of space between them to allow for spreading. With a damp knife spread each spoonful out to a thin disk. Sprinkle each one with slivered almonds.

Bake in an oven preheated to 425°F for 5–7 minutes until they are golden and tinged brown around the edges. As soon as they come out of the oven remove them with a flat knife and drape around a rolling pin with the almonds on the outside. Leave to harden into shape then carefully transfer to a wire rack to cool completely.

Makes approximately 20

Almond Tuiles with Orange Flower Water

Beat a few drops of orange flower water into the butter with the orange zest, sugar and salt.

Choux Pastry

1/2 cup all-purpose flour
4 tablespoons butter, diced
1 teaspoon sugar
2 large eggs, beaten

Sift the flour onto a sheet of waxpaper. Put the butter, sugar and 2/3 cup water in a saucepan over low heat. Stir to dissolve then bring to the boil rapidly. Remove from the heat and immediately pour all the flour in at once and beat vigorously with a wooden spoon to form a stiff paste. Return the pan to the heat and cook for 30 seconds to 1 minute, beating, until the mixture forms a smooth ball. Remove from the heat and leave to cool slightly. Gradually add the eggs, beating well after each addition and making sure that it is incorporated before adding any more. Beat until the mixture is a smooth, shiny, stiff paste.

Spoon the mixture into a piping bag fitted with a straight 1/2 inch nozzle. Holding the bag at right angles to a greased cookie sheet, pipe 1/2–1 inch balls, depending on the size of shell you want. Bake in an oven preheated to 425°F for 10 minutes. Remove the choux balls from the oven and lower the temperature to 325°F. Pierce a small hole in the side of each choux ball and return them to the oven for about 15 minutes to dry. Transfer to a wire rack to cool.

Makes 4–6

Cigars Russe

2 egg whites
1 cup confectioners' sugar, sifted
1/4 cup all-purpose flour, sifted
5 tablespoons melted sweet butter
Few drops of vanilla extract

Lightly grease and flour 2 cookie sheets.

Put the egg whites in a bowl and whip until stiff. Whip in the sugar followed by the flour. Beat in the melted butter and vanilla extract. Drop 2 or 3 spoonfuls of the mixture onto a cookie sheet leaving plenty of room between them. With a wetted knife spread each spoonful out and bake in an oven preheated to 400°F for 5–6 minutes until golden brown.

Meanwhile, place another 2 or 3 spoonfuls on another baking sheet in a similar way and put in the oven halfway through the baking of the first batch. When the first spoonfuls are ready, immediately remove them with a flat knife or pancake turner and wrap them around the handle of an oiled wooden spoon. Leave to harden then slip off. Repeat until all the mixture is used.

Makes approximately 18

Cinnamon-flavored Cigars Russe

Sift 1/2 teaspoon ground cinnamon with the flour before whipping it into the egg whites.

Coupelles

4 tablespoons sweet butter
2 egg whites
1/3 cup sugar
1/4 cup all-purpose flour

Lightly grease a cookie sheet.

Put the butter in a small saucepan and melt over gentle heat, then allow to cool. Whip the egg whites in a bowl until frothy. Whip in the sugar and continue to whip for 2–3 minutes until thick. Gently fold in the flour together with the melted butter.

Drop 3 spoonfuls onto the cookie sheet and spread each one out to a circle 4 inches in diameter. Bake in an oven preheated to 400°F for 5–7 minutes until the edges are golden brown.

Carefully but quickly remove the cookies with a spatula and quickly shape around the bottom of an orange or apple or small custard cup. When set to shape remove from the mold and leave to cool completely on a wire rack.

Bake the remaining mixture, using a cool cookie sheet each time and shape the biscuits as above.

Store carefully in tins or airtight containers.

Makes 8–10

Lightly Spiced Coupelles

Sift 1/4 teaspoon ground mixed spice with the flour and fold into the egg whites with the melted butter.

Almond-flavored Coupelles

Mix 2 tablespoons finely chopped slivered almonds with the flour and butter and fold into the egg whites.

Crêpes

3 tablespoons all-purpose flour
Pinch of salt
1 egg, beaten
1 tablespoon melted butter
1/3 cup milk

Sift the flour and salt into a bowl and form a well in the center. Pour the egg and butter into the well. Using a spoon, stir the egg, gradually drawing in the flour. Stir until smooth. Slowly stir in the milk to make a smooth batter. Leave to stand for 2 hours.

Heat a small frying pan or crêpe pan, grease it and spoon in 2–3 tablespoons of the batter, depending on the size of the pan. Tilt the pan so that the batter coats the base evenly then cook over a medium heat for 1 minute. Turn the crêpe over and cook the other side for 1 minute. Remove the crêpe and repeat until all the batter is used up. Stack the crêpes as they are made and keep them warm.

Makes 6 crêpes

Serving suggestion

Enclose an iced mixture, and perhaps some fruit, inside a small crêpe. Fold the crêpe over and tuck in the ends. Secure with a toothpick and deep fry at 375°F for 2–3 minutes. Serve at once with a sprinkling of icing sugar.

Genoise Cake

4 eggs
1/2 cup sugar
1 cup all-purpose flour, sifted
4 tablespoons clarified butter, runny but not melted

Line two 9 inch cake pans with greased waxpaper.

Put the eggs and sugar in a bowl and beat together until very thick and light. Very carefully fold in the flour. Pour in the butter and fold it into the mixture until just evenly incorporated.

Turn into the cake pan and bake in an oven preheated to 375°F for about 30–35 minutes or until the cake shrinks slightly from the sides of the pan and the top feels springy to the touch. Leave to cool slightly before turning out, removing the waxpaper and leaving to cool on a wire rack.

Coconut Cake

Stir 1/2 cup shredded coconut into the flour and fold into the egg mixture.

Moist Ginger Cake

Stir 1 teaspoon ground ginger into the flour and fold into the egg mixture.

Gingersnap Baskets

1/4 cup light corn syrup
4 tablespoons butter
2/3 cup sugar
1/2 cup all-purpose flour
1 teaspoon ground ginger
1/2 teaspoon finely grated lemon zest
1/2 teaspoon lemon juice

Lightly grease a cookie sheet.

Put the syrup, butter and sugar in a saucepan and heat gently until the sugar has dissolved. Remove from the heat and fold in the remaining ingredients. Drop 3 tablespoons onto the cookie sheet, leaving room for the mixture to spread. Bake in an oven preheated to 350°F for 7–10 minutes until golden brown.

Quickly but carefully remove with a spatula and mold around the base of an orange, apple or a small custard cup. When set, remove from the molds and leave to cool on a wire rack. Bake and shape the remaining mixture in the same way.

Makes 8–10

Gingersnaps

Drop teaspoonfuls of the mixture onto the cookie sheet. Using a spatula, quickly but carefully transfer the baked cookies to a wire rack to cool.

Gingersnap Cones

When the mixture has baked until golden brown, remove from the cookie sheet with a spatula and mold around lightly greased funnel molds. Leave to cool then carefully slip off the molds.

Gingersnaps Shaped Like Cigars Russe

Bake in batches. When the cookies have baked until golden brown, remove from the cookie sheet with a spatula and wrap them around the handle of an oiled wooden spoon. Leave to harden then slip off. Repeat until the mixture is finished.

Ice Cream Cones

2 egg whites
½ cup sugar
½ cup all-purpose flour, sifted
3 tablespoons melted sweet butter

Line cookie sheets with waxpaper or foil.

Put the egg whites in a bowl and whip until stiff. Fold in half the sugar and whip again until stiff. Fold in the remaining sugar, then the flour and butter.

Drop spoonfuls of the mixture onto the cookie sheets and bake in an oven preheated to 400°F for about 3–4 minutes or until light brown around the edges. Carefully remove from the tray with a spatula and mold around lightly greased funnel molds. Leave to cool then carefully slip off the molds.

Makes approximately 14

Coated Ice Cream Cones

Brush the outside of the cones with egg white and dip in colored sprinkles, toasted or colored coconut, very finely chopped nuts or chocolate sprinkles. Or brush the cones with melted semi-sweet chocolate.

Langues de Chat

4 tablespoons butter
¼ cup sugar
1 egg, beaten
½ cup all-purpose flour, sifted
2 squares semi-sweet chocolate, optional

Lightly grease and flour a cookie sheet.

Put the butter in a bowl and cream until well softened. Beat in the sugar and continue to beat until the mixture is light and fluffy. Gradually beat in the egg then carefully fold in the flour.

Spoon the mixture into a piping bag fitted with a ½ inch straight nozzle. Pipe finger lengths on to the cookie sheet, leaving sufficient room in between them to allow for spreading.

Bake in an oven preheated to 425°F for 4–5 minutes until lightly browned around the edges. Carefully remove from the cookie sheet with a spatula and leave on a wire rack to cool.

If using the chocolate, melt it in a bowl set over a pan of hot water and dip the ends of the langues de chat in it. Leave to set on a wire rack.

Makes about 15

Round Cookies

Drop teaspoonfuls of the mixture onto the cookie sheet, spacing well apart. Bake for 5–7 minutes until golden brown. If the edges are too brown, cut them off with a cookie cutter.

Meringues

2 large egg whites
½ cup sugar

Line a baking tray with waxpaper.

Whip the egg whites until very stiff. Add half the sugar, a teaspoon at a time, whipping well after each addition. Lightly fold in the remaining sugar. Spoon the meringue mixture into a piping bag fitted with a straight ½ inch nozzle and pipe 16 balls or swirled shapes onto the tray, or use 2 tablespoons to shape the shells. Bake in an oven preheated to 225°F 2–2½ hours. Remove and cool.

Makes 16

Coconut Meringues

Fold in ¼ cup shredded coconut with the last of the sugar.

Hazelnut or Almond Meringues

Fold in ¼ cup ground hazelnuts or ground almonds with the last of the sugar.

Chocolate Meringues

Fold in 2 tablespoons cocoa with the last of the sugar.

Coffee Meringues

Dissolve 2 teaspoons good-quality instant coffee in very little water and whip into the egg whites with the sugar.

Meringues with Orange Flower Water

Add a few drops of orange flower water with the last of the sugar.

Tiny Meringues

Use a ¼ inch nozzle or 2 teaspoons to shape the shells. Bake for about 45 minutes at 225°F.

Meringue Fingers

Using a straight ½ inch nozzle pipe approximately 2¼ inch lengths. Bake for 1–1½ hours at 225°F.

Meringue Bases

Line a cookie sheet with waxpaper. Mark the size and shape of base you require on the paper. Fill in the shape with piped meringue or lightly spread out the meringue with a flat knife. Bake at 225°F for about 1 hour for small shapes, 2 hours for large ones.

Meringue Basket

Line 6 cookie sheets, or as many surfaces as necessary, with waxpaper. Mark six 8–9 inch circles on the trays. Make the base by filling in one circle with meringue, either by spreading it with a flat knife or piping with a straight ½ inch nozzle in concentric circles. Make the sides of the basket by piping a single circle of meringue on each of the remaining shapes. Bake at 225°F for about 1½ hours. Remove the waxpaper, cool the meringues then stack the rings on the base.

Individual Meringue Baskets

Line a cookie sheet with waxpaper. Mark four to six 3–4 inch circles on the paper. Pipe the meringue onto the lines in concentric circles to make the bases. Then pipe 2 circles, one on top of the other, around the circumference of the base. Bake at 225°F for about 2 hours.

Macaroons

½ cup finely ground almonds or hazelnuts
⅔ cup sugar
2 egg whites
Few drops of vanilla extract

Line a cookie sheet with rice paper or oiled foil.

Mix the nuts and sugar together. Whip the egg whites until stiff then carefully fold in the ground nut mixture with the vanilla extract.

Place small spoonfuls of the mixture on the baking sheet, leaving room in between them to allow for spreading. Bake in an oven preheated to 350°F for about 20 minutes until the tops are lightly browned. Cool on a wire rack.

Makes 15–25 depending on size

Sponge Fingers

3 eggs, separated
⅓ cup sugar
¾ cup all-purpose flour, sifted
2 drops vanilla extract
Sifted confectioners' sugar

Line cookie sheets with greased waxpaper.

Put the egg yolks and sugar in a bowl and beat until very thick and pale. In another bowl, whip the egg whites until stiff then fold into the egg yolk mixture with the flour and vanilla extract.

Spoon into a piping bag fitted with a straight ½ inch nozzle and pipe finger lengths onto the cookie sheets.

Dust with sifted confectioners' sugar and bake in an oven preheated to 350°F for 10–13 minutes. Carefully remove the paper and leave the fingers to cool on a wire rack.

Makes about 20

Sponge Cake

3 eggs, separated
⅓ cup sugar
¾ cup all-purpose flour, sifted
Pinch of salt

Line two 8 inch cake pans with waxpaper.

Put the egg yolks and sugar in a bowl and beat until very thick and light. Whip the egg whites in another bowl until stiff. Fold into the egg yolk mixture with the flour and salt.

Pour into the pans and bake in an oven preheated to 350°F for 20–25 minutes or until a light golden color, springy to the touch and slightly shrunken from the edges of the tin.

Leave to cool slightly before turning out, removing the paper and leaving to cool on a wire rack.

Chocolate Cake

Replace 1½ tablespoons flour with the same amount of cocoa.

Jelly Roll

Spoon the sponge batter into a 9 × 13 inch shallow cake pan and bake in an oven preheated to 400°F for 8–10 minutes. Turn the cake out onto a sheet of waxpaper, sprinkled with sugar, resting on a warm, dampened dish-towel. Peel away the lining paper and roll up the cake with the sugared paper inside and leave to cool. Unroll the cake, remove the waxpaper, spread with the filling and roll up again.

Chocolate Roll

Replace 1½ tablespoon flour with the same amount of cocoa. Follow the instructions for making a Jelly roll.

Chocolate Containers and Decorations

Chocolate Squares

To make simple chocolate squares, break a bar of cooking chocolate into a small bowl and place it over a pan of hot water. Line a cookie sheet with waxpaper and carefully pour the melted chocolate over it. Spread the chocolate quite thickly over the paper with a flat knife and leave it to set. Using a ruler as a guide, mark out the squares and cut them out with the point of a warm sharp knife. Peel off the paper.

Chocolate Boxes

First freeze the ice cream in a square mold. Cut chocolate squares (as explained above). Allow the ice cream to soften slightly in the refrigerator before turning out. Gently press the chocolate squares over the sides. Transfer to a foil-covered tray and return to the freezer. When hard, cover with foil.

Chocolate Cases

Spoon melted chocolate into two thicknesses of cupcake case and swirl around until the sides and base are evenly coated. If the chocolate lining seems too thin, repeat the process. Turn the case upside down and set aside. When the chocolate has set, peel off the paper. Fill the chocolate cases with small scoops of ice cream. Alternatively, fill with the iced mixture after it has been beaten for the last time, transfer to a foil-covered tray and freeze. Wrap in freezerproof foil or plastic wrap and pack in a rigid container to protect from damage.

Chocolate Baskets

Make a Meringue Basket* and roll the sides in melted chocolate. Leave to set.

Alternatively, use a waxpaper piping bag with a ¼ inch nozzle. Lightly oil the inside of a small bowl. Fill the bag with melted chocolate and pipe lines of chocolate over the base and a little way up the sides. Pipe another set of lines crosswise, to form a basketwork pattern. Pipe a line of chocolate joining the ends together. Leave to set then slip the basket out of the bowl.

Chocolate Curls

Scrape a potato peeler along the long edge of a bar of cold chocolate.

Chocolate Shapes

Line a tray with waxpaper. Pour melted chocolate on the paper and spread evenly with a flat knife. Leave to set. Cut out shapes using small aspic cutters.

To make triangles, first cut out squares then cut across diagonally with the point of a warm sharp knife.

To make outlined shapes, draw the outline on a piece of waxpaper. Using a waxpaper piping bag fitted with a fine nozzle and filled with the melted chocolate, pipe out the outline. Leave to set before peeling off the paper. You can use the piping bag to draw more complicated shapes like flowers or butterflies.

Chocolate Leaves

Brush the surface of a washed leaf with melted chocolate. When the chocolate has set, peel off the leaf. Carefully mark the veins on the chocolate leaf with the point of a sharp knife.

Fruits and Herbs

Caramelized Peels

Remove the peel from one large orange, two small or medium-sized lemons or one grapefruit, taking care not to include any pith. Cut it into fine strips or pretty shapes with a sharp knife or aspic cutters. In a heavy-based saucepan, pour 1 cup sugar and 2 tablespoons water and stir to dissolve. Cook the syrup to a mid-amber color. Remove from the heat and stir in the peel. After a few seconds remove the peel with a pair of tweezers or small tongs and dry on a wire rack.

Frosted Decorations

To frost fresh herbs, leaves, flowers, berries and so on, brush them with egg white and dip in sugar. Leave to dry on a wire rack.

Compotes

Fresh or dried fruits, lightly poached in a little water or white wine and sweetened to taste with honey or sugar, are a good accompaniment to iced mixtures.

Remove the pits from fruits such as peaches and plums and cut fruit in half; core and cut in half or slice apples and pears; peel oranges and lemons (removing pith) and divide them into segments or slice them into rounds.

Techniques

Iced desserts provide the ideal opportunity for using your creative flair. The following are the main techniques involved in creating them.

Ice Cream Balls

Scoop slightly softened ice cream into ball shapes. Place on a foil-covered tray and freeze. Conceal a surprise in the center – a liqueur chocolate, for example – to create a real sensation.

To add liqueurs: remove the balls from the freezer and allow to soften slightly. Make a thimble-size indentation on top of each and fill with liqueur, allowing it to dribble down the sides as it is served.

Checkerboard Ices

When cut, these look like checkerboards. Freeze different flavored iced mixtures in loaf pans. Then cut lengthwise into square 'fingers'. Place contrasting flavors or colors side by side and stack on top of each other to make a checkerboard pattern. Return to the freezer.

Coating

Freeze the iced mixture in a cylindrical mold or can or form into balls (see page 152). Soften slightly if necessary then roll in a coating of crushed macaroons, meringues, cookies, finely ground nuts, shredded coconut, chocolate sprinkles or cocoa. Place the coated ice cream on a foil-covered tray and return to the freezer until firm.

Chocolate Coating

Shape the ice cream into balls (see page 152), and return to the freezer to harden. Melt the chocolate in a bowl over a pan of hot water. Remove from the heat. Dip each ice cream ball briefly into the chocolate, turning it over with a metal spoon to coat. Drain off the excess chocolate and place on a foil-covered tray. Freeze the balls and cover with foil when hard.

Layering

This technique combines any number of flavors, textures and ingredients. Use Sponge Fingers*, Langues de Chat* or cookies such as chocolate chip cookies and brownies. Meringues* can be crushed, or make Meringue Bases* and use them to sandwich an iced mixture – or, conversely, use the ice to sandwich a meringue. Crisp breakfast cereals, crushed cookies held together with melted butter, chopped nuts, fruit, and any of the simple toppings on page 145 are other alternatives. All these look especially attractive if the dessert is served in tall glasses. Alternate each layer with scoops of the iced mixture or spoonfuls smoothed to form even layers.

To Layer Ice Cream

The easiest way is to stack the different layers one on top of each other as in three-flavors ice cream, which is made from strawberry, vanilla and chocolate ice creams. Spoon the iced mixture for the first layer into a loaf or cake pan or any other suitable container. Smooth until even, cover and freeze until firm. Soften the ice for the following layer in the refrigerator for 30 minutes. When the first layer is frozen, spoon on the softened ice cream and freeze. Continue to add layers until the dessert is complete. You can also arrange layers vertically side by side.

A more advanced method is to coat an iced mixture with one of a different flavor. Freeze the main ice in a cylindrical mold or can. Soften the coating layer in the refrigerator for 30 to 45 minutes, depending on the type of mixture. (A rich or mousse-type ice cream needs less time.) Turn out the frozen roll and coat with an outer layer of the softened mixture, using a flat knife with a broad blade. Put on a foil-covered tray and return to the freezer. When frozen, cover with foil. Soften in the refrigerator for 30 minutes before serving.

Lining a Mold

Whatever the lining, always soften the iced mixture before spooning it into the center. Then cover the dessert and freeze until firm. Turn out onto a cold plate and leave in the refrigerator to soften for approximately 30 minutes before serving.

Chopped Nuts, Crushed Cookies

Line the mold with buttered waxpaper. Coat the base and sides evenly with crushed cookies or finely chopped nuts, pressing them into the buttered paper. Fill with the softened iced mixture.

Cakes, Cookies

To line a pan with Genoise Cake*, bake the cake mixture in a shallow cake pan and allow to cool. Cut a piece to fit the base of the pan, and cut the remaining cake into strips the length and depth of the sides of the pan. Arrange the base piece in place and fit the strips around the sides. Fill with the softened iced mixture. To make a Genoise Cake 'box', use a square pan and fit a 'lid' of cake over the ice before freezing.

To line a charlotte mold with Genoise Cake or Sponge Cake*, bake the cake mixture in a shallow cake pan, allow it to cool and cut it in half. Cut one half into 11 even fingers, and the remaining sponge horizontally into two strips, each the depth of the mold. Trim the fingers into triangular shapes that will fit together on the base like the spokes of a wheel. Fit the side strips into position, against the sides of the mold. Each should reach halfway around; trim the strips if necessary. Fill with the iced mixture.

To line a charlotte mold with Langues de Chat* or Sponge Fingers*, place a small circle cut from one cookie in the center of the base. Decide how many cookies are needed to fill the rest of the base, then trim their sides to make triangular petal shapes that will fit together around the central disk. Arrange them in place. Square off the ends for the sides and fit them inside the mold, cut side down and with the curved side of the cookie facing inwards. Line them up with the cookies on the base. Fill with the iced mixture and trim the cookies so they are even with the filling.

Ice Cream

Place the container in the freezer and soften the iced mixture which will be used for lining in the refrigerator for 30 minutes. Spoon the ice cream into the cold container and smooth it to an even layer over the base and sides. Cover and freeze until firm.

Soften the ice cream to go in the center and, when the lining is frozen, spoon in the softened ice cream. Freeze again.

To make a second lining as well as the 'jacket', smooth softened ice cream to an even layer over the base and sides once the jacket has frozen, then continue as above. An ice cream lining can also be smoothed onto a jacket of cake or cookies.

Encasing or enclosing: Spread a layer of the lining ice cream over the top of the lined and filled mold.

Bombe: Follow the techniques described above, and encase the filling if you do not have a bombe mold.

Ring molds

Ices that have been frozen in ring molds call out to be made into desserts. Turn the ice out onto a serving plate, put fruit in the center and serve. If you are filling the center with another ice cream, scoop or spoon the softened mixture into the center of the turned-out ring and freeze again until firm. Serve immediately.

Rippling

For a rippled effect, simply fold two softened ices lightly together, or lightly fold a fruit purée or sauce into a softened ice. Proportions are flexible.

Swirling

Freeze one layer until it is still slightly soft and spoon in a second layer of softened ice cream, gently swirling the first few spoonfuls into the base layer with a spoon. Then complete the second layer, freeze until it is still slightly soft and repeat the process with the third layer.

Shaped Containers for Freezing

A very simple way of adding an extra special touch to iced mixtures is to make them in different-shaped containers. Decorative jelly molds, brioche, tube and braided loaf pans are obvious candidates, but are by no means the only ones. Even a plain loaf pan, a square or round cake pan will bring a new look to an iced mixture, whether it is served whole or cut into wedges or slices.

Individual containers such as custard cups, dariole molds, rum baba molds, funnel molds, waxpaper cups and individual pie pans especially if they are fluted or patterned, add a personal touch.

Clean cylinder-shaped food cans may come in handy to make rolls that can then be sliced into rounds.

Cover the open ends with freezerproof foil. Leave dividers in ice-cube trays to make small squares that can be piled up in glasses. Double-thick cupcake cases can be peeled away just before the ice is served to make a change from a scoop.

A special copper mold is not necessary if you are making a bombe. Similar-shaped desserts can be produced with plastic, foil, earthenware or ceramic freezerproof bowls. You can also use cake or loaf pans or charlotte molds.

Turning Out Shaped Ices

Mixtures should be turned out immediately after they are taken out of the freezer and before they are allowed to soften up. Put the serving plate or dish in the freezer or refrigerator well before the iced mixture is brought out. Remove the protective wrapping from the iced mixture and invert the mold onto the serving dish or plate. Then dip a cloth in hot water, wring it out and wrap it around the outside of the mold for 30 seconds if the mold is metal, a little longer if the mold is earthenware. If the cloth cools, dip it in hot water and wring it out again.

Then hold the plate and mold firmly together, and give them a sharp shake to release the ice before carefully lifting the mold from it. If necessary, smooth any blemishes on the surface of the ice with a warm knife that has been dipped in hot water and dried.

If you put the ice back in the freezer, wrap it in freezerproof foil or plastic wrap and pack it in a rigid container to protect it from damage.

Serving Dishes

Small, pretty plates, bowls or glasses are especially attractive if the rims are frosted to give a suitably icy appearance. Dip the rims in lemon juice or beaten egg white, then into sugar, and chill. Try serving two or three scoops of ice cream in a tall, slim wine glass or a bright sorbet in a champagne glass – particularly effective if some sparkling wine is poured over to trickle down and collect at the base of the glass.

Edible containers for serving ices include Meringue* or Chocolate Baskets* and Chocolate Cases*, hollowed-out brioche, Choux* balls, éclairs and Coupelles*, Gingersnap Baskets* and Ice Cream Cones*. You can also fill the centers of rum babas or doughnuts with small scoops of ice cream.

The hollowed-out shells of oranges, lemons, grapefruit, limes, pears, pineapples, etc. make natural dishes – scallop the edges for a final flourish. Remember to chill them well before filling them with the ice cream. Smaller fruits like peaches and apricots can also be used. Remove the pits and enlarge the hollows, then fill them with small scoops of ice cream. Match the flavors or combine contrasting or complementary ones.

Index

Picture acknowledgments

Photographs: Anthony Blake
Photo Library 48, 51, 122,
129; Ian O'Leary 2, 19, 22,
26-27, 31, 33, 37, 40, 54-55,
58, 62-63, 68, 76-77, 80, 82,
86-87, 91, 97, 100, 104-105,
109, 112, 114, 118-119, 126,
141, 160; Charlie Stebbings
10, 44-45, 94-95, 132-133;
Tessa Traeger 73, 144, 153;
Nedra Westwater 136

Cover photographs: Ian
O'Leary
Paintings: Nicki Kemball

The end